This beautifully thoughtful book brings tog[e]... sophical and theological thinking on the concept of loneliness as part of human existence. Whilst its purpose is to understand, explain and debate how loneliness and Christianity is experienced and the impact this can have on a persons' sense of loneliness and their relationship with God, I believe its reach is wider. Reading the chapters that discuss what loneliness is and how it has been conceptualised over millennia through philosophy, psychology and sociology, recognising both the spiritual and existential importance of loneliness, leaves us with a strong sense of what it means to be human and what being in the world means for us, individually and collectively.

The book, in its description of types of loneliness, be it social, emotional, spiritual, reminds me of a quote from Carl Jung in which he says "It is ... only in the state of complete abandonment and loneliness that we can experience the helpful powers of our own nature" (Modern Man in Search of a Soul).

Whatever kind of loneliness we are experiencing, it is within ourselves to search and find for the meaning of our connection and communion in relationship with others, with the self and with a higher spiritual existence. Sometimes a complete state of loneliness feels intensely painful, it is only by facing and bearing the pain that we find our deepest selves.

This book will be a deep source of understanding and comfort to the Christian in their relationship with God. It will also be of importance to anyone who has a personal or scholarly desire to widen their depth of appreciation of what it means to not just exist, but to heal and grow through loneliness.

Sally Kendall, PhD
Professor of Community Nursing and Public Health,
University of Kent, UK

This well-written and informative piece of work will prove to be a very useful tool to individuals, families, and churches for deep reflection on the different kinds of loneliness that can impact people's lives. This feels like a very timely book in an increasingly relationally fractured age.

Stefan Liston
Pastor,
Revelation Church, London, UK

We were created *in* relationship, *through* relationship, and *for* relationship. However, in today's post-COVID reality, the aftermath of isolation and its often silent companion, loneliness, have created a tsunami of consequences impacting mental, emotional, and relational health across the globe. The timely release of *Better than One: A Biblical View of Loneliness*, offers a well-researched and much needed resource on this critically important topic. The authors address every aspect of the subject with a sound and integrated approach, encompassing both psychological and theological principles. Readers will find a message of biblical hope and practical help across its pages, and a pathway of discovery to greater and more meaningful connection with others.

Eric Scalise, PhD
Senior Vice President and Chief Strategy Officer,
Hope for the Heart

Better than One

Langham
GLOBAL LIBRARY

Better than One

A Biblical View of Loneliness

Valeriia Chornobai and Viktoriia Hrytsenko

Langham
GLOBAL LIBRARY

© 2023 Valeriia Chornobai and Viktoriia Hrytsenko

Published 2023 by Langham Global Library
An imprint of Langham Publishing
www.langhampublishing.org

Langham Publishing and its imprints are a ministry of Langham Partnership

Langham Partnership
PO Box 296, Carlisle, Cumbria, CA3 9WZ, UK
www.langham.org

ISBNs:
978-1-83973-536-3 Print
978-1-83973-942-2 ePub
978-1-83973-943-9 PDF

Scripture quotations are from The Holy Bible, English Standard Version® (ESV®), copyright © 2001 by Crossway, a publishing ministry of Good News Publishers. Used by permission. All rights reserved.

Scripture quotations marked (NIV) are taken from the Holy Bible, New International Version®, NIV®. Copyright © 1973, 1978, 1984, 2011 by Biblica, Inc.™ Used by permission of Zondervan.

New King James Version (NKJV). Copyright © 1982 by Thomas Nelson, Inc. Used by permission. All rights reserved.

Scripture quotations marked (TLB) are taken from The Living Bible copyright © 1971. Used by permission of Tyndale House Publishers, a Division of Tyndale House Ministries, Carol Stream, Illinois 60188. All rights reserved.

British Library Cataloguing-in-Publication Data
A catalogue record for this book is available from the British Library

ISBN: 978-1-83973-536-3

Cover & Book Design: projectluz.com

Contents

Preface

We are writing this book at the request of many Christians who either suffer from loneliness themselves or who know people suffering from loneliness and want to help them. The book is the result of more than a dozen years of research on the topic of loneliness since the time of my (Valeriia's) studies in theological seminary. In talking with many believers from various Christian denominations, I wondered why some suffer from loneliness, while others do not feel lonely at all and do not even understand what is at stake – even when they face approximately the same life circumstances (for example, being single), and have the same Christian values. I wondered if this experience of loneliness depends on external circumstances and events in a person's life (for example, a relationship breakdown or the death of a spouse) or internal subjective factors such as a person's self-perception. Do social factors such as marital status or economic stability affect a person's experience of loneliness? Or is it the other way around – is loneliness the driving force, affecting a person's ability to form relationships, and thus social status and emotional well-being? I also wanted to know if our religious beliefs influence the experience of loneliness. It seemed to me that true faith should at least lessen a person's loneliness, if not completely eliminate it (or so I wanted to believe).

Naturally, as we were researching this topic, it became necessary to understand what loneliness *is*. Is it simply a feeling that shifts about with our moods, something that comes and goes swiftly? Or is it our constant human condition at some deep, visceral level, which (for whatever reason) some people do not feel? Finally, is loneliness an alien, unpleasant, and painful experience, which we need to fight against in every possible way, or is it a natural experience, a given of human existence, to which we just have to submit, accept, or even love? Or is loneliness something like light that has a whole spectrum of shades and gradations? And how is it different from solitude and isolation? The first part of this book is devoted to answering these questions. Particular attention in this part of the book is given to biblical narratives that illustrate the various aspects and types of loneliness, as well as the analysis of different types of loneliness found in Scripture.

In this book we cite a number of sources and attempt to consider the topic from multiple angles, in order to see the relationship between various types of loneliness and other phenomena that are similar to loneliness, but, in fact, are not. This might create an impression that this is an academic book. However, it is far from comprehensive academic research and it also does not pretend to be a book of "ready-made recipes on how to get rid of loneliness." Rather, it is an attempt to make the results of our research (and that of other authors) accessible to a wider range of readers. This book was written by ordinary Christians, for ordinary Christians, who want to understand better the strange feeling of loneliness that sometimes overtakes them – or even gnaws at them all the time – in order to learn how better to cope with it.

Acknowledgments

From Viktoriia

The special genius of my dear sister Valeriia made this book possible. I admire her diligence, ethics, and attentiveness to both broad concepts and details! And most of all I admire her genuine love and practical care for people – an unfading desire to help those who are lonely was her motive to write this book and involve me in the process!

None of my writing would be possible without the encouragement of my dear husband Denys Hrytsenko. In particular, I am grateful that taking our children out and entertaining them, he gave me time to concentrate on the book and write. Thanks also to my kids and mom!

I am grateful to Bob Harman for his editorial work on the book. His experience, expertise, and practical advice helped me express my thoughts in a much more reader-friendly way!

From Valeriia

First of all, I want to thank my wonderful family for their support: our mom and sister Anzhela, for always believing in me and encouraging me in all my "crazy" endeavors. Thanks especially to my sister Viktoriia. She is one of those rare people in my life whose support I am sure I can always count on. Her example and diligence inspired me first to write my dissertation, and then this book. In our life, I was usually the one who would get Viktoriia involved in some kind of "adventure." Then she as a more responsible, older (15 minutes) sister would always help me get out of it with dignity. One of these "adventures" was this book about loneliness – I asked Viktoriia, a much more competent specialist in the strategies for overcoming loneliness, to write the second chapter with me. Thank you, Viktoriia, for agreeing to become a co-author of this book and for always supporting me throughout my life! I am happy to have such a twin!

This book would be dry and colorless and perceived by the reader much harder to relate to if it were not for the life stories of real people in it, each of whom we know and witness with admiration how God is creating his "story" in their lives. For the sake of confidentiality, we do not give their real names

xii   Better than One

here, but they know that I am talking about them. Thank you for having the courage to share your story with so many other people who are also going through their valley of loneliness.

I am also very grateful to my supervisors and colleagues, who later became my good friends, for their support in words, advice, prayers, and even finances: Sergei Sannikov, Roman Soloviy, Taras Dyatlik, and Alla Nechiporuk. Thanks also to Pieter Kwant from Langham Publishing for believing in us, for considering this topic important, and for supporting this book's writing. It is my great honor to know and serve the Lord with such people!

I want to give special thanks to my spiritual mentor, teacher, a friend for a couple of decades now, and the first editor of this book, Bob Harman. Bob, your encouragement, advice in the writing process, your support in word and deed, your prayers, and your example as a faithful Christian minister, have shaped me in many ways.

Finally, I express immeasurable gratitude to my Lord Jesus for leading me on the path of loneliness, so that I could better understand what lonely people are going through and how they can be helped, for always being with me, giving me the right people, ideas, and words!

Part 1

Theology of Loneliness

Over the past century or more, under the influence of the ideas of materialist philosophers, many have tried to convince humanity that people are just a clot of matter, instinct, and unconditioned reflexes. The progress of this idea was eloquently evidenced by two world wars, the sexual revolution of the 1960s and the general disappointment with religion that swept Europe in the last century. Despite this, humans are nevertheless not only biological, but also social, and from the Christian viewpoint, spiritual beings. For every human being, the need for other humans is the norm. From the theological point of view, humans are created for communication and interaction with other people and with God. More and more often, however, loneliness is discussed in the media and academia as a widespread problem that causes concern, especially among sociologists, psychologists, clergy, and all those who work with people. It seems that we are becoming lonelier. The Internet provides more than seventy million links within seconds for the keyword "loneliness," which indicates the relevance of this query.

Interestingly, some people perceive loneliness positively as something natural and even desirable, while others see it negatively, because to them it is always associated with pain or loss. The difference lies in the answer to the question: what is meant by "loneliness"? It seems to us that it is impossible to say whether a person is lonely based only on external circumstances or the conditions of life. After all, there are people who, it would seem, have great social support, a wide circle of social contacts, but who still feel terribly and chronically lonely. Vice versa, a person may be without proper social support, which usually includes love, care, and the respect of loved ones, as well as acceptance in a community, but nevertheless not suffer from loneliness. The first chapter of this part of the book examines what exactly loneliness is and what it depends on – internal beliefs or external factors affecting a person, or both of them.

1

Five Types of Loneliness: Emotional, Social, Cultural, Existential, and Spiritual

As the title of this chapter suggests, we see loneliness as a multifaceted phenomenon that can manifest itself in various aspects of a person's relationship with the self, with other people, and with God. We think that loneliness has at least five main types: emotional, social, cultural, existential, and spiritual. Despite the fact that various typologies of loneliness have been actively emerging and developing over the past half-century, loneliness is still often perceived as something monolithic and simple. It is often incorrectly confused with solitude and other phenomena. Therefore, we will begin with a small historical overview of various theories and approaches to the study of loneliness, without which it is impossible to define its "terminological shores." For those readers who find such a jungle of philosophical ideas of little interest, we suggest jumping directly to the conclusions at the end of this chapter for a summary.

Since antiquity, the phenomenon of loneliness has occupied the minds of philosophers, and they mostly had a very negative attitude to it. Aristotle and Cicero, emphasizing the social nature of man, unequivocally asserted that a human is created for communication with others, and therefore loneliness is seen as something contrary to human nature. Aristotle said that a man who considers himself self-sufficient and not in need of others was akin to "a beast or a god."[1]

---

1. Аристотель, *Сочинения, Политика*, Т. 4, пер. О. Кислюка (М.: Мысль, 1983) [Aristotle, Works, Politics, T. 4, trans. O. Kislyuk (Moscow: Mysl, 1983)], 376–644. Aristotle, "Politics," I.2 in *The Complete Works of Aristotle*, ed. Jonathan Barnes (Princeton: Princeton

Later, in the medieval theological tradition of hesychasm,[2] loneliness was considered to be a sign of a "sick soul separated from God."[3] Spiritual recovery was thought to be achieved through a person's unity with God, mainly by an ascetic and (oddly enough) a hermit life, in solitude. In particular, Gregory Palamas, the founder of hesychasm, posits that "the one who seeks . . . to unite with God . . . should choose monastic and solitary living . . . trying to be in the immovable sanctuary of *hesychia* without confusion and worry."[4] Notice that within this approach, the concepts of loneliness and solitary living are distinguished, emphasizing the spiritually negative roots of the former and the re-creational power of the latter.

The humanistic philosophy of the Enlightenment era is also characterized by a clearly negative attitude towards loneliness as an unnatural state for a person. In the understanding of philosophers such as John Locke and David Hume, for instance, loneliness was a practice as odd as fasting or celibacy.[5] In the same train of thought, Adam Smith emphasized the importance of social life, saying that "all the members of human society stand in need of each other's assistance . . . Where the necessary assistance is reciprocally afforded from love, from gratitude, from friendship, and esteem, the society flourishes and is happy."[6]

If for the ancient philosophers, church fathers and philosophers of the Enlightenment, loneliness had mostly a negative connotation, for the transcendentalist (perhaps, for the first time) it began to be thought of in a more positive light.[7] Henry David Thoreau, one of the prominent representatives of

---

University Press, 1995), 2:1988.

2. In Eastern Christianity, monastic seeking of divine quietness through contemplation of God.

3. Following common practice for theological writings, throughout the book, the terms "God," "Divine," "Deity," "Person" in reference to the Trinity, will begin with capital letters.

4. Григорий Палама, *Триады в Защиту Священно-Безмолвствующих* (М.: Канон, 1995) [Gregory Palamas, *Triads for The Defense of Those Who Practice Sacred Quietude* (Moscow: Kanon, 1995)], 322. Hesychasm (greek ἡσυχία – peace, silence) is an ancient Orthodox ascetic tradition and spiritual practice, which is based on solitary, hermitic monasticism (as opposed to life in community), running in silent prayer.

5. David Hume, *Enquiries Concerning Human Understanding and Concerning Principles of Morals* (Oxford: Clarendon Press, 1975), 270.

6. Adam Smith, *Theory of Moral Sentiments*, Sixth Edition (Sao Paulo: MexaLibri, 2006), 77.

7. Transcendentalism was a nineteenth-century movement of writers and philosophers in New England who were loosely bound together by adherence to an idealistic system of thought based on a belief in the essential unity of all creation, the innate goodness of humanity, and the supremacy of insight over logic and experience for the revelation of the deepest truths. See:

transcendentalism, put forward the idea of choosing loneliness to activate the individual's creative powers and to bring men closer to nature and spiritual self-improvement. The main purpose of loneliness in this sense is to awaken the possibilities hidden within the person. In general, Thoreau believed that "a thinking person is always alone. We are for the most part more lonely when we go abroad among men than when we stay in our chambers."[8] For Thoreau, loneliness is not measured by the distance from one person to another. Rather, loneliness is a person's detachment from himself due to the hustle and bustle of everyday social life. Loneliness is viewed here through the prism of the modern man's alienation from nature and himself. Note, however, that in the writings of transcendentalists, loneliness is sometimes understood as a negative painful experience, and sometimes as a state of being alone (in solitude) which is necessary for the restoration of a person's mental resources.[9]

For the philosophy of existentialism, loneliness has a slightly different interpretation. Existentialists see the roots of loneliness in the very nature of man. Because each person is unique and original, it is impossible for another person to fully understand him, and therefore he is "doomed" to loneliness from birth.[10] Loneliness for Søren Kierkegaard, one of the most famous theologian-existentialists, is a closed world of a person's inner consciousness, into which no other person, only God, can enter. Loneliness in this sense is a kind of "homelessness," a restlessness of the human spirit in the universe.[11]

However, existentialism also emphasizes the idea of the usefulness of loneliness. Despite all its pain and horror, if it wasn't for loneliness, how would we each know our uniqueness and originality? Because loneliness is (so to speak) a special space for contemplation, there one can find oneself, and "get

Encyclopedia Britannica, s.v. "Transcendentalism," accessed Dec. 4, 2022, https://www.britannica.com/event/Transcendentalism-American-movement.

8. Henry D. Thoreau, *Walden,* A Fully Annotated Edition (London, New Haven: Yale University Press, 2004), 131.

9. As we will see later, loneliness and solitude are two completely different concepts that should not be confused.

10. The most famous representatives of this approach are Martin Buber, Martin Heidegger, Søren Kierkegaard, Nikolai Berdyaev, Ben Miyuskovich, Clark Mustakas, Jean-Paul Sartre, Vladimir Soloviev, Erich Fromm.

11. Jean-Paul Sartre, *Kierkegaard Vivant: Collogue Organise par Unesko a Paris lu 21–23 april 1964* (Paris, 1966), 108.

closer" to oneself and God. Martin Heidegger emphasizes the same idea when he writes that the path to knowing oneself is through loneliness.[12]

Such loneliness as an escape from the world and society into oneself, according to Kierkegaard, is also "a sign of a person's spiritual maturity."[13] This resonates deeply with the words of the Russian philosopher and representative of existentialism, Nikolai Berdyaev, as he says that "ontologically, loneliness is an expression of longing for God. Loneliness is almost always social because it is actualized not in the absence, but only in the presence of the other."[14] Therefore, from the standpoint of existentialism, one's awareness of one's essential loneliness or separateness is an indicator of personal spiritual depth. Nikolai Berdyaev was also one of the first to introduce the concept of the so-called "prophetic loneliness" which will be discussed below. The origins of this type of loneliness lie not in the person, but in a society which "imposes" alien stereotypes on the person.

Although loneliness is the result of a person's self-realization, a "side effect" of the inner "search for oneself" and one's place in the universe, it is also a social phenomenon. Therefore, at the end of the twentieth century loneliness attracted the attention of sociologists.[15] The main contribution of sociologists to the study of loneliness is an emphasis on the role of socio-cultural factors influencing the formation of loneliness in a person: the process of socialization, education, media, culture, specific life situations, and the like.

If from a sociological point of view loneliness is rooted in external social events or a person's life situation, from the point of view of psychology, the cause of loneliness often lies in the person's individual characteristics. A psychological approach to loneliness helps to determine some of the personality traits of lonely people, as well as identify social (communicative) and emotional (intimate) types of loneliness. Social loneliness is understood as

---

12. Мартин Хайдеггер, *Основные Понятия Метафизики: Мир-Конечность-Одиночество*, пер. В. В. Бибихина, Л. В. Ахутина, А. П. Шурбелева (СПб: Владимир Даль, 2013) [Martin Heidegger, The Fundamental Concepts of Metaphysics: World-Finitude-Solitude, trans. V. V. Bibikhina, L. V. Akhutina, A. P. Shurbeleva (St. Petersburg: Vladimir Dal, 2013)], 29.

13. Ларс Фр. Г. Свендсен, *Філософія Самотності,* Пер. Софії Волковецької (Київ: Ніка-Центр, 2017) [Lars Fr. G. Svendsen, A Philosophy of Loneliness, trans. Sofia Volkovetskoy (Kyiv: Nika-Center, 2017)], 9. See also: Сьорен Кьеркегор, *Страх и Трепет* (М: Республика, 1993) [Søren Kierkegaard, Fear and Trembling (Moscow: Republic, 1993)], 95.

14. Николай Бердяев, *Я и Мир Объектов. Опыт Философии Одиночества и Общения* (Париж: YMCA PRESS, 1934) [Nikolai Berdyaev, Me and the World of Objects. An Experience of the Philosophy of Loneliness and Communication (Paris: YMCA PRESS, 1934)], 87, 89.

15. Among those who have contributed the most to the studies of loneliness as a socio-cultural phenomenon, are Letitia A. Peplau, Daniel Russell, Daniel Perlman, Ami Rokach, Robert Putnam, David Riesman, Philip E. Slater, and others.

the result of a person's awareness of dissatisfaction with the quality or quantity of interpersonal relationships, and emotional loneliness is a subjective feeling of lack of intimacy or attachment to another person.

1. Using attachment theory to explain emotional loneliness

John Bowlby's theory of attachment, which has become especially popular since the 1980s, deserves special attention in connection with our understanding of the difference between social and emotional loneliness.[16] According to this theory, there are four main styles of attachment in relationships between people – one secure and three insecure.

	INSECURE ATTACHMENTS
SECURE ATTACHMENT	Ambivalent-anxious / dependent
	Avoidant
	Disorganized / chaotic

The closest person in one's life is called an attachment figure. The four attachment styles were found to be based on people's basic beliefs about themselves and others. This theory argues that all attachment styles are formed from childhood and, although they can change, they are quite stable and therefore are often carried over into adult relationships, such as marriage or friendship.

People with secure attachment styles tend to show trust in their attachment figures – they seek their company and support, especially during stressful times. The attachment figures, in turn, serve as their "safe haven" and a "secure base" in an uncertain and dangerous world. In particular, people with secure attachments tend to have a positive attitude towards both themselves and those around them. They are comfortable with their interdependence with other people; they freely and easily show love, trust, intimacy and warmth in relationships with their attachment figures and other close people.

---

16. John Bowlby, *Attachment and Loss: Attachment*, Second edition, Vol. 1 (Tavistock Institute of Human Relations: Basic Books, 1982); see also John Bowlby, *Attachment and Loss: Separation*, Vol. 2 (New York: Basic Books, 1973); John Bowlby, *Attachment and Loss: Loss*, Vol. 3 (New York: Basic Books, 1980); Mary Ainsworth, Timothy Clinton, Harry Sibsy, Cynthia Hazan, Philip Shaver, and others further developed and improved this theory. In order to learn more about the essence of attachment theory from a Christian perspective, we recommend Timothy E. Clinton and Gary Sibcy, *Attachments: Why You Love, Feel and Act the Way You Do* (Brentwood: Integrity Publishers, 2002), 166.

The ambivalent-anxious (dependent) style of attachment is characterized by a person's negative attitude to the self and positive attitude to others, and the figures of attachment are perceived as unpredictable – warm, loving and reliable at one time, and cold and distant at another. This style of attachment is formed in children when their parents are inconsistent in their attitude towards them: either they show care, which is often close to overprotectiveness, or they show disapproval, anger and indifference, especially when the child expresses his or her opinion or disagreement. As a result, such children become insecure, preoccupied with feelings of their own unworthiness and inferiority, having a constant need for approval from others. The real problem comes when such people bring this over-dependence into adult relationships, and demand approval of their own worth from their loved ones. These demands of affirmation become quite a burden for their loved ones who then react by rejecting such people and their demands.

In contrast, people with an avoidant attachment style tend to deny their need or desire for emotional closeness and suppress their true deep impulses to protect themselves. They believe they are self-sufficient and invulnerable, and that other people are neither reliable nor worthy of their full trust. In relationships they are constantly emotionally cold and distant. As a rule, this style is formed in children brought up in insensitive family conditions, with overly strict, demanding caregivers who are indifferent to or suppress the feelings of the child.

Finally, there is a disorganized or chaotic attachment style, which is a combination of the two. It is characterized by a person's negative attitude both towards the self and other people, as well as by fear and confusion. This style of attachment is often formed in children who were brought up in abusive and violent family conditions, when parents, due to their, for example, abuse of alcohol and/or drugs, failed to provide the basic needs of children for love and care. Naturally, such children become used to shying away from intimacy because of mistrust and fear, and are afraid of those very people from whom they seek security and protection. As adults, they tend to question their own and others' sense of worth. As a result, this completely disorganizes their ideas about love and security in the world and puts their interpersonal relationships into chaos.

This theory is of particular interest to us because its developers established a connection between the attachment styles of people in interpersonal relationships, and loneliness.[17] Their conclusions are consistent with the results of our recent study, the purpose of which was to determine the level and types of loneliness among Christians in Ukraine.[18] In particular, those able to form secure attachments were significantly less lonely, of any type without exception, whereas those who had any of the insecure attachment styles experienced much greater loneliness. Thus, we can conclude that Christians who have the secure attachment style in relationships with other significant people are generally less prone to experiencing loneliness.

2. Using attachment theory to explain spiritual loneliness

After studying attachment theory for the first time, a new thought came to me (Valeriia): what if we try to apply its main conclusions to the relationship between humans and God? After studying the issue in more detail, I found that this was not at all as original as I thought; others had researched and developed it before me.[19] As it turned out, a certain group of researchers did see that some aspects of religiosity, such as a person's close relationship with God, can best be described in terms of attachment theory.[20] These researchers suggested that in the intimate relationship between people and God there are all the criteria necessary for healthy attachment: the desire for closeness with the figure of attachment, the perception of God as a "safe haven" in times of need or danger, and a "secure base" that provides freedom of choice and all the necessary resources for life. For example, researchers Lee Kirkpatrick and Philip Shaver in their article "Attachment Theory and Religion" argue that in most Christian traditions, God is conceptualized as an adequate attachment figure.[21] Empirical evidence that most Christians see God as a figure of attachment can be found

---

17. See: Phillip R. Shaver and Cynthia Hazan, "Adult Romantic Attachment: Theory and Evidence," in *Advances in Personal Relationships*, eds. W. Jones and D. Perlman, Vol. 4 (London: Jessica Kingsley, 1992), 300.

18. The survey was conducted in 2019–2020, in which 333 respondents, representatives of different Christian denominations throughout Ukraine, took part.

19. Our main ideas about the connection between attachment theory and religiosity are presented in the article "Attachment to God as a Deterrent against Loneliness," which is partially reproduced here. Valeriia Chornobai, "Attachment to God as a Deterrent against Loneliness," *Modern Science – Moderní věda* 1 (2018): 79–85.

20. Matt Bradshaw, Christopher G. Ellison, Jack P. Marcum, "Attachment to God, Images of God, and Psychological Distress in a Nationwide Sample of Presbyterians," *The International Journal for the Psychology of Religion* 20.2 (2010): 131.

21. Lee Kirkpatrick and Philip Shaver, "Attachment Theory and Religion: Childhood Attachments, Religious Beliefs, and Conversion," *Journal for the Scientific Study of Religion* (1990): 329.

in other scholarly writings. For example, a study by Kenneth Pargament and colleagues (1988) showed that during times of stress and difficulty people usually turn to God for help.[22] This behavior of a believer, which seeks intimacy with God as someone more powerful and at the same time loving, can clearly serve as an example of the security function in attachment. Scholars have even tried to measure attachment styles in the relationship between people and God by developing questionnaires. An example of such a method is the Attachment to God Inventory, a questionnaire developed by Angie MacDonald and Richard Beck in 2004.[23]

From our point of view, a lack of secure attachment to God indicates that a Christian is experiencing spiritual loneliness to some degree. What do we mean by spiritual loneliness – what are its main features and the criteria by which one could recognize it? We define spiritual loneliness as a lack of a sense of connection and closeness with God. How might we determine how close a Christian is to God? Surprisingly, our research shows that it is not so much a Christian's doctrinal beliefs or manifestations of outward religiosity (participation in church services, the number of hours spent in prayer or reading Scripture, etc.) that determine the quality and closeness of a believer's relationship with God. Indeed, as researchers Zahl and Gibson aptly noted, what Christians *should believe* about God and what they personally *really experience* in their relationship with him can be very different in practice.[24] It seems that there is a connection between Christians' representations of God and their style of attachment to him.

We will turn to the description and examples of all types of loneliness in more detail in the next chapter. At this point, having made a very short review of various philosophical, theological, sociological, and psychological approaches to understanding the nature and causes of loneliness, we can see

---

22. Kenneth Pargament, Joseph Kennell, William Hathaway, Nancy Grevengoed, Jon Newman, and Wendy Jones, "Religion and the Problem-Solving Process: Three Styles of Coping," *Journal for the Scientific Study of Religion* 27.1 (1988): 90–104, https://doi: 10.2307/1387404.

23. For further information, see Richard Beck and Angie McDonald, "The Attachment to God Inventory, Tests of Working Model Correspondence, and an Exploration of Faith Group Differences," *Journal of Psychology and Theology* 32.2 (2004): 92–103.

24. Bonnie Poon Zahl and Nicholas J. S. Gibson, "God Representations, Attachment to God, and Satisfaction with Life: A Comparison of Doctrinal and Experiential Representations of God in Christian Young Adults," *International Journal for the Psychology of Religion* 22.3 (2012): 225. See also: Beck and McDonald, "Attachment to God Inventory," 100.

that it is a multidimensional phenomenon that can manifest itself in several aspects of a person's life.[25]

3. Types of loneliness

In the most general sense, loneliness is a break in relationships. As mentioned before, it can manifest itself in three dimensions. First, in a person's relationship with another close person, with groups of people, or the whole of society; second, it is a break of a person's relationship with the self; and third, with God. The following main types of loneliness can be distinguished: social, emotional, cultural, existential, and spiritual.

The first type – the *social* or, as it is often called, the communicative type of loneliness – is a consequence of deprivation of meaningful communication at the level of understanding ideas. A person can experience such loneliness when there is no communication with the usual circle of friends, relatives or church, as well as during a more or less lengthy stay among strangers or almost-strangers. It is this kind of loneliness that a newcomer to a group most often experiences. This type of loneliness can be accompanied by cultural loneliness, which we will talk about below, in the case of a long-term business trip to an unknown area, or moving abroad, when new social ties have not yet been formed, and the cultural norms are unfamiliar, alien or unacceptable for a person.

Emotional or intimate loneliness arises when there is an absence or a break of deep emotional or intimate ties with another significant person or several close people. It comes from the lack of a sense of heartfelt understanding, unity, and emotional closeness, sometimes even despite communication with these closest people. The term "intimate loneliness" is used here not in the sense of sexual intimacy, but rather in the sense of friendship and affection. Thus, emotional loneliness is not the same as social loneliness. Indeed, there is a difference between the feeling of loneliness experienced by a newly widowed woman and that of a newly married couple when they miss their friends. In the first case, it is emotional loneliness associated with emptiness and loss, and in the second, it is communicative, akin to boredom.

---

25. It would be fair to note that the concept of loneliness as a multidimensional phenomenon is not supported by all scholars. Among the opponents of this theory are L. Peplau, D. Russell, D. Perlman, K. Cutrona, and others.

We can also distinguish the *cultural* – or prophetic – type of loneliness.[26] This is a feeling of a person's alienation from cultural and social values, and of deep dissatisfaction with the society the person is considered to be part of. Such an experience of alienation and rejection of social norms is to a certain extent a part of the life of almost all biblical prophets, reformers, creative initiators, philosophers, and fighters for justice. This internal rejection of the cultural and social norms of the era is expressed by a person either in attempts to change society or in an attempt to psychologically or physically "withdraw" from it. Historically, the extreme examples of the latter have been monasticism and anchoritic life. Later we will discuss this at greater length.

Often a person's rejection of the existing social and cultural values and norms subsequently causes a backlash of mutual rejection of this person by society, which itself excludes and rejects such a person, depriving the person of the opportunity to communicate or even belong to the community. In this case, the person will experience partial or complete isolation, which can be in the form of exile, ostracism, exclusion from the church, rejection by a group of peers, and the like. Such rejection and isolation on society's part may be justified and even necessary, provided they are a response to man's sinful nature, rather than a reaction to the man's calling from God to "go against the tide." For example, it can take the form of solitary confinement of the offender.

Social, emotional, and cultural types of loneliness can be called "loneliness in a crowd" because these types of loneliness can arise even when a person is surrounded by people, yet lacks deep connection and understanding with them. Perhaps precisely because of being surrounded by people, the person experiences loneliness even more.[27]

There is also *existential* loneliness, which we define as a person's loss of a sense of harmony, a loss of unity with oneself and nature, a kind of self-alienation or isolation from oneself. A person can experience such existential loneliness in the form of disappointment in life, or lack of understanding of the meaning and purpose of life. Accordingly, the more a person becomes aware of a fundamental "otherness," one's uniqueness, place and role, and identity from God, the less existential loneliness that person experiences.

---

26. Бердяев, *Я и Мир Объектов* [Berdyaev, Me and the World of Objects], 23.

27. Гузалия Р. Шагивалеева, "Культурологическое и Психологическое Понимание Феномена Одиночества," *Концепт*, Спецвыпуск 1 (2013) [Guzaliya R. Shagivaleeva, "Culturological and Psychological Understanding of the Loneliness Phenomenon," Concept, Special Issue 1 (2013)]: 10.

Finally, there is *spiritual* or metaphysical loneliness, which is a break in a person's relationship with God, a lack of connection and trust, and a feeling of being abandoned by God. According to Berdyaev, not everyone experiences this type of loneliness, but only the one who has come to realization that "the depth of human existence is spiritual." Berdyaev continues: "Only in this depth loneliness, which can be a sign of this depth, is overcome."[28] This desire, this longing for God that no other person can fill, is felt because this place is intended only for God to dwell in. St. Augustine said about this experience that "the whole life of a good Christian is a holy desire . . . so God, by deferring our hope, stretches our desire; by the desiring, stretches the mind; by stretching, makes it more capacious. Let us desire, therefore, my brethren, for we shall be filled."[29] Although we all as Christians will experience this longing for God while here on earth, such loneliness in our hearts in some cases may indicate a certain problem in our relationship with God, and perhaps a disappointment with faith. We can also assume that spiritual loneliness may spill over into existential loneliness, because faith and relationship with God are factors that give the life of a believer coherence and guidance for most Christians. Speaking about his experience of overcoming existential loneliness by faith, Berdyaev emphasizes: "My loneliness is overcome because there is God. God is my victory over loneliness, the fullness and meaning of my existence."[30]

Sometimes loneliness is perceived by some people as a positive even desirable state to which they voluntarily strive (for example, solitude or monastic life). However, in essence, neither solitude nor monasticism is loneliness and does not cause a feeling of loneliness if chosen by a person voluntarily and consciously. So, loneliness and solitude are not interchangeable concepts. In this case, solitude has a positive flavor for the person, and it is a desirable and sometimes even necessary step since it is associated with several positive therapeutic effects, which will be discussed in more detail in the following sections of the book. There is also involuntary, compulsory even forced conditions that elicit loneliness. Examples of such can be compulsory isolation, expulsion, punishment in the form of solitary confinement, quarantine due to some infectious disease, and the like. These conditions almost always cause loneliness, negative feelings, anguish, and suffering.

---

28. Бердяев, *Я и Мир Объектов* [Berdyaev, Me and the World of Objects], 116.

29. St. Augustine, "Homily 4 on the First Epistle of John," in *Nicene and Post-Nicene Fathers*, trans. H. Browne, ed. Philip Schaff, Kevin Knight, Vol. 7 (Buffalo: Christian Literature Publishing Co., 1888), <http://www.newadvent.org/fathers/170204.htm>.

30. Бердяев, *Я и Мир Объектов* [Berdyaev, Me and the World of Objects], 113.

The duration of loneliness can also differ. It can be short-term, situational, or chronic loneliness. Loneliness for some can be like an unexpected guest that comes and quickly goes away; while for others it can settle and make its dwelling for years. It is believed that short-term and situational kinds of loneliness most often occur due to life circumstances (moving to another city, divorce, death of a spouse), while chronic loneliness originates in the person him or herself.

It is important to note that, practically, these types and forms of loneliness are often combined, and we can experience them in the social, emotional, cultural, spiritual, and existential realms simultaneously.[31] For example, based on several scientific studies, it has been proven that the suffering of people due to chronic loneliness is associated for them with existential loneliness – disappointment due to the absence of a clear goal and understanding of their purpose in life; or spiritual loneliness, that is, a feeling of a split in relationships with God. Loneliness becomes especially unbearable when a person experiences it chronically and in several dimensions at once. The more broken ties with the outside world and the self a person experiences, the sharper the feeling of loneliness. Conversely, strong, satisfying connections at all levels lead to the fullest disclosure of holistic personality traits. A threat to such connections gives rise to suffering from loneliness.

In real life it is not always possible for a person to maintain balance and be satisfied with relationships in all areas. We can, of course, argue about this, but as we study the Bible, we notice that the more people understand their destiny, vocation, and close relationship with God, the more this leads to a split in their relationships with the mainstream of society as a whole.[32] We notice such events unfolding in the life of almost all the prophets and Christ himself. Thus, we can assume that solving the problem of existential and spiritual loneliness in the life of an individual can sometimes lead to an intensification of cultural and social loneliness. Conversely, a person's excellent relationships with other people, which imply no cultural and social loneliness, do not guarantee a lack of existential and spiritual loneliness.

As you can see, loneliness has a multi-faceted nature. The experience of loneliness by a person may well be simultaneous in several dimensions,

---

31. Елена А. Мазуренко, "Одиночество как Феномен Индивидуальной и Социальной Жизни" (Автореф. дисс., Архангельск: Поморский государственный университет имени М. В. Ломоносова, 2006) [Elena A. Mazurenko, "Loneliness as a Phenomenon of Individual and Social Life," (Abstract diss., Arkhangelsk: Pomorsky State University named after M.V. Lomonosov, 2006)], 22.

32. See for instance: Matt 10:34–35; 2 Tim 3:12.

in the social, emotional, and spiritual realms of life, and mutually influence each other. At the individual level, loneliness is generated by a person's loss or confusion about the meaning of life, and at the social level by dissatisfaction with communication.[33]

Below we will try to outline the "terminological shores," that is, to give a definition of "loneliness" and some other related concepts.

4. What loneliness looks like and what it is not

From the previous brief review of various scientific approaches to the study of loneliness, we see this topic considered from two sides: as an objective reality of one's physical and social separation and as a subjective awareness of one's loneliness. Moreover, sometimes loneliness is perceived as a necessary and even desirable condition and sometimes as a painful inner experience, accompanied by suffering, various mental disorders, and other problems. In our opinion, people have such an ambiguous, sometimes polarized perception of loneliness not only because of the complex nature of the phenomenon itself but also because there is a certain confusion in understanding what is meant by loneliness. For example, until the mid-twentieth century, loneliness was considered primarily as a physical state of complete or partial isolation, and so there is still a confusion of the concepts of "solitude" and "loneliness" in the literature on this issue. Therefore, it is necessary to define clearer boundaries, highlighting the difference between loneliness, solo-living, retreat, solitude, hermitage, isolation, alienation, and deprivation.

Let us start our analysis by defining isolation. The Merriam-Webster Dictionary gives the following definition: "to isolate is to set apart from others." "An isolate" means an individual socially withdrawn or removed from society," deprived of the possibility to contact or communicate with others (speaking of infectious patients, prisoners, etc.) – which is identical to quarantine.[34] The *Encyclopaedia of Sociology* complements this definition by emphasizing that isolation "is characterized by a minimum of social contacts and a maximum of social distance concerning the rest of the society" or community.[35]

---

33. Елена Мазуренко, "Одиночество как Феномен Индивидуальной и Социальной Жизни"[Elena Mazurenko, "Loneliness as a Phenomenon of Individual and Social Life"], 22.

34. "Isolate," Merriam Webster Dictionary, accessed December 6, 2022, https://www.merriam-webster.com/dictionary/isolate.

35. "Энциклопедия Социологии," Академик ["Encyclopedia of Sociology," Academician], accessed August 8, 2019, https://dic.academic.ru/dic.nsf/socio/1177.

Isolation can be absolute or complete (the kind of sensory deprivation when a person is totally deprived of contact with the outside world) – for example in the situation of Robinson Crusoe, or imprisonment in solitary confinement. Isolation can also be partial. It can be expulsion from the community, excommunication, or involve certain types of occupation (such as a seafarer). Isolation is close to deprivation, which is generally understood as "the state of being kept from possessing, enjoying, or using something significant."[36] Thus, social loneliness as a lack of communication is social deprivation.

Note that social and cultural types of loneliness differ from complete isolation. In the case of social and cultural loneliness there are people within reach, so interaction or communication with them is lacking due to an inability to communicate or unwillingness to understand each other. Perhaps in the conditions of global social isolation and distancing which have swept the whole world as a forced measure to prevent the spread and aggravation of the COVID-19 pandemic, social loneliness is the most common and widespread type of loneliness.

Further, note that the nature of isolation mainly depends on what meaning a person gives to this state. It is usually assumed that isolation is involuntary and compulsory, and so, painful. That is why it is still used as a form of punishment in most pedagogical and penitentiary practices. Indeed, through all human history, it seems there was no greater punishment than by forced isolation, expulsion, and deprivation of communication.[37] Such punishment for violation of the basic church dogmas or norms occurred in the form of anathema and excommunication, which would leave a person outside the community, depriving the person of communication with others. Likewise, at the state level, imprisonment or a prohibition to reside in a certain area was applied for violation of certain laws. In many family traditions, isolation of children is in the form of a temporary prohibition to move around the room. We probably all know phrases such as: "Time out!" Or "You won't go out until you do your homework!" Such punishment is very common and often quite effective. All these forms of punishment are types of isolation because they mean the complete, if short-term, separation from the usual social circle, from the level of culture, or various benefits or conveniences.

---

36. "Deprivation," Merriam Webster Dictionary, accessed December 6, 2022, https://www.merriam-webster.com/dictionary/deprivation.

37. Игорь С. Кон, *Многоликое Одиночество, Популярная Психология, Хрестоматия* (М.: Prosveshchenye, 1990) [Igor S. Kon, Many Faces of Loneliness, Popular Psychology, Reader (Moscow: Enlightenment, 1990)], 162–70.

In this regard, it is important to note that isolation is related to alienation. While isolation is society's rejection of the unacceptable or threatening behavior of its members, alienation is a person's internal emotional reaction, the inability to accept the norms and values adopted in the society, and rejection of other people or society as a whole. By definition, alienation is a break of the original unity between something whole and its part. Such a gap leads to the impoverishment of the whole and the degeneration of its alienated part or function.[38] In this sense, alienation is akin to cultural loneliness, which is characterized by internal rejection and the break of the person's initial unity with the society and its norms of which this person is considered to be a part, which leads to the impoverishment of the society.

On the other hand, from the end of the twentieth century, philosophers began to pay special attention to the topic of human alienation from oneself, when a person, deprived of some essential characteristics, seems to lose his or her nature or "humanity."[39]

Returning to the concept of isolation, let us try to distinguish between isolation and loneliness. In a general sense, we understand loneliness as an acute negative experience of a real or imagined split or absence of significant connections, which leads an individual to dissatisfaction with his or her relationships with significant other people, with the self and with God. In contrast to isolation, which is an objective, externally conditioned, and somewhat more controllable state, loneliness is a subjective inner experience. They are not identical concepts. It is no secret that many people felt the loneliest not in isolation, but in some kind of community, even with family or friends. On the other hand, history knows many Christians who, being strictly isolated, persecuted, imprisoned, and rejected for their faith, nonetheless did not feel lonely, finding comfort and peace of mind in close fellowship with God.

It is important to emphasize a significant difference between isolation and solitude. They are similar because both solitude and isolation most often

---

38. Александр А. Ивин, ред., *Философия: Энциклопедический Словарь* (М: Гардарики, 2004) [Alexander A. Ivin, ed., Philosophy: Encyclopedic Dictionary (Moscow: Gardariki, 2004)], accessed August 25, 2019, https://dic.academic.ru/dic.nsf/enc_philosophy/890.

39. Ивин. The main indicator of such self-alienation, according to Professor Alexander Ivin, are the following dominants in the worldview of a modern person: a sense of powerlessness when the future seems to be totally out of control of the individual; meaninglessness and the irrationality of a human's existence; perception of the reality as a world in which people's mutual obligations to adhere to certain social norms and values have been lost; loneliness, "detachment" of a person from existing social ties, i.e. marginalization of a person in society; the loss of the individual's "true I" and identity disorder. In our opinion, all of the above are signs of existential loneliness.

mean a person is alone, not in the presence of other people. But solitude is a temporary avoidance or restriction of communication, motivated by the individual's voluntary desire to be completely alone or with certain people only. Thus, an important feature that separates solitude from isolation is the will of a person. Therefore solitude is most often associated with positive feelings. It is for many a desirable state, for which they voluntarily and consciously strive, which is necessary for a person's healthy development.

One of the modern forms of solitude is the retreat, which is a short period of personal or group withdrawal for spiritual or psychological work on oneself in a calm and safe atmosphere, a time for rest and study. Such spiritual practice is used in many religions. In Christianity in particular it is a time of fasting, prayer, focusing on spiritual issues, contemplation, and avoiding trivial life to meet with God and to restore peace of mind and balance.

A more radical form of solitude is a hermitage, which is the voluntary and complete renunciation or avoidance of relationships with people. It is about living alone, avoiding secular affairs and the physical separation of a person from life in society for some higher, often religious purpose.[40] A synonym for hermit is anchorite (from the Greek *ana* "to the side" and *choreo* "I am going"). The word "hermit" is derived from the Greek meaning "solitary" or "living in the desert," that is, a person who for some religious reasons spends his or her life separately, in complete solitude. From the end of the third century Christian hermits began to settle in Egypt and the surrounding desert lands. Some of them (for example, St. Anthony the Great, Pachomius and St. Basil the Great) had considerable influence, attracting pilgrims and popularizing ascetic and monastic life.[41] Hermitage or the ascetic desert life, it seems, never lost its popularity, from the time of ancient Christianity in the fourth century when it became widespread, till now, especially among representatives of the Catholic and the Eastern Orthodox Church.

We may wonder whether such practice of solitude, and even more so, hermitic life, contributes to loneliness. After all, a person deprives him or herself of the most elementary thing – communication with one's own kind! Thomas Merton, a famous modern Catholic Trappist monk of the twentieth century, pays much attention to the role of solitude in the hermit life. In his

---

40. "Hermit," Oxford Learner's Dictionary, accessed December 6, 2022, https://www.oxfordlearnersdictionaries.com/definition/english/hermit.

41. See: Сергій В. Санніков, *Популярна Історія Християнства. Двадцять Століть у Дорозі* (К: Самміт-Книга, 2012) [Serhii V. Sannikov, Popular History of Christianity. Twenty Centuries on the Road (Kyiv: Summit-Knyga, 2012)], 83, 96, 117.

"Philosophy of Solitude," he assures us that the solitary life must also be a life of prayer and meditation if it is to be authentically Christian. He continues:

> solitude, the riches of his [the hermit's] emptiness . . . is simply an established fact . . . In fact, it is inescapable. It is everything. It contains God, surrounds him in God . . . He is lost in God and lost to himself. He is never far enough away from God to see Him in perspective, or as an object. He is swallowed up in Him, and therefore so to speak never sees Him at all.[42]

Note that in his essay, Thomas Merton perceives solitude both as a fact of being and as a necessity for everyone who has completely devoted him or herself to God. The well-known Christian historian Sergei Sannikov believes that the rapid development of the hermit form of monasticism was caused by the protest of many Christians against the secularization of the church of that time.[43] Suppose the motive for this avoidance of society is the protest of an individual Christian against certain socio-cultural norms or values. If so, such solitude can also be considered an external manifestation of internal cultural loneliness. However, the last part of this book will discuss more the connection between the hermitic way of life as one of the forms of solo living and celibacy with loneliness.

Conclusion to part 1

Having made a brief analysis of the closely related concepts of loneliness, retreat, solitude, recluse, isolation, alienation, and deprivation, we can draw several conclusions.

First, loneliness is a multidimensional phenomenon that is rooted in a deficit of an individual's emotional, socio-cultural, cognitive and spiritual connections with the outside world, which is accompanied by suffering, sadness, oppression, and anxiety. Accordingly, we identified the following types of loneliness: emotional (or intimate), communicative (or social), cultural (or prophetic), existential, and spiritual. Usually, loneliness is a subjective inner state or experience that does not always coincide with the external circumstances of a person's social isolation.

---

42. Thomas Merton, *Disputed Questions* (New York: Farrar, Straus and Cudahy, 1960), 202–203.

43. Сергій Санніков, *Популярна Історія Християнства* [Serhii Sannikov, Popular History of Christianity], 83, 96, 117.

Second, loneliness is practically independent of solitude. These concepts are not identical and therefore are not interchangeable. As L. Svendsen puts it, it is not so important who or how many other people surround you, but what is your emotional connection with those others.[44] "It's not good to be alone and lonely," a well-known proverb says; but it is even worse to be among other people, and still lonely. It turns out that the quality of social relationships is more important than their quantity.[45]

Third, loneliness is often perceived negatively as generating suffering, while solitude, on the contrary, is usually seen as desirable and necessary for the best functioning of a person. As Anthony Storr argues, the capacity for solitude is a valuable resource: "Learning, thinking, innovation, and maintaining contact with one's own inner world are all facilitated by solitude."[46] Solitude can be accompanied by loneliness; however, loneliness is overcome more easily when solitude is a result of a person's free choice.[47]

Fourth, we can conclude that there is a positive aspect to loneliness itself. As a rule, people tend to enjoy spending time with others more than alone because they are unable to use effectively the opportunities that are provided by solitude. Even so, loneliness has its own advantages, since it drives a person to seek communication, love and close relationships with other people. Thus, loneliness, on the one hand, helps us reassess our values and be aware of how much we need other people; on the other hand, it creates an excellent opportunity for understanding our own uniqueness, difference and identity. This is true provided that loneliness does not become chronic.

Now let us turn to the nature of human loneliness as found in the pages of Holy Scripture.

---

44. Свендсен, *Філософія Самотності* [Svendsen, A Philosophy of Loneliness], 25.

45. See: Harry T. Reis, "The Role of Intimacy in Interpersonal Relations," *Journal of Social and Clinical Psychology* 9.1 (1990) 15–30, https://doi.org/10.1521/jscp.1990.9.1.15.

46. It allows you to improve communication with others, better understand your own feelings, accept some kind of loss or defeat, and change your attitude towards certain circumstances in your life. Anthony Storr, *Solitude* (London: Flamingo, 1989), 28.

47. Мазуренко, "Одиночество как Феномен Индивидуальной и Социальной Жизни" [Mazurenko, "Loneliness as a Phenomenon of Individual and Social Life"], 23.

2

God Is Not Lonely.
Why Should We Be?

The question of loneliness as a feeling of alienation from God and other people, from the biblical point of view, is as old as humanity itself. It is rooted in the history of the creation of the world.

1. The relational nature of God

As we read the Bible carefully we find communication, unity, and interaction from the very first lines of Genesis. The notion of a relational God, seen in the interaction of all three persons of the Trinity, is traced in the process of the creation of the world, from which we conclude that loneliness is not something inherent in God.[1] The first verse of the first chapter of Genesis says: "In the beginning, God created the heavens and the earth . . ." (*bereshith bara Elohim*).[2] An interesting detail, which may escape readers unfamiliar with the original language, is the use of the general word "God" (Hebrew *elohim*), a plural noun, in combination with the verb "created" (Hebrew *bara*) in the singular. Since the time of the church fathers, theologians have seen in this peculiarity the

---

1. As Razumovsky puts it, relationality is a basic condition for existence, a feature, and a common property of all objects that are able to reflect the other in them. Without it and outside of it there is no world, no movement, no space, no time, and no knowledge. See: Олег С. Разумовский, "Реляционизм и Изоляционизм: Пролог к Теории Систем," *Полигнозис* 4 (1999) [Oleg S. Razumovsky, "Relationism and Isolationism: A Prologue to Systems Theory," Polygnosis 4 (1999)]: 1–30.

2. All passages from the Old Testament in the original language are cited according to the Leningrad Code of the Old Testament (WTT) in the ESV translation unless otherwise indicated separately.

first indication of the multiple persons of the Godhead and a foreshadowing of the doctrine of the Trinity.[3]

The modern era, however, largely rejected the viewpoint that the author of Genesis was trying to reflect the Trinitarian nature of God's essence. One of the explanations for this grammatical peculiarity was that the use of the plural in relation to God was a polite form of "we" as in addressing earthly rulers. But, according to the prominent exegetes and experts of ancient Jewish texts, Karl Keil and Franz Delitzsch, such explanation has no confirmation in other texts of Scripture.[4]

A similar Trinitarian idea can be traced in verse 26 of the same chapter of Genesis: "Then God said, 'Let *us* make man in our image, after *our* likeness.'" Likewise, it uses the word *elohim* together with the verb "said" in the singular and the verb "let us make" in the plural, and in addition, the pronoun "our" in the plural. There are interesting interpretations of such vocabulary. Some commentators (for example, Aben Ezra, Franz Delitzsch and Philo of Alexandria) believe that here "God takes counsel with the angels" or with the earth (Moshe B. Maimonides), or with himself (Markus Kalisch).[5] The idea that God is consulting here with angels or the earth, however, is unlikely. Karl Barth in *Church Dogmatics* asserts that whoever is addressed in the phrase "make man in our image," he must share the image and likeness of God, and no one else. However, the exaltation of angels or any other creature to such a high level of God is unacceptable in Scripture.[6] The notion that God here consults with himself is also questionable because in similar passages of Scripture concerning God we see the use of a pronoun and a verb in the singular.[7] So in our opinion, taking into account the unity of the books of the Bible and the absence of such ideas in other places in Scripture, these passages should be

---

3. Among them, for example, Irenaeus of Lyons, Theophilus of Antioch, Justin. Also, of a similar view was M. Luther, J. Calvin, J. Cocceius, P. Lombard, R.S. Candlish, et al. "Genesis," *The Pulpit Commentary*, Electronic Database, accessed January 17, 2018, http://biblehub.com/commentaries/pulpit/genesis/1.htm.

4. See Carl F. Keil and Franz Delitzsch, "Commentary on Genesis," *Keil and Delitzsch Old Testament Commentary* (1854–1889), accessed August 31, 2019, https://www.studylight.org/commentaries/kdo/genesis-1.html.

5. *The Pulpit Commentary*, "Genesis."

6. Karl Barth, *Church Dogmatics, The Doctrine of Creation*, Vol. 3, Part 1. The Work of Creation, transl., J. W. Edwards, O. Bussey, H. Knight, ed. G. W. Bromiley, T. F. Torrance (London: T&T Clark International, 1958), 192.

7. See for example: Genesis 18:17, Hosea 11:8 etc. For a more detailed analysis of the various Old Testament passages that use the plural in relation to God (Genesis 3:22; 11:7, for instance), see David T. Williams, "Who Will Go for Us? (Is.6:8): The Divine Plurals and the Image of God," *Old Testament Essays* 12, 1 (1999): 173–90.

understood as expressing for the first time a unique interaction between the persons of the Godhead in the process of creation. Commenting on this passage from Genesis, Karl Barth believes that it is a shadow of the Christian Trinitarian doctrine – a picture of God, who is one and only of his kind, yet who for this very reason is not alone, but includes the differences and relationships between me and you.[8]

This notion that God, existing in three persons, is one but not alone, is very important, although it is not consistently supported by all theologians. In particular, Wesley Wildman, professor of religious studies at Boston University, considers it impossible to draw the exceptional conclusion that loneliness is not part of the nature of God.[9] However, most Christians traditionally believe that God is triune in nature, and that all the persons of the Trinity from eternity shared communication in love, eternal dynamics in their differences, and participation in the actions of each other.

It is impossible to reflect fully everything that Scripture reveals to us about relationships within the Trinity even in a separate book, let alone a single chapter. Nevertheless, we will mention in passing that the interaction of the persons is reflected not only in the process of creation but also in the fact that "the Spirit searches everything, even the depths of God" (1 Cor 2:10); and the Spirit is God who expects to be worshiped "in Spirit and truth" (John 4:23). The Spirit of the Lord is called the "Spirit of truth" proceeding from the Father (John 15:26), the Spirit of wisdom and understanding, counsel and might, knowledge, and the fear of the Lord (Isa 11:2), he is sent by the Son, comes from the Father, testifies of the Son, and glorifies the Son (John 16:14). Just like the Son, the Spirit glorifies the Father, and the Father glorifies the Son (John 12:28; 17:1, 5).

In trying to comprehend and find proper words to describe the nature of one God in three persons, the early church fathers, beginning with the Cappadocians, used the Greek word "perichoresis" which means "rotation." The term "perichoresis" was always understood by the church as "mutual penetration without loss of individuality." Protestant theologian Jürgen

---

8. Karl Barth, *Church Dogmatics*, 192. Much depends on how the notion that God is one is understood. As Robert E. Harman puts it: "The Hebrew of the Old Testament has two words for 'one': 'yacheed' means an absolute one while 'echad' means a compound one, as in one cluster of grapes. When the oneness of God is written about, the word used is 'echad,' for instance in Deut.6:4, 'The LORD our God is one LORD.'" See Robert Harman, *One Sure Thing: The Power of a Life Grounded in Assurance* (Williamsburg: Wellhouse Publishers, 2016), 17.

9. Wesley J. Wildman, "In Praise of Loneliness," in *Loneliness: Boston University Studies in Philosophy and Religion*, Vol. 19, ed. Leroy S. Rouner (Indiana: University of Notre Dame, 1998), 35.

Moltmann considered that the interpenetration and communication of the Persons of the Holy Trinity implied their participation in the actions of each other. He wrote: "Perichoresis denotes that . . . by virtue of their eternal love, Divine Persons exist so intimately *with* one another, *for* one another and *in* one another, that they constitute themselves in their unique, incomparable and complete unity."[10]

The Eastern tradition goes even further in defining divine relationships in the Trinity. One of the most influential modern Orthodox theologians, metropolitan John Zizioulas, suggests understanding the very essence of God as a communion of three divine persons, arguing that "there is no true substance without communion."[11] So, according to Zizioulas, communion is a part of the essence of God. Each of the persons of the Trinity does not live for himself, but they interpenetrate and abide in each other. Thus, the being of Triune God is realized as love, in which the individual's own existence is identified with self-giving.[12]

Thus, in God himself there are all the elements to overcome loneliness. In him, there is a distinction in the persons of God which provides eternal dynamics in interaction; proximity, that is, unity and constant longing for communion; and love and harmony in their relationship. The triune God is one, unique, and he has no equal. And he is not lonely. Loneliness becomes impossible due to the fellowship of the equal persons of God. Loneliness is conquered by equality and fellowship.

John Sailhamer follows the same train of thought in his commentary on Genesis saying that: "The divine plurality of persons . . . can be seen as an anticipation of the human plurality of persons reflected in man and woman, thus casting human personal relationships in the role of reflecting God's own personhood."[13] Thus, it can be argued, Scripture indicates to us that God is one, though he is never alone; and communication and interaction between the persons of God are his essential inherent qualities.

---

10. Jürgen Moltmann, *The Trinity and the Kingdom*, trans. Margaret Kohl (San Francisco: Harper and Row, 1981), 175.

11. John D. Zizioulas, "Human Capacity and Human Incapacity: A Theological Exploration of Personhood," *Scottish Journal of Theology* 28.5 (October, 1975): 408.

12. Олег Давыденков, *Догматическое Богословие. Курс Лекций* [Oleg Davydenkov, Dogmatic Theology. Course of Lectures], accessed December 5, 2022, https://azbyka.ru/perixorezis.

13. John H. Sailhamer, *Expositor's Bible Commentary: Genesis*, Vol. 1, ed. T. Longman III, D. E. Garland, rev. ed. (Grand Rapids: Zondervan, 2008), 70. Quoted in Andreas J. Köstenberger, Margaret E. Köstenberger, *God's Design for Man and Woman: a Biblical–Theological Survey* (Wheaton: Crossway, 2014), 29.

Why is this important for us? Because it means that within God himself there is a fellowship, a fellowship the three persons have been enjoying, into which he invites us. These insights on God's nature are essential for a better understanding of the nature of a man who was created to be an image of God, after his likeness. It also helps us understand better the essence of loneliness.

2. The relational nature of humanity

Returning to the biblical text of the first and second chapters of the book of Genesis, we read:

> So God created man in his own image,
>   in the image of God he created him;
> male and female he created them.
>   And God blessed them . . . And God saw everything that
>   he had made, and behold, it was very good. (Gen 1:27,
>   28, 31)

Note that in the creator's own assessment, all of his creation became not just "good," but "very good," once people – not just one man, but a man and a woman – were placed into the world.

The biblical narrative continues: "The Lord God said, 'It is not good for the man to be alone. I will make a helper suitable for him'" (Gen 2:18). There are several views as to why it was not good for a man to be alone. The rabbinic tradition suggests a certain imperfection of a man, his inability to exist without a woman.[14] But given that God's assessment "it is not good for a man to be alone" was in the context of Adam's governing the earth, when there was no suitable assistant for him found, other theologians suggest interpreting God's "not good" from a functional point of view; that is, "ineffective" as to his task to subdue the land. Probably it was not good for a man to be alone because then he would not be able to populate the earth; or because it is just unpleasant, awkward, and abnormal due to his social nature.[15]

Reading the story of the creation of Eve, one gets the impression that the "helper" was given to the man at the initiative of the creator, and not the man himself. It seems that Adam was not against governing the creation by himself. But God, having his purpose in mind, was against it. Keil and Delitzsch agree that "a helper corresponding to him" (Hebrew *ezer kenegdo*) can literally be

---

14. Keil and Delitzsch, "Commentary on Genesis."
15. Keil and Delitzsch, "Commentary on Genesis."

translated as "a helper standing opposite (and sometimes against) him, that is, an appropriate and suitable one."[16] This thought fits with the complementary pairs God has been creating: light and darkness, heavens and earth, sea and dry land, and so on. Apparently, this expression reflects the principle of correspondence: a woman, a future helper, had to have his nature (to be bone from his bone), have a similar yet independent character, be suitable, and in every possible way adapted to be his partner and companion, to fulfill the task assigned by God for both of them.

We agree here with the researchers Andreas and Margaret Köstenberger when they say that the word "helper" (*ezer* in Hebrew) denotes rather the difference in the roles of men and women than a woman's subsidiary role or inferiority of her nature,[17] since the Old Testament repeatedly renders God himself as our helper.[18] Here in the union of the first man and woman, in the unity of two in one, is laid the foundation for the divine institution of marriage, which was subsequently intended for their descendants and which is a reflection of the great mystery, in the words of the apostle Paul – the union of Christ and the church (Eph 5:32). We may also look at these lines a little more broadly, seeing in them an indication of the initial social nature of all persons, created with basic needs of communication and belonging. This social nature of man is a reflection of the divine nature of the triune creator.

If we consider these two narratives about the creation of humanity from the first and second chapters of Genesis as complementary parts of one story, it is obvious that three main ideas form their core: first, the creation of humanity in the image and likeness of God; second, the creation of humanity as sexually differentiated; and third, the creation of humanity as social beings. Each of these thoughts is extremely important and suggests that the original divine plan for a person included communication with both God and with another person.

This raises several questions related to the understanding of loneliness. What of God's image were the social and sexual natures of humans intended to reflect? And if the man was created perfect from the very beginning, before the fall, having a close personal relationship and fellowship with God, why was there the need to create another person, moreover, of a different sex? In other words, was it not enough for Adam to have fellowship with God so as not to feel lonely? Also, is a human's sexuality related to their loneliness? All these questions have to do with human identity.

---

16. Keil and Delitzsch, "Commentary on Genesis."

17. Köstenberger and Köstenberger, *God's Design for Man and Woman*, 36.

18. See: Exod 18:4; Pss 33:20;70:5; 115:9–11; 121:1–2; 146:5 and others.

Roman Catholic theologian Sebastian Moore believes that the creation story from Genesis 2:7 says that first God created a man of indefinite sex (Adam), and then (in verses 22–24 of the same chapter) he "split" him into two sexes: a man (Hebrew *ish*) and a woman (*isha*).[19] From our point of view, however, such an interpretation seems questionable. The biblical text does not show us any change in Adam's secondary or primary sexual characteristics after the "surgery" of a woman's creation. Only the number of his ribs has changed. And the use of the word "Adam," which means "a man" in Hebrew before the creation of Eve, simply indicates that the woman shared the same human nature with the man.

It is quite possible that Adam was not fully aware of his masculine identity and sexuality, as well as his need "not to be alone," until the woman appeared. Theologian Stanley Grenz notes that by describing the modeling of a woman who was greeted by Adam with great enthusiasm, the author reveals the fundamentally sexual nature of his loneliness as an embodied being. Only in the presence of a woman did Adam become able to discern that loneliness was part of him as a sexual being.[20] Obviously, here Grenz is referring to the emotional loneliness of Adam, which according to the perfect plan of God the creator, should dissolve with the appearance of a woman corresponding to Adam. So, Grenz continues, sexuality is closely related to the social nature of human existence.[21]

And yet, why did God decide to create people in this way – of two sexes – male and female? For reproduction, you may answer. But couldn't God have created people so that they reproduce in some other way, let's say, like plants – by budding!? But he invented intimacy. The story of the creation of the universe ends with the words: "And the man and his wife were both naked and were not ashamed" (Gen 2:25). I wonder if I am the only one who was always surprised by this ending of the story of the creation. "Naked. . . What a happy end!!!" But here the author of Genesis wants to tell us something very important: their nakedness means the power to be seen as they are and accepted, the courage to be vulnerable, and the joy of knowing and being known by others [22] And in this ideal world designed by God, such closeness, complete openness, and trust

---

19. Sebastian Moore, *The Inner Loneliness* (New York: Cross Road, 1982), 58.

20. Stanley J. Grenz, *The Social God and the Relational Self. A Trinitarian Theology on the Imago Dei* (London: Westminster John Knox Press, 2001), 276.

21. Ibid.

22. Rob Toonstra, *Naked and Unashamed: Exploring the Way the Good News of Jesus Transforms Sexuality* (Oro Valley: Doulos Resources, 2014), 27.

on a spiritual, mental, and physical level – were very good because it reflects his essence like nothing else.

Regarding how human sexual nature is called to reflect God, the most popular and traditional viewpoint for Christianity is the belief that the God of the Bible goes beyond gender differences, and, accordingly, gender-role images found in the Bible in relation to him must be understood metaphorically. Karl Barth, in turn, emphasizes that in the very essence of God there is a kind of unity of opposites: "real and harmonious self-expression and self-disclosure; free coexistence and interaction; open communication and reciprocity. Man is an exact copy and echo of this Divine life."[23] Catholic theologian Hans Urs von Balthasar also adds that in the Trinity, as well as in men and women, we "have distance for the sake of intimacy, individuality for the sake of relationship and love, difference for the sake of true unity."[24]

Conclusion to chapter 2

Having analyzed the first chapters of the book of Genesis containing the first examples of human loneliness, we can draw several basic conclusions.

First, a man was created in the likeness of God as a perfect and whole person (Eccl 7:29). The fact that even before the creation of a woman from his rib, Adam had communion with God and was fulfilling his functions of a ruler over creation, indicates that human identity is not limited to the sphere of his sexuality only, but exists in God and has its fulfillment in a God-inspired calling. Sebastian Moore in his book *Inner Loneliness* aptly spoke about human identity as follows: "To a man who is finding God within himself, the woman is not just a mysterious other-half but a person anchored in the eternal."[25] It is possible to find one's identity in God beyond sexuality, as the doctrine of true celibacy explains, which we will explore in more detail in the third chapter of our book.

Secondly, a person's self-awareness, that is, the recognition of uniqueness, creates the desire to be "for-the-other,"[26] because it is only in the presence of this "other" that uniqueness makes sense. Along with this, self-awareness requires

---

23. Barth, *Church Dogmatics*, 185. Quote in: Grenz, *The Social God and the Relational Self*, 297.

24. Hans Urs von Balthasar, *The Theology of Karl Barth*, trans. John Drury (Garden City : Doubleday, 1972), 106.

25. Moore, *The Inner Loneliness*, 59.

26. The term "for-the-other" was borrowed from Moore.

being recognized and accepted by others in communication or interaction. These two basic needs of each person – recognition of uniqueness, and belonging – are inherent human needs given by God, because they reflect the image of God and God's original plan for all humankind.

From this follows the third conclusion: that although initially a man was created in the likeness of God as a whole and complete person, yet he was not a self-sufficient one. We have an internal, innate need to form close bonds, for belonging to our own kind (Gen 2:18). Building such close emotional ties is possible in godly friendships. We think the best way to form such strong intimate emotional ties and have the need for recognition and acceptance met, occurs within the framework of the nuclear family – in a dedicated mutual relationship between a man and a woman, which we usually call marriage. Also, the fact that humans were created as female and male in bodies and will remain such for eternity, indicates that a person's sexuality is a basic integral part of identity. And in the longing for the union of a man and a woman – so similar and different, equal and free, in this dynamic of the unity of opposites – the image and likeness of the creator in people is also manifested and multiplied.

Fourth, the New Testament says that believers in Christ have been given fullness in Christ (Col 2:10; Eph 1:23; John 1:16). It seems to us that this refers to the essence of human identity from a social perspective. It is in Christ, in the last Adam, that Christians as a community of those who belong to him have the opportunity to regain the integrity of their personality, despite gender or status differences, like the first man before the fall, for "There is no . . . male and female, for you are all one in Christ Jesus" (Gal 3:28). In this "fullness," everyone who is "in Christ" has not only everything necessary for salvation, life, and sanctification, but also the fullness of personality, and an understanding of one's role and place in the church, "which is his body, the fullness of him who fills all in all" (Eph 1:23). For Jürgen Moltmann "in Christ" is a social concept. To be in Christ is to have discovered the true community.[27] So, this fullness of human identity "in Christ" is practically realized in the social, relational nature of man.

Although in the Scriptures we find individual cases when the physical needs of people were satisfied through communication with God directly (Moses on Mount Sinai, the prophet Elijah, Jesus in the desert when he fasted for forty days), this was an exception. As a rule, God meets our natural human earthly needs, especially social ones, mainly through another person, friend,

---

27. Jürgen Moltmann, *The Coming of God: Christian Eschatology*, First Edition, transl. by Margaret Kohl (Minneapolis: Fortress Press, 1996), 267.

community, or church. The same idea is reflected in Psalm 68, which asserts that it is God who is "A father to the fatherless, a defender of widows . . . in his holy dwelling. God sets the lonely in families, he leads forth the prisoners with singing" (Ps 67:5–6, NIV). The phrase "God sets the lonely in families" carries the idea of belonging to a family, acquiring the right to settle in the house, to be accepted into the community, protected, and provided for by God himself. For this reason, when people find fellowship with God in friendship, community, and church, then God's plan for us as social beings that can form strong devout spiritual bonds and thus multiply God's image on earth is realized.

Lastly, when these basic human needs are unmet, it causes loneliness. Intimate loneliness, for example, comes with an unfulfilled need for intimate affection, acceptance, and belonging. When we don't understand our identity, our place in the world, or who God is, and we have a distorted image of God in our minds, it leads to the destruction of communication with God and gives rise to a feeling of existential and spiritual loneliness. These types of loneliness, in turn, can cause social loneliness associated with problems in relationships with other people. The biblical narratives to which we turn in the second part of the book perfectly illustrate all types of loneliness. The story of the fall is a vivid example that reveals to us the origins of loneliness.

3

Biblical Narratives of Loneliness

1. Loneliness of sin: spiritual loneliness as a result of the fall and Cain's social isolation

The first two chapters of the book of Genesis tell us about the ideal world in which the first people were created and lived. But as we know, this idyll soon came to an end because of Adam and Eve's sin. The biblical story of the fall is rich in deep themes and meanings that cannot be exhaustively examined within this small volume, but even a brief look can reveal much. For it profoundly shows us how a negative image of God in the minds of people breaks the relationship between them and God, giving rise to human loneliness and isolation. Sebastian Moore describes the story of the fall as "the beginning of cosmic loneliness."[1]

The story begins with satanic deception and the desire of people to possess knowledge and rule independently of God. Talking to Eve, Satan (which in Hebrew means "accuser") uses doubt to undermine her confidence in the good character and intentions of God: "Did God actually say, 'you shall not eat of any tree in the garden'?" (Gen 3:1). Further, we read: "the serpent said to the woman . . . 'For God knows that when you eat of it your eyes will be opened, and you will be like God, knowing good and evil'" (Gen 3:4–5). Note how here Satan is trying to sow in Eve the thought that God is hiding something good from them. "Satan's first attack upon the human race was his sly effort to destroy Eve's confidence in the kindness of God. Unfortunately for her and for us he succeeded too well. From that day, men have had a false conception of God."[2] Further, doubting the good character of God leads to Eve's values changing: "the woman saw that the tree was good for food, and that it was a delight to

---

1. Moore, *The Inner Loneliness*, 67.
2. Aiden W. Tozer, *The Best of A. W. Tozer* (Baker Book House Company, 1980), 120.

31

the eyes, and that the tree was to be desired to make one wise." Eve suddenly saw some special value in the forbidden fruit and, of course, wanted to possess it. This deception automatically led to disobedience, despite the prohibition: "she took of its fruit and ate, and she also gave some to her husband who was with her, and he ate" (Gen 3:6).

As you can see, people's distrust of God is based on their negative image of God, as someone who deprives them of something good. Relationships cannot be built without trust; mistrust always leads to the destruction of relationships, and finally to loneliness. In this biblical story, after their disobedience Adam and Eve begin to see their nakedness, be ashamed, and hide from God. Instead of the promised wisdom that would make them like God, on the contrary they lose this glorious likeness, and with it, the understanding of God as the one who knows everything and is present everywhere.

Christian psychologist Craig Ellison concludes that in the end, the sin of the first people undermined not only their relationship with the creator but also between themselves. He explains:

> Because absolute love requires absolute integrity, Adam and Eve could no longer receive God's love as before. Neither could they give love to God or each other. Their sin made them hide because of shame. Intimacy was crushed because integrity was lost. Right into the present day, sin drives us self-centered people to hide, protect and isolate ourselves from others. Thus, due to our sinful nature, we can no longer allow ourselves to be seen and known for who we really are because who we are is truly shameful.[3]

The narrative of the fall ends with God, who reaches out to take the initiative in restoring communication with people, although it was people who disobeyed God and broke off their relationship with him (Gen 3:8–9). A. W. Tozer once said: "If we think of Him [God] as cold and exacting, we shall find it impossible to love Him, and our lives will be ridden with servile fear."[4] So, we can say that the root cause of sin was a change of the image of God in the minds of people, and the inevitable price for sin was spiritual loneliness as a result of the destruction of trust between us and God, and eventually with other people. In some exceptional cases the payment for sin was social isolation.

---

3. Craig W. Ellison, *Saying Good-Bye to Loneliness and Finding Intimacy* (San Francisco: Harper and Row Publishers, 1983), 48.

4. Aiden W. Tozer, *The Root of the Righteous* (Camp Hill, Pennsylvania: Christian Publishing Inc., 1985), 5.

As we know from the biblical story of the fall, a serious violation of God's decrees and the laws of conscience resulted in a severe punishment – exile of the first couple from the garden of Eden. The seeds of sin sown by the disobedience of Adam and Eve bore fruit in the lives of their descendants. Cain, their firstborn son, cunningly and unjustly murders his younger brother Abel. For the committed fratricide, God punishes Cain by exile, saying: "You shall be a fugitive and a wanderer on the earth" (Gen 4:12). It is difficult to find in English the exact translation of these two words "fugitive and wanderer" (in the original: *na'-va-nad*). The word translated as "fugitive" means the "one who weaves or sways from weakness, instability or fatigue," and the word "wanderer" carries a connotation of aimless wandering, going aimlessly from place to place. That was Cain's curse.[5]

Two aspects should be noted in this punishment of Cain. First, he is kicked out of the cultivated soil (tillage was his main activity before he murdered his brother). In other words, now he is exiled into the desert, away from his familiar and calm settlement on earth, from society and communication with its inhabitants; in particular, he was expelled from the area where he was born and raised, where he worked, and where his relatives lived. Homeless, insecure, and restless, he is now banished to a foreign land, uninhabited, and at a distance from those with whom he used to live. From now on, he must lead the life of not a farmer, but a wandering nomad of the desert. Secondly, his nomadic life is not the result of his own conscience reproaching him, but a divine judgment. This was the most painful punishment for him. "Cain said to the Lord, 'My punishment is greater than I can bear'" (Gen 4:13). Here the word translated as "punishment" (Hebrew *avon*) can mean both "punishment for sin" (as in 1 Sam 28:10), and "crime, sin, guilt" (as in 2 Sam 14:9). Some commentators believe that Cain's reaction signifies his belief that the sin he committed was too great to be forgiven;[6] but most commentators agree that here Cain does not so much regret the seriousness of his own sin as complains about the disproportionately heavy judgment of God. This is confirmed by the following words of Cain: "Behold, you have driven me today away from the

---

5. "Genesis," Cambridge Bible for Schools and Colleges, accessed September 1, 2019, https://biblehub.com/commentaries/genesis/4-12.htm. It seems interesting to me that in the Russian language there is an expression "wandering like a ne-pri-cain-ny," which literally means "to walk around not knowing what to do because of anxiety, not finding a place, restlessly, rushing from place to place, being unsettled." It is a cognate word with the verb "cayatsya" meaning "to repent, blame yourself." The roots of this Slavic word may stem from the biblical personage Cain.

6. Such a translation of this verse, although used in the Septuagint and Vulgate, is unlikely, given the following verse (Gen 4:14). For more detailed information, see: "Genesis," *The Pulpit Commentary*.

ground (Hebrew *adama* – cultivated soil, ground), and from your face I shall be hidden. I shall be a fugitive and a wanderer on the earth (Hebrew *arets*, the place of life of man and animals, land, country); and whoever finds me will kill me" (4:14). Apparently, Cain is tormented here not by the realization of the horror of his crime, but mainly by the worry for his own life and safety. The real reason for his despair was that he saw God's judgment as unjustly heavy retribution, which so unexpectedly fell on him, and which he understood as his exile from God's presence: "from your face I shall be hidden." Note that Cain did not seem to have the slightest idea about the omnipresence of God. Fleeing from his native land, which he had previously toiled, he thought that now it would be impossible to enjoy the divine presence and protection anywhere else. He was unlike Enoch, who was said to "walk with God," being constantly in his presence, contemplating God (Gen 5:22, 24), and unlike King David, who exclaimed: "Where shall I go from your Spirit? Or where shall I flee from your presence? If I ascend to heaven, you are there! If I make my bed in Sheol, you are there!" (Ps 139:7–8). Therefore, Cain perceives his punishment as an undeserved one, and comes to the conclusion, "from your face I shall be hidden." That is quite remarkable. He does not consider it an option to call on God in the land of exile, while David, on the contrary, believes in the omnipresence, power, and goodness of God, and does not know where to hide from the sight and hand of the Lord. Even in hell David is convinced he would find him.

The stories of the fall and the fratricide of Cain show us how the distorted image of God as distant, limited, cruel, and evil destroys relations with God and with other people, and how this negative image of God leads to spiritual loneliness and social isolation. Further, isolation and exile as a way of punishment were often used in human history.

The prophet Jeremiah, who was thrown into a lonely pit for his fearless proclamation of a prophetic word, was one of the biblical examples of absolute temporal isolation. "They lowered Jeremiah by ropes into the cistern; it had no water in it, only mud, and Jeremiah sank down into the mud" (Jer 38:6 NIV). Typically, isolation is excruciating because it is forced or violent. That is why it is used as a form of punishment. Cain's partial isolation was a consequence of the sin he had committed, whereas Jeremiah's absolute isolation in the form of imprisonment was a result of his cultural loneliness, which will be discussed below, and which is often an integral part of the life of everyone who follows God.

2. Loneliness of the elected: the cultural loneliness of God's chosen people

The truth is that loneliness or social isolation can be experienced not only due to a lack of a close relationship with God, but sometimes because of it. Indeed, a person who has made a firm decision to follow God may face misunderstanding and even opposition from society, experiencing cultural loneliness.

Cultural loneliness is sometimes called "prophetic" loneliness precisely because it is often experienced by people called to serve God (for example, prophets) because of their "otherness," their difference from the world, and their rejection of society's values. Cultural loneliness is also associated with a certain mutual rejection of such "prophets" by society and is often accompanied by a feeling of abandonment, misunderstanding, even betrayal. It is probably this type of loneliness and rejection that Christ had in mind when he said that no prophet is accepted in his own country (Luke 4:24; John 4:44). New Christians experience this type of loneliness when they reject their sinful habits and communities and are emotionally and physically abandoned by non-Christian friends and relatives. We think it is not an exaggeration to say that cultural loneliness, to one degree or another, was familiar to almost all the great ministers of God, whose names appear on the pages of the Bible, from Joseph to the apostle Paul.

During the stormy life of Moses as it appears before us in the pages of the Bible, quite often we find him in a lonely confrontation. After his birth, he was alone at the Egyptian royal court aware of his national identity, alone as he stood up for his fellow Jew before the Egyptian, alone in a vain attempt to reconcile two quarreling Jews. As Elie Wiesel aptly notes, "Disillusioned, betrayed, heartbroken, he leaves Egypt and his newly found Jewish community and family for another forty years!"[7] In his further striving to fulfill his mission of the liberator of God's chosen people, Moses more than once must have felt lonely and misunderstood among the wayward and rebellious people, who grumbled, questioned, rebelled, and even threatened to kill him. Also, Moses was alone in his intercession for his people before God himself, who in his righteous anger more than once wanted to wipe them away completely (Exod 32:11–14; 33:15–16).

Perhaps David, who like Moses was not only a shepherd but also the leader of the people of God, had similar experiences of cultural loneliness. Like Moses,

---

7. Elie Wiesel, "The Lonely Prophet," in *Loneliness, Boston University Studies in Philosophy and Religion*, ed. Leroy S. Rouner, Vol. 19 (Notre Dame: University of Notre Dame Press, 1998), 127–42.

David urged God not to leave him or withdraw from him, as his psalms vividly testify. In particular, David asks the Lord: "How long, O LORD? Will you forget me forever? How long will you hide your face from me?" (Ps 13:1). He asks God to "consider and answer" him (Ps 13:4). In Psalm 25, David directly calls himself "lonely and afflicted" (25:16) because of the hostility and fierce hatred of the people around him. We find a similar thought in Psalm 35: "Malicious witnesses rise up . . . They repay me evil for good; my soul is bereft . . . Rescue me from their destruction, my precious life (Hebrew 'only one') from the lions!" (Ps 35:11–12, 17). Because of his relationship with the Lord, David feels like a stranger among his own, rejected and shamed by those whom he considered friends, and even his own family:

> More in number than the hairs of my head
>> are those who hate me without cause;
> mighty are those who would destroy me,
>> those who attack me . . .
> I have become a stranger to my brothers,
>> an alien to my mother's sons,
> for zeal for your house has consumed me,
>> and the reproaches of those who reproach you have fallen
>>> on me
> Psalm 69:4, 8–9

Further, we see David suffering from bullying and neglect on the part of both those who "sit in the gate" and "drunkards" (that is, both noble people and the most "degraded" people in terms of social status). King David does not find support or compassion from anyone: "Reproaches have broken my heart so that I am in despair. I looked for pity, but there was none, and for comforters, but I found none" (Ps 69:20).[8] Events in David's life, described in the first book of Samuel, indicate that David's youth was marked with persecution by King Saul and disrespect from his own family, at least until he ascended to the throne. Also, during David's rule over Israel (which was not irreproachable), many people were dissatisfied with his reign, including his son Absalom. But despite all kinds of rejection, persecution, his mistakes, and inner loneliness,

---

8. It is possible that this psalm was written by David towards the end of his life, although the events described in the psalm far exceed anything David personally experienced. Based on the New Testament understanding, we know that in many ways the psalm is prophetic, messianic, fulfilled in the life of Jesus Christ (for example, verses 10, 22). "Psalm 78. Probable Occasion When Each Psalm Was Composed," accessed December 5, 2022, https://www.blueletterbible.org/study/parallel/paral18.cfm.

David put his hope on the Lord, saying "Cast me not off; forsake me not, O God of my salvation! For my father and my mother have forsaken me, but the LORD will take me in" (Ps 27:9–10).

We have already mentioned the story of the prophet Jeremiah who definitely felt alienated from the rest of the people. Because of his fearless proclamations of the word of the Lord, he was put in a solitary pit at the royal court. Knowing that according to his calling he had to "go against the tide," Jeremiah laments: "Woe is me, my mother, that you bore me, a man of strife and contention to the whole land! . . . all of them curse me . . ." (Jer 15:10). And again: "O LORD, you know . . . that for your sake I bear reproach" (Jer 15:15). He also speaks of his loneliness in verse 17: "I did not sit in the company of revelers, nor did I rejoice; I sat alone because your hand was upon me." In chapter 20 of the book of Jeremiah we read: "Then Pashhur[9] . . . beat Jeremiah the prophet, and put him in the stocks" (Jer 20:2). Perhaps at this moment, the prophet experienced some disappointment in the Lord, when he faced rejection from both religious and state authorities, disbelief from the people, as well as persecution, bullying, public torture, and imprisonment for his service to God. Turning to the one who has sent him to serve, the prophet exclaims: "O LORD, you have deceived me, and I was deceived; you are stronger than I, and you have prevailed. I have become a laughingstock all the day; everyone mocks me" (Jer 20:7). Most commentators point out that this Hebrew word "deceive" can be also translated as "persuade" or "entice."[10] One way or another, Jeremiah's service to the Lord turned out to be something totally different from what he had imagined at the beginning when God promised to put him over kingdoms to "pluck up and to break down, to destroy and to overthrow, to build and to plant." God had promised his servant that "they shall not prevail against you, for I am with you, declares the LORD, to deliver you" (Jer 1:10, 19). Expressing his indignation and disappointment before God, and reminding himself of God's promises, Jeremiah seems to understand that the Lord did not promise to keep him *from* all troubles and difficulties, but to strengthen the prophet *among* them, to make him strong and able to overcome any opposition because

---

9. The temple priest.

10. The same verb is used in Hosea 2:1. It is also used in the story of Samson and Delilah (Judg 15:5), and in the story of the deception of King Ahab by the false prophets (1 Kgs 22:20; 2 Chr 18:19), in Proverbs 25:15 and other passages. Its meaning is to "seduce someone speaking softly and persuasively to win them over or force them to do something." For a more detailed analysis, see: "jeremiah-20," John Gill's Exposition of the Bible, accessed February 27, 2020, https://www.biblestudytools.com/commentaries/gills-exposition-of-the-bible/jeremiah-20-7.html.

of God's presence with him. Jeremiah declares: "But the LORD is with me as a dread warrior; therefore my persecutors will stumble; they will not overcome me" (Jer 20:11).

Further, we learn from the Scriptures that such a great prophet as Elijah also felt extremely depressed and alone despite his recent victory over the false prophets. We read "I, even I only, am left, and they seek my life, to take it away" (1 Kgs 19:10, 14). God's answer shows that Elijah's complaint was the somewhat hypertrophied reaction of an exhausted minister. It was far from reality. God replied to Elijah that in Israel at that time, besides the prophet himself, there were at least 7000 other people faithful to God (1 Kgs 19:18). The prophet was not as alone in his struggle against the apostates as he felt.

In this regard, we can also recall the apostle Paul's imprisonment. At the end of his ministry, Paul was abandoned by all his companions and had to appear before Caesar's judgment without any human support. He writes: "At my first defense no one came to stand by me, but all deserted me. May it not be charged against them! But the Lord stood by me and strengthened me" (2 Tim 4:16–17; see also 2 Tim 4:10; Acts 18:10).

Cultural or prophetic loneliness often characterizes the people whose ideas go way beyond their lifetime, and who, under God's calling, have to go against the mainstream. Moreover, this loneliness can relate to both an individual and an entire nation. The chosen people that have not yet come to embrace their "chosenness" are, in fact, what most of the historical and poetic books of the Old Testament are about. Even at the very beginning of the formation of the Jewish nation, a prophecy was uttered by the somewhat contradictory prophet Balaam that characterizes God's chosen people as a nation dwelling alone (Hebrew *badad* – "by one, alone, separately"), not counting itself among other nations (Num 23:9). This is the main feature of God's people – its "separateness." The way the Israelites were supposed to live their lives, provide for their families, raise children, serve God – in everything they had to be different, separated from all other peoples.[11] This was their main purpose and the meaning of their election – to reflect the character of God himself by their "otherness," holiness, and separateness from the rest of the sinful world. This most important theme, the loneliness of the nation because of its "chosenness" and rejection by other nations, would pass further through the entire history of the Israeli people, and subsequently of Christians, too.

---

11. Shubert Spero, "A People That Shall Dwell Alone: Curse or Blessing?" *Jewish Bible Quarterly* 43, 2 (April – June 2015): 1.

Thus, cultural loneliness includes such concepts as separateness, peculiarity, uniqueness, and alienation. It contributes to Christians' awareness of their uniqueness and divergence. It helps people crystallize their identity and reassess their values. This is the positive aspect of such loneliness. Craig Ellison expresses this thought clearly: "If there is any form of alienation that we might argue ought to be part of the Christian's experience, it would be cultural alienation – being cut off from the core values of our secular society. You'll find yourself rejected if you're too good. Christ did."[12] The loneliness of following Christ is especially painful because it is the least expected. But this conflict of values and worldviews, followed by the cultural loneliness of a Christian who is whole-heartedly devoted to God, is inevitable. Every Christian should be prepared for this loneliness.

Cultural loneliness is often used by God for a specific purpose. It benefits both the Christians who experience such loneliness and those to whom they carry the message on behalf of the Lord, fulfilling their calling and ministry. Yet cultural loneliness is different from social loneliness, which we will discuss next.

3. Social loneliness in the book of Ecclesiastes

In the book of Ecclesiastes, whose authorship is traditionally attributed to Solomon, the preacher recognizes certain advantages of social relations, which save a person from social loneliness. He says,

> There was a man all alone;
> he had neither son nor brother.
> There was no end to his toil,
> yet his eyes were not content with his wealth.
> "For whom am I toiling," he asked,
> "and why am I depriving myself of enjoyment?"
> This too is meaningless –
> a miserable business! (Eccl 4:8)[13]

Here, in his extensive reflections on the meaning of life, the preacher turns his gaze to the lonely and stingy person and concludes that the accumulation of material wealth without cooperation, family ties, or friendships is a useless thing. He further supports his thought with the following arguments:

> Two are better than one,

---

12. Craig W. Ellison, *Loneliness: The Search for Intimacy* (NY: Christian Herald Books), 98.
13. Here and below the NIV translation of Ecclesiastes is used.

> because they have a good return for their labor:
> if either of them falls down,
>> one can help the other up.
> But pity anyone who falls
>> and has no one to help them up! (Eccl 4:9–10)

These verses can be applied both to moral failures as well as stumbling due to natural obstacles. Scripture repeatedly warns us of the dangers of deliberately isolating ourselves or avoiding relationships with other believers (Heb 3:13; 10:24–25; 1 Pet 5:8–9). Also in the Old Testament, Proverbs 18:1 says: "Whoever isolates himself seeks his own desire; he breaks out against all sound judgment." Note that here Scripture warns us that separation for self-indulgence is a sign of arrogance and selfishness. Belonging to church, brotherly and sisterly fellowship, and having the support of others, has proved to help resist temptation in a spiritual war. We find a similar thought in 1 John: "But if we walk in the light, as he is in the light, we have fellowship with one another, and the blood of Jesus his Son cleanses us from all sin" (1 John 1:7). Of course, such fellowship implies a certain openness, trust, and accountability in the relationship between believers, which for various reasons not everyone likes because it always requires some risk.

The preacher goes on to illustrate the benefits of companionship: "Also, if two lie down together, they will keep warm. But how can one keep warm alone?" (Eccl 4:11). As Targum interprets it, this verse means husband and wife, especially when they warm each other during the cold season, lying together.[14] Figuratively, this verse can also be applied to warm soul ties that arise from social relationships, warmth, and affection of friends, especially those united by a common faith and purpose (1 Sam 18:1; Acts 4:32; Eph 4:2–6 etc.).

Next, Ecclesiastes underlines a sense of protection and security as advantages of fellowship: "Though one may be overpowered, two can defend themselves. A cord of three strands is not quickly broken" (Eccl 4:12). Therefore, two are better than one because they "afford each other protection and help, and mutually render life agreeable. The isolated man on the contrary must work in vain, since he is destitute of enjoyment in life, and without protection in danger."[15] So, the lack of close, trusting relationships with other people due

---

14. The Targum mentioned here is the Aramaic translation of the Old Testament. Quote from: The Pulpit Commentary, "Genesis". This practice of "warming up" was apparently widespread in the East (see: 1 Kgs 1:2).

15. Ernst Wilhelm Hengstenberg, *Commentary on Ecclesiastes with Other Treatises* (New York: Sheldon and Company, 1890), 130.

to certain character traits, such as insularity, a tendency to isolate yourself, and inability or unwillingness to build and maintain such relationships, creates a sense of social loneliness. The studies of loneliness show that people who separate themselves from communication are rarely aware and even less likely to recognize themselves as socially lonely. Yet, in fact, they are. Conversely, open people who are capable of creating trusting emotional connections rarely experience social loneliness because others are drawn to them.

Summarizing the main thoughts in these passages of the book of Ecclesiastes, the following key principles can be distinguished. The preacher emphasizes the social nature of a person and the importance of companionship for a sense of well-being, while the selfish ambitions dominating this world and manifesting themselves in the form of pride and greed make it difficult to form meaningful mutual friendships, without which a person is doomed to experience social loneliness.

4. The loneliness of shattered intimacy: Hosea's emotional loneliness

As we mentioned before, there is a big difference between social and emotional loneliness. Social loneliness occurs when there is a lack of contact and communication with friends or relatives, while emotional loneliness is associated with a sense of disconnection or a lack of mutual understanding in relationships with friends and loved ones. It has nothing to do with the number of contacts, but with the quality of these relationships. According to Robert Weiss, who was the first to draw the distinction between emotional and social types of loneliness, social loneliness springs out of a lack of social connections or integration, whereas emotional loneliness is a person's subjective reaction to the absence of close emotional attachment or understanding of one other significant person.[16] Sadly, loneliness in this form is usually experienced as a result of broken friendship or love relationships due to betrayal, disloyalty, or death of a spouse or a close friend.

Perhaps the best illustration of this type of loneliness in Scripture is the striking story of the prophet Hosea and his wife, Gomer. Of course, we will not find emotional loneliness or attachment mentioned directly here, but a closer look allows us to see in this story all the necessary components of attachment: sincere concern and participation in the life of a loved one, desire for close

---

16. See: Robert Weiss, *Loneliness: The Experience of Emotional and Social Isolation* (Cambridge: MIT Press, 1975), 236.

mutual relations with the object of one's affection, recognition of freedom, and respect of the other person's free choice.

The events of the book of the prophet Hosea unfold intensively from the very beginning, astonishing the reader with God's command to a pious and decent prophet – to marry Gomer, a prostitute. The prophet Hosea did as he was told, out of obedience to the Lord but also because he fell in love with Gomer. He loved her with all his heart. Despite everything, Hosea accepted this woman, officially married her, brought her to his house, gave her his name, and took care of her and her children. Perhaps he had hoped that now her infidelity would be over, that his love would be enough for her. But he was wrong. Despite all his care, love, and loyalty, Gomer left Hosea and returned to her former career. The Lord reveals that the reason for this behavior was "the spirit of whoredom within" her, and lack of knowledge of the Lord (Hos 5:4; 4:12). Paradoxically, despite the voluntary choice of Gomer to leave her husband for her lovers, Hosea continued to take care of her secretly. In fact, she mistakenly thought that the allowance and the gifts she had been receiving were the payment for her "services" from her lovers (Hos 2:8). We can only imagine what Hosea was feeling.

The climax of this tragic marital relationship, poisoned by infidelity and ingratitude, torn apart by the loss of trust, was God's command to Hosea to find Gomer anyway, love her again, and bring her back at any cost. And in the third chapter of the book, we see that Hosea finally finds his wife Gomer, humiliated and on sale as livestock in the market. He literally ransoms her back for a lot of money, perhaps from some brothel.

Perhaps the most amazing thing about this story of a faithful prophet and his wicked harlot wife is that the story of their relationship was a living illustration of God's relationship with his people at that time. It is striking that God himself uses such an explicit language of matrimonial relations when speaking of himself and his chosen people. He is jealous, indignant, laments their unfaithfulness to him and compares their idolatry with adultery: "For I desire steadfast love and not sacrifice, the knowledge of God rather than burnt offerings. But like Adam, they transgressed the covenant; there they dealt faithlessly with me" (Hos 6:6–7). In the book of Hosea, like nowhere else except for a few chapters – in the books of Isaiah (chapter 54), Ezekiel (chapters 16 and 23), and Jeremiah (chapters 2 and 3) – we see God as a rejected, deceived husband eager to restore his relationship with his "wife" – the people of Israel – because he still loves her so much.

However, there is a happy ending in the book of Hosea. It is full of hope for a relationship restoration. Despite their stubborn refusal, God repeatedly calls the people of Israel to return to him (Hos 6:1; 12:6; 14:2, 3). Moreover, it is he who initiates the restoration of relations. He says: "I will allure her, and bring her into the wilderness, and speak tenderly to her" (Hos 2:14). Here the verb "allure" is used to convey the idea of concern in building trustful close relationships.[17] Further, God promises: "And I will betroth you to me forever. I will betroth you to me in righteousness and justice, in steadfast love and mercy. I will betroth you to me in faithfulness. And you shall know the LORD" (Hos 2:19–20). The triple use of the verb "betroth" signifies an eternal marriage covenant, dedication, and lifetime devotion in close relationships. Such rhetoric suggests that God longs to find a reciprocal desire in his people and not simply obedience out of fear. He is interested in their voluntary love, in their knowing him closely, in personal relationships, in short, in their secure attachment to him.

Undoubtedly, infidelity undermines trust, destroys emotional closeness, causes a desire to take revenge, punish, or at least reject, in response to betrayal and disloyalty (see Hos 8:13; 9:1, etc.). Obviously, such a reaction of the hurt spouse is fully justified and even necessary to help the guilty one realize his or her mistake, loneliness, and, finally, return and restore relations: "Come, let us return to the LORD; for he has torn us, that he may heal us . . . that we may live before him. Let us know; let us press on to know the LORD" (Hos 6:1–3).

So much emotional warmth is heard in the words of the Lord: "How can I give you up, O Ephraim? How can I hand you over, O Israel? . . . My heart recoils within me; my compassion grows warm and tender. I will not execute my burning anger" (Hos 11:8–9). The book of Hosea, as an illustration of emotional loneliness due to broken intimate attachment, is encouraging, holding prophetic touching promises of the restoration of the relationship.

Now we will talk about existential loneliness, which indicates, first of all, a Christian's misunderstanding of our place and calling in life.

5. The loneliness of emptiness: the existential loneliness of Ecclesiastes

The book of Ecclesiastes is considered one of the most controversial and philosophical parts of the Old Testament, which deals with the existential and moral foundations of human existence far more than the doctrinal ones. Probably, this is one of the best books to reveal the essence of existential loneliness as a person's misunderstanding of the meaning of life and his

---

17. This verb is used in Exod 22:16 and Judg 14:15 in a sense "to deceive" someone.

place "under the sun" (Eccl 1:3). The book describes this type of loneliness very vividly and (in the language of the original) in "words of delight . . . and truth" (Eccl 12:10). The American philosopher Ruth Putman believes that, most likely, the book reflects the deep existential loneliness of the author that manifests itself, first of all, in the inability to wonder, admire or see anything new "under the sun," that is, on earth (Eccl 1:9); and second in the fact that life in all its manifestations seems to him an insignificant "vanity of vanities" and "vexation of the spirit" (Eccl 1:2; 4:6; 1:17 KJV).[18] David Moore, author of a commentary on the book of Ecclesiastes, notes that the word vanity (Hebrew *havel*) can also be translated as "fog," that is, something empty, obscure, and fleeting. The phrase "vexation of the spirit," as the King James translation renders it, could be translated as "striving after wind," because "wind" in the biblical literature of wisdom often means something fleeting and insignificant, having no lasting value in itself.[19]

At the same time, one can fully agree with the author that in one sense "there is nothing new under the sun" (Eccl 1:9), for the cyclical nature of life, the need to work, and the desire for pleasure, as well as injustice and violence proceeding from the sinful nature of man – nothing has changed since the time of the fall. Moore believes that this is the author's main idea: "to draw our attention to the fact that power, wealth and pleasure – all the same things in the pursuit of which people have always sought to find a 'good life'"[20] when gained, give only bitter disappointment, because in themselves all these things are vanity. This is when existential loneliness is born: when a person attains a certain success in life, has breathtaking achievements, all kinds of pleasures, riches, fame, and power, and suddenly realizes that *nothing of this makes him happy*. Such a person asks the question: "So what is the meaning of life?"

As we read the book of Ecclesiastes, we see that the preacher appears before us with all the signs of existential loneliness: in search of the meaning of life (Eccl 1:2), in the realization of the futility of his worries and efforts (Eccl 2:22; 3:9), in a certain disappointment and even hatred with life (Eccl 2:17–20), in helplessness and uncertainty in the face of death which makes everyone equal – rich and poor, wise and foolish, righteous and wicked (Eccl 2:14–15; 3:19–21; 8:8, 10; 9:2). At the same time, we can feel his alienation not only from

---

18. Ruth A. Putman, "The Loneliness of Koheleth," in *Loneliness*, Boston University Studies in Philosophy and Religion, ed. Leroy S. Rouner, Vol. 19 (Notre Dame: University of Notre Dame Press, 1998), 145.

19. David G. Moore, "Ecclesiastes, Song of Songs," in *Holman Old Testament Commentary* (Nashville: Holman Reference, 2003), 3–4.

20. Ibid.

himself or other people but also from God. Although he seems to be involved in all the aspects of Jewish religious life (Eccl 5:1), none of this suggests that the author has a personal relationship with God: he often talks about God and never with him personally, recalls him only as creator and a strict judge, who should be remembered and feared, and never as a protector or a loving father. The preacher not even once in this book calls God by name, which, considering the attributed authorship of Solomon (to whom God appeared twice in a dream), is rather strange and surprising.

So, in his book the author pays attention to the important philosophical issues of human existence, such as the role and meaning of a human's life, the frailty, and volatility of it, the impossibility of achieving complete satisfaction on this earth, the vanity of life's labors and the inevitability of human death. These thoughts are totally natural when there is no personal and trusting relationship with God. The conclusion to which the author of Ecclesiastes comes at the end of his reasoning about the meaning of human life is the realization that the ability to have wealth, see the good, use, and enjoy it – this is God's gift (Eccl 5:18). And the main goal in life is to "honor God and obey his commandments" because God knows everything and will judge everything that people do (Eccl 12:13). Thus, here in the book of the preacher, we see a certain principle: the cause and solution to the problem of existential loneliness lie in the realm of faith and relationship with God since they are the main factors to give meaning to life.

In the next section, we will consider the role of human suffering and the image of God in fostering feelings of existential loneliness.

6. The loneliness of suffering and loss: Job's existential loneliness

Suffering, which is the main theme of the book of Job, can be a catalyst for existential loneliness. One of the most famous ancient stories in the entire Bible is also one of the least understood, never failing to puzzle the reader. In this story, Job appears before us as a righteous, famous, and influential man, whom God blessed in every possible way with large income and property, a wife, ten children, health, and power – but who lost it all (except for his wife) in a matter of days. Note that God himself evaluates Job as a blameless and upright man, who fears God and turns away from evil, and "there is none like him on the earth" (Job 1:8). Therefore, it seems that Job was the last person to deserve such suffering that fell to his lot. This very thing – the undeserved sufferings of righteous men, given that God is just – is what makes Job's story so difficult to comprehend and at the same time so attractive.

Suffering is a painful experience, and people often tend to perceive their suffering as a punishment from God. They seek to find the meaning of their suffering, wondering what they have done to deserve it. When suffering occurs in the lives of righteous, so to speak, "good" people, it seems especially incomprehensible, suggesting the thought: "If God is so Almighty, loving and just, why does he allow the suffering of these good people"? Such questions are raised in the book of Job.

The plot of the book unfolds in such a way that in his misfortunes Job was absolutely misunderstood by everyone and completely alone, which undoubtedly intensified his suffering. We learn that all his servants and family have left Job, disappeared from him, and, as it seemed to him, conspired against him (Job 6:15; 16:10; 19:13–17, 19). Even his breath has become repulsive, strange to his wife. Because of her contempt for her husband or out of despair, she suggested Job curse God and die (Job 2:9). Hearing about his misfortunes, Job's friends first came to support him, but instead of offering sympathy and help, they laugh at him and criticize him (Job 12:4), using this situation to accuse Job of various sins, to reconcile these terrible events in the life of their friend with their own concept of God (Job 15:4–6; 22:5–7; 34:7–8).

We should mention that suffering is experienced by each person quite individually, in a particular way. It seems to most people that no one else suffers as they do. Even the same circumstances can be perceived by one person as an unpleasant complication with which one can live, or as an obstacle that must be overcome, while for another it means the end of life. Loneliness experienced by a suffering person further enhances this feeling of the uniqueness of suffering. Support from significant people for those who face life-threatening or health-threatening circumstances is of paramount importance. Aviva Meyers and Martin Svartberg, researchers of existential loneliness among HIV-infected people, state:

> Significant others in our lives, such as parents, friends, partners, and society serve to validate our existence through our ability to communicate with them and feel their affirming and reassuring presence and interest. This reciprocal relationship allows one to perpetuate the belief that one is not alone and can count on others to protect one from death and vulnerability . . . thereby enabling

one to maintain an integrated self and minimize the emergence of isolation, anxiety, and existential loneliness.[21]

The most difficult thing to understand in the book of Job, perhaps, is that throughout the entire story of Job's mental and physical tortures, God remains silent almost to the very end. Job, as can be seen from the text, felt that God, in whom he always believed and whom he revered, yet who allowed all these misfortunes, seemed to turn away or hide from him. He even considers Job to be his enemy (Job 13:24; 19:11), he broke and abandoned him (Job 16:11–14), accused and hated him (Job 16:9). Job is shocked; he does not know what all this is for. Where can he find God to talk to? How to justify and defend himself before God? How to prove his innocence (Job 23:3–8; 31:6)? Although Job, despite all this, still expresses his hope in God as redeemer (Job 19:25), witness and intercessor (Job 16:19), he also frankly expresses his doubts about the just and merciful nature of God (Job 9:22–29; 10:3, 6; 9:17–18; 24:12).

In addition to incredible misunderstanding and loneliness in his grief, Job suffers from injustice, naturally perceiving his sorrows as an undeserved punishment from God, who deprives him of the opportunity to receive at least some consolation in life. Therefore Job begs God to back down and turn away from him (Job 10:20; 14:6). In general, according to Craig Ellison, the suffering of "good" people runs counter to our sense of justice, causing some to doubt God.[22] However, the question of justice is removed if suffering is perceived not as a punishment for sin but as a test of fidelity, as was the case with Job.

Interestingly, God did not tell Job what the meaning of his suffering was almost until the very end. Job, perhaps, did not understand this, but having passed such a test of his faith, he received twice as much blessing, making up for his loss of family, property, and health (Job 42:11–17). But perhaps the most important thing that Job gained from these sufferings is a better understanding of God as almighty, sovereign (Job 38:27–41; 42:2–6), omniscient (Job 42:2), and as a good God. Job became humbler and stronger in his trust in God. From the eternal perspective, theologian Stephen Lawson concludes, Job's eternal spiritual wealth outweighed his temporary physical losses and mental suffering

---

21. Aviva M. Mayers and Martin Svartberg, "Existential Loneliness: A Review of the Concept, Its Psychosocial Precipitants and Psychotherapeutic Implications for HIV-Infected Women," *British Journal of Medical Psychology* 74 (2001): 544.

22. Ellison, *Saying Good-Bye to Loneliness and Finding Intimacy*, 57.

because he realized that even in the midst of suffering he was not alone. For God knew him, saw, and answered him.[23]

Thus, on the pages of Scripture, we find not only explanations of the essence and role of social, emotional, and existential loneliness in life, but also instructions on how a believer can avoid falling into the "trap" of such types of loneliness even in the face of crisis, life blows, and suffering. However, practical experience shows that such blows bring some people to a feeling of God-forsakenness and the shipwreck of their faith. To the question of why some believers lose their faith under the pressure of suffering, while others do not, we will try to answer from a biblical perspective below in the next two sections, which are devoted to revealing the essence of spiritual loneliness and the feeling of being forsaken by God.

7. The loneliness of the Messiah: the many faces of Christ's loneliness. Hell as an extreme form of spiritual loneliness

In the psalms of King David of the Old Testament, we find a new and fundamentally deeper reflection of loneliness – spiritual loneliness. In order to understand the essence of spiritual loneliness, it is necessary to take a closer look at those Scriptures that most clearly describe it.

There are several passages in Psalms where David, experiencing loneliness, cries out in prayer to God. For instance, Psalm 25:16 says: "Turn to me and be gracious to me, for I am lonely and afflicted." In this psalm, David repents and grieves, expressing his need to restore a right relationship with God. Here, as in many other places in the book of Psalms, loneliness is related not as a loss of communication with other people, but a feeling of alienation from God.

The most striking example of spiritual loneliness, perhaps the most vivid mention of it in the book of Psalms, is the twenty-second psalm: "My God, my God, why have you forsaken me? . . . Deliver my soul from the sword, my precious (only) life from the power of the dog!" (Ps 22:1, 20–21). This is considered one of the Messianic psalms, and Jesus quoted it on the cross. It is logical to conclude that it was not by chance that Jesus quoted this particular text of the Holy Scripture, and not just to fulfill the ancient prophecy, but rather because these prophetic words accurately expressed exactly what the Son of God was experiencing at that moment on the cross, namely, the feeling of being forsaken by God.

---

23. Steven J. Lawson, *Holman Old Testament Commentary: Job* (Nashville: Broadman & Holman Publishers, 2004), 366.

Some Jewish commentators believe that in this psalm David directly described his own experience, while others believe that it refers to the people of Israel in captivity. It is indisputable, in our opinion, that this psalm describes the suffering of the Messiah. Even one ancient rabbinical Midrash of the eighth century, Pesikta Rabbati[24] relates the words from this psalm to descriptions of the suffering of the Messiah: "our true Messiah . . . your skin stuck to your bones, and your body was dry – like a dried tree . . . and your strength – dried up like a shard . . . All this suffering was for the sins of our children."[25] So, the twenty-second psalm is a visual description of the execution of the Messiah: his bones are out of joint (Ps 22:14); he is dehydrated, exhausted (Ps 22:15); and is surrounded by enemies who cast lots to divide his garment among them while he was dying (Ps 22:16–18). Moreover, to intensify his public humiliation, he is nailed to a tree and stripped naked – for all to stare and make fun of him (Ps 22:16–17). All of these descriptions strangely fit with the peculiarity of execution by crucifixion, which was not known to the Jews when the psalm was written! Hence, in this psalm, David prophetically looks at the events he himself did not experience, which are not similar to anything that he personally went through. Yet, as a prophet, he speaks of the future sufferings of the Messiah on the cross.

We can also find other prophetic passages in Scripture that foretell the death, suffering, and glorification of the Messiah.[26] Comparing the words of the ancient prophecy recorded by David in Psalm 22 many centuries before the events, with the text of the Gospels describing the last minutes of Jesus's life, it is really striking how accurately they come true (see the table below). The first words of this psalm, quoted by Jesus, should have reminded the scribes, who were standing there reviling him, about that prophecy. Their very words of scorn, his bloody pierced body and the death penalty that caused dehydration and suffocation, the stripping of his garments and the casting of lots by Roman soldiers – all these happened and were carefully recorded so as not to leave the reader in any doubt that it is he, Jesus, who is the hero of this psalm.

---

24. Midrash (Hebrew "interpretation") is the explanation of the Written Torah in allegories and parables. Pesikta Rabbati (Hebrew "Great Sections") is a medieval collection of sermons or lessons of festivals of the year, "Pesikta Rabbati," Encyclopedia.com, accessed December 14, 2022, https://www.encyclopedia.com/religion/encyclopedias-almanacs-transcripts-and-maps/pesikta-rabbati.

25. *Pesikta Rabbati: Homiletical Discourses for Festal Days and Special Sabbaths*, trans. William George Braude, 2 Vol. (New Haven: Yale, 1968), 685–86.

26. See, for example, Zech 13:7; Ps 2:1–3, etc. Thought borrowed from Robert Harman, *Foundations of Faith: Understanding the Doctrines of Salvation, Baptism, and Eternal Judgment* (Global Vision Ministries Antikva, 2003), 77.

Fulfilled prophecies from Psalm 22

Verse in Psalm 22	Verse in the Gospels
1 My God, my God, why have you forsaken me?	Matt 27:46 And about the ninth hour Jesus cried out with a loud voice, saying, "Eli, Eli, lema sabachthani?" that is, "My God, my God, why have you forsaken me?"
6 But I am a worm and not a man, scorned by mankind and despised by the people.	Matt 27:44 And the robbers who were crucified with him also reviled him in the same way.
7 All who see me mock me; they make mouths at me; they wag their heads;	Matt 27:39 And those who passed by derided him, wagging their heads.
8 "He trusts in the LORD; let him deliver him; let him rescue him, for he delights in him!"	Matt 27:43 He trusts in God; let God deliver him now, if he desires him. For he said, 'I am the Son of God.'"
14 I am poured out like water, and all my bones are out of joint; my heart is like wax;	John 19:34 But one of the soldiers pierced his side with a spear, and at once there came out blood and water.
15 my strength is dried up like a potsherd, and my tongue sticks to my jaws;	John 19:28 After this, Jesus, knowing that all was now finished, said (to fulfill the Scripture), "I thirst."
16 For dogs encompass me; a company of evildoers encircles me; they have pierced my hands and feet.	Luke 23:33 And when they came to the place that is called The Skull, there they crucified him, and the criminals, one on his right and one on his left.
17 I can count all my bones – they stare and gloat over me;	Luke 23:35 And the people stood by, watching, but the rulers scoffed at him, saying, "He saved others; let him save himself, if he is the Christ of God, his Chosen One!"
18 they divide my garments among them, and for my clothing they cast lots.	Matt 27:35 And when they had crucified him, they divided his garments among them by casting lots.

What did the Son of God actually experience on that cross? The fact that Jesus quotes Psalm 22 during his sufferings testifies first of all to the fact that he saw himself as the one who fulfills this prophecy about the Messiah, says

Tim Hegg, author of numerous books on the Hebrew sacred texts.[27] Jesus's exclamation "My God, My God! Why have you forsaken me?" was not just so the words of prophecy would come true, but rather that the prophecy was the shadow of the reality to come – the death of Jesus on a cross. Thus we can see in the psalm an insight into the inner anguish of the savior. He really was experiencing an extreme degree of physical, mental and spiritual suffering, especially during the last three hours on the cross. It would be logical to conclude that at that moment Jesus actually was going through complete devastation and spiritual loneliness, which reached its climax – the feeling of being forsaken by God.

Thus, being betrayed, ridiculed, spat upon, and finally crucified on the cross for the sins of all mankind, Jesus experienced almost every form of loneliness imaginable. Indeed, during his earthly life, he was alone when tempted in the wilderness (Luke 4:1–2), misunderstood in his own family (John 7:5), rejected by the religious and secular rulers and people of his time (John 19:15), and then betrayed and abandoned by his own disciples (Mark 14:50). So, from the human perspective, he was truly alone. American theologian Rutledge Fleming also notes that the flight of the disciples was another demonstration that such a shameful death was seen by them as a sign of God's displeasure with him since a real hero is never abandoned by all his followers. At that moment, the disciples saw in his humiliating and meaningless death neither obedience to God, nor fulfillment of his mission, nor a heroic martyrdom of self-sacrifice. On the contrary, precisely because it was a crucifixion, they could see in it only a complete discrediting of the whole ministry of Jesus before people and a sign of a curse from God.[28]

Let us note that although the betrayal of his disciples and friends was not a surprise to Jesus but the fulfillment of an ancient prophecy, until the last moment at Calvary, the realization that God the Father did not leave the Son alone comforted and strengthened Jesus. "Behold, the hour is coming, indeed it has come, when you will be scattered, each to his own home, and will leave me alone. Yet I am not alone, for the Father is with me" Jesus warned his disciples as if reminding himself of this truth during the last supper (John 16:32). Therefore, perhaps the most terrible and most painful experience for him was not even that rejection by people or his disciples' betrayal, but the

---

27. Tim Hegg, "Studies in the Biblical Text: Psalm 22:16," accessed January 17, 2021, https://torahresource.com/psalm-2216-like-lion-pierced/.

28. Rutledge Fleming, *The Crucifixion: Understanding the Death of Jesus Christ* (Grand Rapids / Cambridge, U.K: Eerdmans, 2015), 89.

feeling of abandonment by God the Father himself. He, the sinless Son, had to endure this abandonment, inherent in every sinful person, identifying himself with sinful people. I believe this was the very feeling that Jesus experienced in his death agony on the cross of Calvary, exclaiming: "My God, My God! Why have you forsaken me?" (Matt 27:46; Mark 15:34).[29] As Rutledge Fleming notes,

> There can be no honest interpretation of this event without an account of this uniquely terrible saying from the cross – the only saying to be reported by not just one but two evangelists. Jesus at this moment on the cross embodies in his own tormented struggle all the fruitlessness of human attempts to befriend with the indifferent silence of space – especially religious attempts.[30]

John Stott put it this way:

> I have entered many Buddhist temples in different Asian countries and stood respectfully before the statue of the Buddha, his legs crossed, arms folded, eyes closed, the ghost of a smile playing round his mouth, a remote look on his face, detached from the agonies of the world. But each time after a while I have had to turn away. And in my imagination I have turned instead to that lonely, twisted, tortured figure on the cross, nails through hands and feet, back lacerated, limbs wrenched, brow bleeding from thorn-pricks, mouth dry and intolerably thirsty, plunged in God-forsaken darkness. That is the God for me! He laid aside his immunity to pain. He entered our world of flesh and blood, tears and death. He suffered for us.[31]

If we fail to understand what exactly happened on the cross and after it, the distinctiveness of Jesus's death, it will be difficult for us to understand the greatness of the redemption and reconciliation of mankind with God in Christ. After all, what happened there allowed us to overcome the cause of spiritual loneliness – man's separation from God because of human sin. The horror of Jesus's crucifixion shows how serious God is about sin. Scripture says: "For the wages of sin is death" (Rom 6:23), that is, separation from God. Sin once separated the first people from God and eventually forced God the Father to turn away from his only Son, when "he himself bore our sins in his body on

---

29. See: Fleming, *The Crucifixion*, 97.
30. Ibid.
31. John Stott, *The Cross of Christ* (Downers Grove: InterVarsity, 1986), 335–36.

the tree that we might die to sin and live to righteousness. By his wounds you have been healed" (1 Pet 2:24). In his letter to Galatia, Paul also writes: "Christ redeemed us from the curse of the law by becoming a curse for us – for it is written, 'Cursed is everyone who is hanged on a tree'" (Gal 3:13).

Fleming notes:

> Paul's mysterious utterance in 2 Corinthians 5:21 "For our sake he made him to be sin who knew no sin, so that in him we might become the righteousness of God," has never been fully understood, but many commentators have noted its relationship to the cry of dereliction. God made Jesus to be sin even though he knew no sin, and in that indescribably terrible and unique transaction, Jesus apparently felt the full force of utter separation from the Father. That is what he underwent in order to remake our human nature – not to improve it, not to accept it, not even to perfect it, but to regenerate it altogether. He "became sin"; we "become the righteousness of God."[32]

By becoming sin and curse, holy Jesus destroyed the power of sin. He overcame our eternal spiritual alienation to bring us to the Father.

In our opinion, Scripture reveals that Christ's suffering for the redemption of mankind did not end with the cross, but he had to descend into hell for our sake (1 Pet 3:18–20; Eph 4:9). After all, physical death would not be enough for the accomplishment of redemption, since when Scripture says that "the wages of sin is death," it is not talking only about physical death, but about spiritual death, which eventually means hell. Calvin puts it this way:

> If Christ had died only a bodily death, it would have been ineffectual. No – it was expedient at the same time for him to undergo the severity of God's vengeance to appease his wrath and satisfy his just judgment. For this reason, he must also grapple hand to hand with the armies of hell and the dread of everlasting death.[33]

The concept of hell in the Bible is revealed gradually. In the Old Testament, the word "Sheol" is used which means a certain place in the center of the earth, where the dead were believed to have been, the underworld (Deut 32:22; 1 Sam 2:6, etc.). In the Jewish understanding, Sheol was understood as the realm of

---

32. Fleming, *The Crucifixion*, 533.

33. John Calvin, *Institutes of the Christian Religion*, Vol. 2, ed. John T. McNeill, trans. Ford Lewis Battles, Illustrated edition (Louisville: Westminster John Knox Press, 2001), 414.

the dead where there is no knowledge of God, no glorification of God, no deeds, no memory, no communication, no light, and from where there is no return (see Job 7:9; 17:13; Ps 88:12; Isa 38:18; Eccl 9:5, etc.).

The term "hell" (Greek *hades*) is more often used in the New Testament and reflects the idea that it is not so much the realm of the dead as the damned, the place of those who endure punishment. In the New Testament, the terms "hell" and "lake of fire" are used interchangeably, meaning a place completely defiled, unclean, dark, set apart, and prepared for the punishment and torment of dead sinners in fire (Matt 5:22, 29, 30; 13:42; Luke 13:28, etc.).[34]

Therefore the image of a descent into hell by the crucified Christ would mean that he entered the realm where God was not, says Fleming. This idea is emphasized by Hans Urs von Balthasar, arguing that such an unprecedented separation of God from God, such a self-identification of Christ with fallen humanity to the end, was a necessary condition of redemption.[35] In this sense, the death and descent of Jesus Christ into hell should be understood as his experiencing "the second death" (Rev 20:14), having undergone total separation from God the Father.

In Christian theology, both hell and death are interpreted as forces capable of imprisoning human souls forever, as if in a cell of solitary confinement, without any hope of liberation. Perhaps this understanding of death as a great enemy, as separation from loved ones, explains the strength of Jesus's emotional reaction at the tomb of Lazarus (John 11:33–38).[36] In the end, we can say that the concept of death and, ultimately, hell as separation should be understood, according to Berdyaev, as absolute loneliness.[37] In the words of T. Moore, "Dying is the loneliest thing we shall ever do."[38] Therefore, when Jesus fights Satan (for example, during his temptation in the wilderness and Gethsemane), he also fights death and loneliness.

---

34. The word "Gehenna" itself comes from the name of the valley of the sons of Hinnom – a place to the south of Jerusalem, where during the time of the extraordinary apostasy, Jewish people and kings sacrificed their children, thereby defiling, and bringing God's judgment on the entire nation (2 Kgs 23:10; 2 Chr 33:6; Jer 7:31–32; 32:35).

35. Hans Urs von Balthasar, *Mysteriurn Paschale: The Mystery of Easter* (San Francisco: Ignatius, 2000; orig. German ed. theologie der Drei Tage, 1970). Quoted in: Fleming, *The Crucifixion*, 407.

36. Fleming, *The Crucifixion*, 405.

37. We understand physical death as the separation of the soul and spirit from the body, while spiritual death is the separation of the soul and spirit of a person from God. See: Бердяев, *Я и мир объектов* [Berdyaev, Me and the World of Objects], 87, 89.

38. Sebastian Moore, *The Inner Loneliness* (New York: Cross Road, 1982), 81.

Therefore, by his resurrection, Jesus proclaims the victory over this "last enemy" of death, which since the time of the fall separated people but which one day will be completely destroyed (1 Cor 15:26). Just as the sin of the first people led to a split in their relationship with God, resulting in spiritual death, so the rebirth of a new human nature overcomes the "great split," that is, spiritual death and man's alienation from God. And this split is overcome only in Christ. In him, there is no longer any separation between God and men. The curtain in the temple was torn in two, from top to bottom, as evidenced by all the synoptic Gospels, "indicating that God had acted and the way into his holy presence was open at last" and forever.[39]

Conclusion to chapter 3

Having surveyed biblical narratives, we are able now to see that the root cause of social, cultural, and existential loneliness is spiritual loneliness, which, in fact, springs from the break of a person's relationship with holy God, due to human sinfulness. The Bible also points to spiritual loneliness as a feeling of God-forsakenness, homelessness, alienation, and lostness of the human spirit without God. This type of loneliness was caused by the fall and is overcome by the sacrifice of Jesus Christ on the cross.

We have also noted that various crises, in particular, illnesses, temptations, and sufferings, force people to reconstruct their worldview, in which God becomes its center. A person will either draw near to him, conquering spiritual loneliness, or move away from him. After much research, our conclusion is that the most important factor that determines whether the movement will be toward or away from God is the image of God one holds in mind. Our relationship with God is based on our perception of God.

We also concluded that while cultural loneliness, like any other type, mostly evokes negative feelings, one positive aspect of this type of loneliness is that it promotes the crystallization of Christian identity and the reassessment of social values and norms. In a sense, this type of loneliness is a normal and necessary part of the true Christian experience. This type of loneliness has been a part of the lives of almost all of God's servants mentioned in the Bible

---

39. It is remarkable that the phrase "And the curtain of the temple was torn in two, from top to bottom" is in the passive aorist, signifying that God is the agent. For a more detailed discussion on this topic, see Philip Edgcumbe Hughes, *A Commentary on the Epistle to the Hebrews* (Grand Rapids: Eerdmans, 1977), 407.

and is, to some extent, a common experience for every Christian who seeks to live up to the highest biblical moral standards.

On the other hand, existential loneliness as reviewed in the books of Ecclesiastes, Job, and Psalms, is revealed by such signs as the meaninglessness of life and the search for one's place in life, especially in times of misfortune and suffering.

We also noted that human sinfulness is the main source of spiritual loneliness, and without a trusting relationship with God, people will inevitably suffer from spiritual loneliness, which is often felt as if one was "forsaken by God." The problem of spiritual, existential, social, and emotional loneliness can be solved only through the atoning death of Christ. It breaks the vicious cycle of enmity with God and other people, the cycle of misunderstanding and loneliness.

Part 2

Biblical Approaches to Overcoming Loneliness

In this part of the book, we want to highlight the most significant causes of all five types of loneliness and the most effective strategies for overcoming them from the biblical point of view.

4

Causes and Factors of Loneliness

A person's experience of loneliness is influenced by various reasons and factors, which we have combined into several groups: social, psychological, and theological.

1. Social factors of loneliness

The first group of risk factors for loneliness is associated not so much with a specific person or life circumstances, rather with the whole of society. First, these are the processes taking place mostly in developed Western societies: urbanization and individualization, the prevalence of technology over interpersonal communication, all kinds of political crises, socio-economic instability, natural disasters, and pandemics. Today we can confidently say that the COVID-19 pandemic has aggravated the loneliness people experience, especially in conditions of mandatory social isolation and distancing.

Let us try to figure out how all these processes increase the loneliness of a modern person. Numerous sociological studies convincingly prove that modern urbanization and technological development, as well as high mobility, so typical for Western society, destroy the sense of community necessary for support between people. Paradoxically, a person is forced to interact with many people at a surface level, and can lose close and deep relationships along the way, ending up being lonely in a crowd!

You may be wondering: wait, but don't social networks and technologies, specially created for communication and keeping in touch, help overcome loneliness? Yes and no. Apparently, social media use reduces feelings of loneliness only when there is active, meaningful communication, interaction, and feedback between social media users. On the other hand, when a person simply passively uses social media – for example, scrolling, viewing other people's pages, liking or commenting on someone's photos or videos without any feedback – this only aggravates the feeling of emotional loneliness. To prevent and overcome loneliness, we must feel that we are acknowledged, and are part of something bigger. This sense of belonging can only develop in the context of mutually enjoyable and long-term caring relationships with other people.[1]

Second, such factors as age, gender, cultural and religious affiliation, income level, marital status, and solo living can also influence a person's experience of loneliness.[2] Let us take age as an example. Who do you think is most at risk of loneliness: young people, middle-aged, or older people?

One would think that only people who are socially isolated would be at risk for loneliness, for example, elderly people who live alone and isolated from friends and families, or people with mental disorders or chronic diseases that limit their ability, communication, and mobility. We also would surmise that stigmatized groups suffer the most from loneliness. The truth is all of us are vulnerable to feeling lonely at any time. Loneliness can manifest itself in people surrounded by family or friends on social networks. Surprisingly, according to statistics, the loneliest generation is the young and adolescents, even though this generation is the most active on social networks and modern technologies.[3]

Another contributor to loneliness is low income. In Western societies, unemployed people with low income are 7 percent more likely to suffer from loneliness than those who are employed with a high income.[4] We think this is quite easy to understand. After all, a person who is financially secure with a stable financial situation is usually psychologically more relaxed, satisfied, and has more opportunities to choose the time, place, and company of people with whom to spend leisure time. Unemployed and financially insecure people, on the other hand, are anxious, tense in communication, and have to spend

---

1. Roy F. Baumeister and Mark R. Leary, "The Need to Belong: Desire for Interpersonal Attachments as a Fundamental Human Motivation," *Psychological Bulletin* 117.3 (1995): 500.

2. Вікторія А. Гриценко, "Соціально-Педагогічні Умови Подолання Стану Самотності Студентів Вищих Навчальних Закладів I-II Рівнів Акредитації" (Дис. канд. пед. наук, ун-т ім. Бориса Грінченка, Київ, 2014) [Viktoriia A. Hrytsenko, "Social and Pedagogical Conditions for Overcoming the Loneliness of Students of Higher Educational Institutions of I-II Levels of Accreditation" (Dissertation of Candidate of Pedagogical Sciences, Borys Grinchenko University, Kyiv, 2014)], 54, https://nolonely.info/socio-pedagogical-conditions-overcoming-loneliness.pdf.

3. Cigna 2018 U.S., "Loneliness Index," accessed May 15, 2019, 2, https://www.cigna.com/static/www-cigna-com/docs/about-us/newsroom/studies-and-reports/combatting-loneliness/loneliness-survey-2018-full-report.pdf.

4. Béatrice D'Hombres, Sylke Schnepf, Martina Barjakovà, and Francisco Teixeira Mendonça, "Loneliness – an Unequally Shared Burden in Europe," Science for Policy Briefs: European Union (2018): 3, https://ec.europa.eu/jrc/en/research/crosscutting-activities/fairness.

almost all their time surviving or searching for work. Their communication is pressured due to circumstances. That's why loneliness comes. So, solving the problem of social loneliness may require a person to have an adequate income. Research has shown that the impact of unemployment on loneliness is twice as great in Eastern and Southern Europe as in the rest of Europe.[5]

Ethnic origin also influences how people experience loneliness. Traditionally, in collectivist societies in Southern and Eastern Europe, families are larger, family ties are stronger, and people seem to pay more attention to their extended family. In such societies, older parents tend to live with their adult children, so that three generations live together. This is much less common in the USA, Western or Northern Europe. When people from collectivist societies have these strong family relationships removed by modern pressures, they are more likely to experience social loneliness. On the other hand, when people in the South and East of Europe are forced to interact often and only because of the need to live together, this creates tension, discontentment, and, as a result, a feeling of emotional loneliness.

The question of who are more lonely – men or women – remains open, as several studies have come to opposite conclusions.[6]

Another factor is marital status. It has been proven that a person's marital status affects emotional loneliness, because intimate partners, as a rule, are the main object of affection, emotional attachment, and support.[7] If this emotional attachment is absent because there is no object of attachment, the person will feel emotionally lonely. This is how singleness contributes to emotional loneliness. This is a whole huge topic on its own, and therefore we will defer more detailed discussion about the connection between loneliness and singleness until the third part of our book.

Another thing that influences people's experience of loneliness is how often they voluntarily participate in social groups. For example, it has been

---

5. Ibid.

6. Michael Flood, "Mapping Loneliness in Australia," The Australia Institute February 1 (2005), https://australiainstitute.org.au/report/mapping-loneliness-in-australia/; Валерія Чорнобай, "Богословське Осмислення Феномена Самотності" (Дис. канд. філос. наук, Київ: НПУ Драгоманова, 2020) [Valeriia Chornobai, "Theological Reflections on the Phenomenon of Loneliness" (PhD Diss. of Philosophical Sciences, Kyiv: Drahomanova National University, 2020)], 192, 202; Cigna 2018 U.S., "Loneliness Index," accessed May 15, 2019, 2, https://www.cigna.com/assets/docs/newsroom/loneliness-survey-2018-full-report.pdf.

7. Чорнобай, "Богословське Осмислення Феномена Самотності" [Chornobai, "Theological Reflections on the Phenomenon of Loneliness"], 207.

proven that if a Christian makes little or no use of gifts and talents in ministry in church or community, the risk of feeling lonely is much higher.[8]

Apart from the frequency of a person's contacts, an obvious factor of social and emotional loneliness is the quality of relationships with friends, family members, and church. Later in the chapter we will touch on the role of friendships in overcoming loneliness.

Factors such as racism, ostracism, discrimination on any grounds, or a feeling of exclusivity and superiority over someone can be the cause of cultural loneliness. Representatives of different ethnic groups and races, migrants, or Christians interacting with the secular value system are at risk of cultural loneliness.

Third, loneliness often arises due to some tragedy in a person's life, such as the loss of close relationships due to death, illness, divorce, or relocation. It is clear that such life crises often mean the destruction or change of those social and emotional ties that previously supported a person. They can also lead a person to lose a sense of the meaning of life, and to doubts about the goodness of God or his existence. All of these can be the cause of social, emotional, existential, and spiritual loneliness.

Of course, these social factors and even serious life turmoil do not necessarily lead a person to loneliness. Psychological factors play a much more significant role in whether a person will feel lonely or not; and scientific research confirms this.

2. Psychological causes of social, emotional, existential and cultural loneliness

Let us take a closer look at the causes of each type of loneliness from a psychological point of view.

A situation where a person experiences only one type of loneliness is quite rare. More often than not, different types of loneliness are mixed in different proportions in each lonely person. That is, everyone experiences loneliness differently, and the reasons for each of the types of loneliness can overlap.

Such individual characteristics of people as introversion, shyness, poor communication skills, and low self-esteem, are psychological factors of social loneliness. Insecure attachment styles in relationships with people also play a role in the formation of loneliness, as we mentioned in the first part of the book.

---

8. Валерія А. Чорнобай, "Стратегії Подолання Самотності Християн: Соціально-Релігійний Аспект," Практична Філософія 68. 2 (2018) ["Strategies to Overcome Loneliness of Christians: Socio-Religious Aspect," Practical Philosophy 68. 2 (2018)]: 193–99.

Psychological causes of social loneliness

Perhaps a real story from life will help us understand better what social loneliness is. We would like to introduce you to Guram,[9] a seemingly shy, but very friendly and companionable man in his forties. Guram has been a Christian from his student years, is a professional in his field, and a wonderful family man. He has a wife and two children.

Despite all his achievements in life, Guram suffers terribly from social loneliness due to the peculiarities of his profession. Guram is a very experienced seaman and he often goes out to sea for five to six months in a row, which means he has to miss his family, relatives, and friends for half a year. When he's at work, there are only three shades of gray, he says: gray ocean, gray cargo ship, and gray sky. And the constant hum of working machines and units. Monotony. Grayness. Responsibility weighs on him as on a senior officer, and yet there is no one to communicate with. Not that no one else is there: there is a crew, sailors, but they are all of different nationalities, and different mentalities. Their jokes seem stupid to Guram and they seem interested only in wine, films, and playing cards. That's it. There is nothing else to talk about. Guram stays alone with his thoughts.

The last business trip was especially difficult for Guram. Suddenly, instead of the usual six months, his shift continued for the whole of nine months due to the widespread quarantine because of COVID-19. It seemed to him that lockdown would never end. "I felt like a trapped animal," Guram told me (Valeriia) thoughtfully,

> walking around my cabin from corner to corner or on the deck for twenty kilometers a day. I was thinking and reading a lot, was angry that nothing had been getting solved for months. I kept appealing, demanding, believing. I tried to fool my brain, imagining that it was as if a new term of my business trip had just begun . . . The only things that helped me not to go crazy and slightly reduce my loneliness were communication on Skype with my family and my prayers to God.

After three additional months in lockdown, social isolation, and sensory deprivation Guram was finally allowed to return home. As soon as he arrived at the airport he was seized by the shock of the variety of screaming sounds, annoying flashing pictures of advertisements and shop windows, and chaotically moving people everywhere. Upon his arrival home, his shock only

---

9. All the stories we're using in our book are true stories of the real people we know, whose names we may have changed to maintain confidentiality.

intensified. He was surprised to find his children grown so much, changed in appearance, and their interests also changed.

> I had to get used to them again, to this crazy rhythm of life and the chaos at home (compared to the orderly life on the ship), to the reality that I now need to take responsibility for the day-to-day stuff, that my wife had to deal with in my absence. It still feels like I'm not catching up, not keeping up with everyone.

Sometimes our subjective attitudes and negative thoughts contribute to loneliness. Lonely people can be their own worst enemy, and experience a downward spiral of negativity. Fundamental distrust of other people, flighty behavior, lack of common interests in relationships, narcissism, and selfishness, can all stand in the way of close relationships. For example, take the lack of trust and expectations of rejection that lonely people often have. For them it's easy to believe other people are against them, even when they are not. The more we accept such thoughts at face value, the more we begin to avoid social interaction with people, refusing invitations to coffee, a party, or to go out. Therefore, the invitations come less and less often, which the lonely person interprets as proof that no one is interested, and the spiral continues downward.

The consequences of false beliefs are vividly described by Patimat Hasanova:

> A person often prefers voluntary loneliness as a way to avoid another misunderstanding, rejection, and pain. He chooses loneliness as less painful, hoping one day to meet someone who would at least hear and understand him. Fear drives a person to limit contacts, reduce trust, and, as a result, deprive him of emotional, truly human communication. Thus, a vicious circle is created: the inability to get the necessary emotional response leads to loneliness, loneliness – to limitation of communication built on trust and affection, and the limitation – to even greater loneliness, in which no one will come to help because there is just no one around.[10]

Psychologist Guy Winch compared this loneliness with the weakness of our social muscles:

---

10. Патимат Г. Гасанова, Омарова Марина К., *Психология Одиночества* (Киев: Общество с ограниченной ответственностью "Финансовая Рада Украины", 2017) [Patimat G. Gasanova, Omarova Marina K., Psychology of Loneliness (Kyiv: Limited Liability Company "Financial Rada of Ukraine," 2017)], 23.

As a result, the fibers that make up our "social muscles": our social and communication skills, the ability to look at things from another person's perspective, to empathize and understand the feelings of others – become weak and let us down when we need them most.[11]

At the root of this loneliness, as we have already said, lies a basic distrust of people and fear of rejection, expressed in the corresponding thoughts, expectations, words, and behavior, which provoke others to reject us. Therefore, changing such self-destructive thoughts and developing "social muscles" are the main therapeutic methods for overcoming social loneliness.

Psychological causes of emotional loneliness

The pain of rejection is a common cause of emotional loneliness as well. When the person who rejects us is significant to us, emotional loneliness as the result of rejection is more likely. As we emphasized in the first part, everyone needs to be accepted. If this natural need is not met, people are overcome with emotional loneliness. People need more than just the presence of others; they need significant others they can trust. Moreover, more than just their physical presence is needed. To avoid feeling emotionally lonely, we need to feel well connected with significant other people.[12] Accordingly, we can temporarily be alone but not feel lonely, if we still feel a strong connection with spouse, family, or friends – even from a distance. At the same time, if we feel insufficiently acknowledged and accepted by other important people, even if this is not the case, we will still feel emotionally lonely. Our experience of loneliness is influenced not so much by real relationships as by our ideal picture of what they should be. So, "loneliness is in our head: only recognizing himself as lonely can a person feel lonely. And vice versa, if a person does not recognize himself as lonely even facing the most obvious external factors, he will not experience this feeling," says Patimat Hasanova.[13]

Another cause of emotional loneliness is the pain of loss and grief. Shocking life events such as the death of a loved one inflict deep mental wounds,

---

11. Гай Винч, *Первая Психологическая Помощь* (ООО «Попурри», 2014) [Guy Winch, Emotional First Aid, rus. transtl. (LLC Popurri, 2014)], 22.

12. Stephanie Cacioppo, Angela J. Grippo, Sarah London, Luc Goossens, and John T. Cacioppo, "Loneliness: Clinical Import and Interventions," *Psychological Science* 10.2 (2015): 239. Doi: 10.1177/1745691615570616.

13. Гасанова, Омарова, *Психология Одиночества* [Gasanova, Omarova, Psychology of Loneliness], 17.

causing a range of negative feelings such as anger, helplessness, longing, fear, hopelessness, depression, and loneliness, especially if the emotional wounds inflicted by the loss were not treated in time or treated wrongly.

Alex, a talented young man under thirty with beautiful sad eyes, went through some shocking life events. When we first met, he was working as a physical therapist. He told me (Viktoriia) that he lost his mother in her fight with cancer when he was twelve years old. After some time, his father got married again. However, according to Alex, the relationship with his father and stepmother, as well as with his siblings, was not very trusting and close.

Later I learned that when he was studying medicine at university, he met a girl to whom he became engaged. However, shortly before the wedding, the bride died in a car accident leaving him devastated. At the time of my first acquaintance with him, Alex had been emotionally stuck in acute grief for the past five years, often being depressed and feeling chronic loneliness. On top of that, Alex had undergone major heart surgery. All those serious tragedies in life undoubtedly influenced Alex's health. As a result of all the stress, Alex developed type 1 diabetes and had been gradually losing his hearing. The loss of his loved ones and his health, his shattered hopes and dreams, turned Alex from a cheerful, sociable person into a nostalgic, devastated, and lonely pessimist.

Psychological causes of existential loneliness

Experiencing grief and rejection can also lead to existential loneliness. Such life situations as death, illness, and tragedy are ultimately always experienced alone. These circumstances make us meet our fears face to face. This is the loneliness of suffering. It is Job's loneliness, which we wrote about in the first part. And even if, unlike Job, a person receives maximum support from other people in such circumstances, he still has to go through the tragic situations of his life on his own, only with God's help.

When Christians lose what was near and dear to them, and lose what made life make sense, it can lead to shipwrecked faith, to the destruction of their foundation, if their foundation was something passing, perishable, and earthly. That is why the apostle Paul writes: "Let each one take care how he builds . . . For no one can lay a foundation other than that which is laid, which is Jesus Christ" (1 Cor 3:10–11). Until we answer the question of who we are and why we are here, we are doomed to suffer from existential loneliness.

But we are often afraid to ask ourselves these questions. We turn on our system of defense mechanisms, which constantly encourage us to establish new contacts, to have supposedly fruitful activity for the sake of the activity, and thus we alienate ourselves from finding answers to the main questions of human existence, such as: "Who am I?" "What is the meaning of my life?," and so on. Having many contacts and constant communication with other people, we create a mere appearance of a meaningful life, while in reality we lack understanding of ourselves, our motives and goals in life as God sees us. One day we will certainly experience disappointment and apathy, which is called "existential loneliness."

Recently, I (Valeriia) had the opportunity to speak with a successful and quite ambitious young man who, having learned about our writing a book about loneliness, enthusiastically responded to the invitation to share his experience of dealing with existential loneliness. Let's call him Daniel.

Daniel faced the idea that he was completely alone in his existence for the first time back in his teenage years. These thoughts matured gradually in Daniel's mind. He was completely different in character from his elder brother, and different from the expectations of people close to him about what a "macho," "tough guy," or "real man" should be like. The image of a tough guy by no means suited Daniel. He was a super-extrovert and life of the party, yet deep down was quite a gentle, vulnerable and creative young man. He and his brother grew up without a father, who suddenly and tragically died when Daniel was only two years old, so Daniel did not remember him. In general, Daniel realized he could not and would not correspond to all the stereotypes imposed by society. It was then the questions arose which later brought him into an existential crisis: If I feel so different from everyone else, then who am I? What is my real self? What does it mean to be me? Or maybe they are right, and I don't need to strive to be myself or be led by my feelings and desires? Where am I in this social coordinate system? Why am I here in this world? Daniel kept asking himself.

In his description of his existential crisis, Daniel noted two features typical of this kind of loneliness. On the one hand, it is frightening to realize that you are different, unlike others, and cannot match the stereotypes accepted in society. It makes you feel so alone. Daniel notes: "The closer someone became to me, say, a close friend, the more I felt existentially lonely with him. That is why I often had to change my circle of friends." When I asked him why existential loneliness would intensify as he became emotionally close to other people, Daniel replied thoughtfully: "I guess, because I was afraid they would find out who I am, and, having found out, they would reject me." That is, existential loneliness may cover the fear of rejection. It is a feeling that there is no one in the whole world who could truly understand you – including yourself! You feel as if you are a shapeless speck of dust in the endless galaxy, which does not matter and is of no use to anyone – pointless, empty, nothing. Such loneliness usually intensifies when we are left all alone in our thoughts.

On the other hand, the same feelings of dissimilarity to others and your uniqueness can help us realize our originality, individuality, identity, meaning, and purpose in life. This is a positive aspect of existential loneliness.

We are convinced that at the root of existential loneliness lies identity confusion. Moreover, existential loneliness is solved not just by giving random answers to the important questions, but by the true answers that we can receive only through the knowledge of God in his Scripture, through the revelation of who we are in God's eyes, of who we are in Christ.

This does not mean, however, that we should completely ignore our aspirations, desires, and feelings. Simply doing something out of religious duty, without acknowledging your feelings, thoughts, and needs leads to boredom, apathy, depression, mental dullness, or rebellion. We need to understand our inner desires and feelings, so we can see our own, even sinful nature, and through this, admit our need for God's grace, which alone can help us change. We see an excellent example of readiness to bring desires and thoughts into line with God's will in Jesus when he prayed to his Heavenly Father: "Abba, Father . . . everything is possible for you. Take this cup from me. Yet not what I will, but what you will" (Mark 14:36).[14]

Also, understanding of our true inner aspirations, desires and feelings helps us recognize our purpose and vocation in life. After all, not all desires and aspirations in us are carnal, sinful, and devilish. Many of them God put inside us from the very beginning to guide us through life. As Thomas Merton once put it, "The will of God, accomplished as it is uttered, identifying us at once with him who speaks and with what he says in us, makes our entire being a perfect reflection of him who desires to see his will done in our hearts."[15] But, one may ask, how can I discern what is actually God's will for my life?

Jesus knew from the Scriptures who he was, why he came, and what he must do on earth. He even knew his future – when, where, and how he

---

14. We are aware of the ongoing debate in theological circles about what exactly Jesus meant by "this cup." Traditionally, most theologians believe that the "cup" means the suffering of the Savior on the cross, which he, knowing in advance what should happen to him, humanly wanted to avoid. However, some are still inclined to believe that here Jesus is praying not to avoid his suffering on the cross, but to be saved from premature death, so he could endure the cross. In favor of the latter interpretation, Hebrews 5:7 is usually cited, where it is said that Christ's petition to be saved from death was heard. In any case, what is important for us here is the very willingness of Christ to surrender his feelings, thoughts, and desires to the will of the heavenly Father.

15. Thomas Merton, *No Man is an Island* (New York: Barnes & Noble Books), 69.

would die, and what would happen after his death (John 18:4; Luke 18:31–33). Standing before Pilate, Jesus clearly stated: "for this reason I was born, and for this purpose I came into the world – to bear witness to the truth" (John 18:37). He never had any confusion about who he was and what his mission on this earth was. But how often we Christians don't know who we are in God, and what is our purpose and calling in life! Our true values, the purpose of life, and ideas about ourselves are often replaced by false, perishable ideas imposed on us by the world, which crumble like a house of cards in times of crisis, leaving nothing but a gaping void behind. In this regard, solitude gives us the opportunity for reflection to know ourselves and our true purpose, if, of course, we stop running away from the big questions of life.[16]

Identity confusion is at the root of all types of loneliness, especially existential loneliness. In addition, our distorted ideas about ourselves (and about other people), as we wrote earlier, result in insecure attachment styles.

Attachment theory and personality theory provide us with a deeper explanation of why we experience existential loneliness. We identify ourselves with something – we hold something near and dear – or alienate ourselves from something making it distant and alien. These two dispositions operate at all stages of a person's life from early childhood. The deeper and longer the identification and alienation, the more significantly they affect a person's mental state. This process of constant isolation/identification is associated with a person's experience of existential (and emotional) loneliness. Let us try to explain how.

When we do not have a clear idea of who we are in God, there is a danger of *identifying* ourselves with other people too much. When that happens, the need for identification and merging with some other person arises up to the point when we might lose our own "self," our personality. Often, in Christian terms, this leads to the formation of unhealthy soul bonds, which are insecure attachments, or "idols" that control our lives.

When the *alienation* mechanism dominates, we, on the contrary, strive to avoid close attachments, thereby depriving ourselves of the opportunity to discover in others and ourselves such qualities as kindness, openness, generosity, vulnerability, etc., which cannot be learned outside of human relationships. In either case, we end up suffering from emotional and/or existential loneliness. Remember that although any type of loneliness can be provoked by external factors (situations and events), it always stems from

---

16. By solitude here, we mean rather a state of mind and heart than some place where one can be alone.

intrapersonal mental processes. Moreover, difficult life circumstances do not always lead us to loneliness, but identification confusion always does.[17]

As Christians, we are called to keep ourselves from idols (1 John 5:21), finding our identity in Christ (Phil 3:9) and always maintaining our "self" complete in Christ (Col 2:10). Hence, discovering that we are overly absorbed by someone or something in a way that interferes with our personal development or harms any other area of our life, we are potentially able to fix the emotional distortions in our lives. Sometimes this requires the support of loved ones, qualified counseling, or professional help. If we do not fix the distortion, or such support and help are not provided, we can develop depression and all kinds of psychosomatic illnesses stemming from loneliness and emptiness. Such distortion is seen in one of the insecure attachment styles.

For example, people with an anxious or dependent attachment tend to identify themselves with other people, social groups, or ideas too much, accepting and trying on someone else's personality, or someone else's life and values, without any reflection on them. Identification confusion, self-rejection, and a person's self-dissatisfaction trigger this process. Comparison with others and lack of self-acceptance prompt a person either to engage in a search for true identity in God (which is difficult and requires courage and commitment); or it makes a person imitate someone whose life seems successful. However, people faced with their imperfection and emptiness often run away from themselves and God, trying to fill the void with someone else's existence, someone else's life, until their own "self" dissolves and is completely lost. This means people renounce themselves. They strive for communication with other people, hoping in their acceptance to find validation of being in the world, significance, and purpose. When this fails, anxiety and fear of loneliness result. And it cannot but fail, because, as Hasanova put it, such a lonely person "has nothing to communicate with. After all, communication presupposes an individual with his personality and consciousness."[18] But it is impossible to experience unity with someone if you are empty inside and existentially lonely!

It is worth noting that when we fill the emptiness of our soul with God, it does not lead us to loneliness. Why? The answer, in our opinion, lies in the understanding of the nature and identity of humanity. To fill the void with God means allowing God through his Scripture to define our identity, our

---

17. Гасанова, Омарова, *Психология Одиночества* [Gasanova, Omarova, Psychology of Loneliness], 34.

18. Гасанова, Омарова. *Психология Одиночества* [Gasanova, Omarova, Psychology of Loneliness], 41.

place and purpose in life; and God as our creator, who created us for a specific purpose, knows best who we are and what our purpose is. The creator of the iPhone or the MacBook knows the purpose and potential of its creation. When some fake program is loaded into Apple, which is not intended for this device, it damages the iPhone or causes it to malfunction. Likewise, when a person allows something – the creation instead of the creator – to define identity, then this causes failures in function, spiritual emptiness, and existential loneliness.

The restoration of our true identity does not leave us in loneliness, but rather, it frees us from loneliness and leads us to the best we can be. It helps us understand our potential and meaning, and gives us sense of purpose. Thus, self-discovery and self-knowledge is an important aspect in overcoming existential loneliness. However, it is important to understand that this process of self-discovery begins with our knowledge of God, and restoration of our identity in him, in line with the Scriptures!

People with avoidant attachment style, on the contrary, suffer from loneliness caused by the predominance of alienation mechanisms. These are when people alienate themselves from other people, objects, values, norms, groups, etc., which were previously close, needed, and dear. Such alienation is accompanied by the loss of emotional connection with familiar and dear people, places, situations, memories, and experiences. Gradually, such a person begins to consider the relationship with them as meaningless, as Daniel did in our story. He allowed no possibility of psychological closeness with them, always keeping the established distance. Underneath there often lies a basic distrust of everyone. The more such alienation progresses in strength and time, the less other people, the objects of alienation, reach out to make contact and offer their participation in the life of this lonely person, in turn alienating themselves. At the same time, a lonely person begins to feel inexplicable anxiety, fear, loss, skepticism, aggressiveness, and of course, loneliness.[19] Sadly, often such alienated people with avoidant attachment never dare admit to themselves how lonely they are.

Chaotic attachment is the most difficult and destructive for people and their relationships with loved ones. In such people, the mechanism of identification-alienation jumps sharply from one extreme to another, often within a short time and concerning the same person.[20] This quickly exhausts both the person and the relationships. Chaos is manifested when from idealizing their potential loved ones at the beginning of their relationship, such people quickly switch

---

19. Гасанова, Омарова. *Психология Одиночества*, 38.

20. Гасанова, Омарова. *Психология Одиночества*, 41.

to rage and suspicion. They may become angry, manipulative, and start to humiliate their partner. This abrupt jump from idealization to the devaluation of relationships reflects their black-and-white thinking when others are often seen only as "good" or "bad." Such people experience intense fear or anger when they feel they have been ignored or rejected. For example, they may panic or get furious when someone important to them cancels an appointment or is a couple of minutes late. In such a case, they see themselves as being rejected and unworthy. They are afraid of being abandoned and lonely. In general, people with chaotic attachment styles have tremendous difficulty controlling their emotions and empathizing with others. In interpersonal relationships, they usually turn out to be open or hidden manipulators, provocateurs, or jealous and possessive types. They often struggle with a sense of their inadequacy, emptiness, and (naturally) from emotional and existential loneliness.

Stephen J. Sandage, Craig Childress, Peter Jankowski, and others link chaotic attachment with narcissism. Through their research, they found that people with narcissism are prone to authoritative, vengeful, and calculating attitudes: "they have low self-awareness and believe others exist to meet their needs."[21] People with a chaotic attachment style are characterized by a utilitarian approach in their relations with other people. At the same time, they are very sensitive, touchy, and manipulative, yet deep inside they are filled with anxiety and guilt. They are lonely because they are unable to build close trusting relationships, although they are unlikely to admit it. Unsurprisingly, people with narcissism and chaotic attachment styles suffer more from existential, social, and emotional loneliness, than people with secure attachment.

Psychological causes of cultural loneliness

Cultural loneliness rises when we experience a discrepancy between the ideal patterns of communication and relationships that exist in our minds and those considered "correct" in our society. As a result, we feel we differ from the majority and do not fit into what is imposed on us by society. Then we begin to experience cultural loneliness, emptiness, and rejection, which torment us. We feel as if we are an ugly duckling, alien among our own.

---

21. See: Steven J. Sandage, Peter Jankowski, Sarah A. Crabtree, and Maria Schweer, "Attachment to God, Adult Attachment, and Spiritual Pathology: Mediator and Moderator Effects," *Mental Health, Religion and Culture* 18.10 (2015):796, https://doi.org/10.1080/136746 76.2015.1090965.

There was a period in my life when, quite unexpectedly, I (Valeriia) began to experience cultural loneliness. While writing my dissertation, I was given an opportunity to go away for six months to one of the prominent evangelical universities in Europe to work on literature. Maybe for some it might seem strange, but I did not want to go. I did not want to be away from my family, friends, and church for so long – but it was necessary to go, for the sake of science! I was in the company of four other Ukrainian students like me. We all lived in a university campus that looked to me like a sixteenth-century catholic monastery. I had my spacious "cell." All our expenses for food and accommodation were paid by sponsors. One would expect me to think, cool! Live and be happy! Write yourself a dissertation!

But finding the strength to write – especially write a dissertation – was very difficult for me. I felt unusually lonely. At first, I was feeling terrible social loneliness because although there were five Ukrainians including me, we did not know each other, so we did not communicate with each other. Actually, we did not communicate with anyone. For the entire first month, I was practically stuck in my "cell." Having no kitchen in my room, only a microwave in the hallway of my floor, I learned how to cook everything in the microwave, even to boil eggs! I found myself missing Ukrainian food so badly! When my campus neighbor (who was also from Eastern Europe and had lived in that country for several years) showed me a store that was selling products from Eastern Europe, it was wonderful to find cottage cheese and buckwheat! I was as happy as a child to taste this food again.

At first, I didn't want to waste my time on making new friends, and I was missing my old friends and family, although I communicated with them from time to time via social networks. But that was not enough. What I missed most then was a simple friendly human touch. This was social loneliness, which, besides everything else, was intensified by cultural loneliness.

We can feel cultural loneliness especially acutely when living in a foreign land, where we can't get used to the customs and mentality of local people. It is not that our mentality is more right or better – it just feels dearer, closer to us. For example, every Sunday I went to a recommended church, where the service was in English. It was a good international church, open to new people and inviting them to participate in their home groups and other church activities. But I did not go to any of those activities because the entire time, no one personally approached me, and no one got to know me or invited me, except for one elderly lady. At that moment I was not eager to spend my time with local grandmothers, so I had to kindly decline her invitation. There were very nice people in the church who smiled at me, asked "how are you," even prayed for me once, but no one asked my name. And though by that time I had already gone to that church for a month and a half, such superficial communication only aggravated my loneliness. For me, who grew up in Eastern European culture, their communication seemed too formal, too alien, when even with a friend you can meet for coffee only after his/her prior written consent! Maybe our Slavic style of communication is too chaotic sometimes, and too spontaneous, but it is sincere. And I missed it a lot!

When experiencing cultural loneliness, we usually choose one of three reactions. If we obey the models of behavior and relationships imposed on us by society but do not share them internally, we avoid rejection by society but sacrifice our "true self" and set ourselves up for existential loneliness. If we separate ourselves from the models imposed on us by society without any attempt to change them, this usually results in a withdrawal, hermitic or secluded lifestyle, and often social loneliness. An example is monasticism at the dawn of the Christian era which is believed to be the way many Christians protested against church secularization at that time. But sometimes a person tries to create a new social ideal. In this case, we are witnessing a fighter, a revolutionary, a reformer who will surely experience a certain amount of cultural loneliness.

In any case, a divergence from socially accepted standards requires an act of courage from a person and voluntary consent to loneliness. It is not always the case, but often it happens that the clearer Christians realize their identity, the more they understand their role in life and vocation from God and follow it, the more often they run the risk of being misunderstood and rejected by other people, including, unfortunately, Christians. Such people may find themselves in loneliness.

The basic reason for the cultural loneliness of Christians is their awareness of their dual identity. They simultaneously live in this world and belong to the kingdom of God, the values of which are often directly opposite to worldly values. So it is natural when Christians alienate themselves from the worldly value system. And against such alienation and cultural loneliness, we do not fight. That is, a Christian should not try to really fit in every aspect of the world. However, when Christians find themselves lonely and alienated as a result of disappointment with other Christians and the church, then it becomes a problem. Because when acceptance and understanding are lacking, a Christian, experiencing such loneliness and alienation, can come to a very serious crisis of faith and such disastrous consequences as apostasy, disappointment not only in people and church but also in God himself, which leads to spiritual loneliness.

3. Causes and factors of spiritual loneliness

Factors in spiritual loneliness include a negative image of God, a believer's misunderstanding of self-identity, as well as certain religious customs and beliefs reflecting an insecure attachment to God. Let us look at these factors in more detail.

Pehr Granqvist argues that a secure attachment to God serves as a protector, preventing mental and physical health risks such as anxiety, depression, and indigestion.[22] Christians with a secure attachment to God have a higher level of spiritual community in terms of friendship, a sense of support from their spiritual community, and a sense of purpose in life. These Christians tend to have more intimate relationships and more positive relationship experiences than insecure attachment styles.[23]

How are a Christian's secure and insecure attachments to God formed? What do they depend on? Independent research confirms that the experience of the parent-child relationship is often reflected in the future experience of a person's adult relationships both with other people and with God.[24] The more negative our childhood experience of attachment to a significant person is, the more difficult it is for us to perceive God as caring, merciful, and good. This means that if we had abusive, inconsistent, hypocritical, or rejecting parents, it may have fostered disorganized, dependent, or avoidant attachments in our relationships with others, and now makes it difficult to form a trusting relationship with God. This is especially difficult for people whose parents or caregivers in childhood were not only inadequate attachment figures but were also actively religious.[25] For example, if such Christians preached about a loving God, it would be difficult to believe in him. If they were to preach about an angry God, on the other hand, and were themselves angry or unpredictable, insensitive or ignorant of their children's needs, then the children would have every reason to believe in such a God. Attitudes and deeds

---

22. Pehr Granqvist, "Mental Health and Religion from an Attachment Viewpoint: Overview with Implications for Future Research," *Mental Health, Religion and Culture* 17.8 (2014): 785, https://doi.org/10.1080/13674676.2014.908513.

23. Todd W. Hall, Annie Fujikawa, Sarah R. Halcrow, Peter C. Hill, and Harold Delaney, "Attachment to God and Implicit Spirituality: Clarifying Correspondence and Compensation Models," *Journal of Psychology and Theology* 37.4, (2009): 241, https://doi:10.1177/009164710903700401.

24. Victor Counted, "God as an Attachment Figure: A Case Study of the God Attachment Language and God Concepts of Anxiously Attached Christian Youths in South Africa," *Journal of Spirituality in Mental Health* 18.4 (2016): 320, https://doi.org/10.1080/19349637.2016.1176757.

25. Granqvist, "Mental Health and Religion," 789.

speak louder than words! We tend to project the image of our earthly father onto our heavenly Father.

Another life story illustrates this process. "My attitude to faith in God was influenced by some of my closest people!" Maria told me (Viktoriia) with a slight sadness in her voice. Maria's disappointment in her faith in God began in her adolescent years with a situation she considered critical. Maria grew up in a Christian family where her parents were religious and very active in the church. But when Maria needed the understanding and support of her parents the most, she received criticism, and physical and emotional abuse. "To say that back then I felt my parents had let me down and disappointed me is to say nothing!" Maria shared with me in a conversation. The worst thing was that the ministers of the church that the family attended knew about the violence and the crisis in the family, but there was no satisfactory intervention or help from them.

> Then it seemed to me that God did not answer my prayers either. Then, over time, I began to rationalize everything, read critical books about Christianity. Now I'm not sure if there is a God. I have neither emotional nor intellectual strength to answer this question to myself. But, if he does exist, he has the right to be the way he is. I decided that intellectual faith is probably good. But I don't want to believe in him in my heart!

Maria's relationship with one of the parents began to improve only recently.

Legalistic religiosity and insensitive parenting have a tremendously destructive effect on the development of an unhealthy image of God and an insecure attachment to God in their children. An insecure attachment to God is a model of our broken relationship with God, which we usually take from our relationships with parents or significant adults, formed in childhood. We often do it based on internal, implicit, or unconscious beliefs.

The insecure attachment to God correlates with the concept of spiritual instability, which, according to David Paine and Steven Sandage, manifests itself in spiritual anguish, emotional distress, insecurity, and distrust.[26] The characteristics of a believer's insecure attachment to God are a negative image of God and a feeling of being forsaken by God. People with an insecure attachment to God feel fear of punishment, distrust, and insecurity in their

---

26. David R. Paine and Steven J. Sandage, "More Prayer, Less Hope: Empirical Findings on Spiritual Instability," *Journal of Spirituality in Mental Health* 17.4 (2015): 224, https://doi.or g/10.1080/19349637.2015.1026429.

relationship with God. He seems to them indifferent, distant, impersonal, cruel, and punishing.[27] Of course, having such a negative image of God, along with spiritual instability and insecure attachment, negatively affect a person's mental health, exacerbating despair, hopelessness, and loneliness, especially spiritual loneliness. At the same time, Todd Hall and colleagues argue that the Christians' external religiosity has nothing to do with their attachment to God, while their internal beliefs, their understanding of God, and their experience with him (what we have defined as their image of God) are directly reflected in their attachment to God.[28]

Adults with an avoidant, anxious, or chaotic attachment to people often have an avoidant, anxious, or chaotic attachment to God. This is proven by the results of our empirical study: it turns out that Christians who have any insecure attachment to other significant people are more than twice as likely to have a negative image of God. That is, it is twice as difficult for such Christians to rely on God and believe that he is loving, just, kind, and close to them personally.

This was the problem Chloe had. Chloe, a fairly successful, pretty, middle-aged woman, was raised without a father by an extremely insensitive mother. Chloe was often physically or emotionally abused by her mother, who almost always ignored her needs and wishes. Chloe's opinion was never asked. Chloe's mom, who worked as a kindergarten babysitter, always "knew better" what Chloe needed and what she did not. For example, Chloe had a toy gnome over her bed, given by her mother. Chloe loved it very much. Once, when guests came to them, her mother simply gave that gnome to a guest boy, without even asking her daughter's approval. Her mother simply ignored Chloe's crying and demands. The mother would often compare Chloe with other children, and those comparisons were never in Chloe's favor. She could tell Chloe what a loser she was, harshly criticizing her actions and appearance. Chloe never felt safe with her mother.

Once, as a fourteen-year-old teenager Chloe was waiting with her mother for a tram at the stop. A man approached Chloe and began to pester her and touch her already fully formed breasts. Chloe's mom was looking at all this but did not react in any way. Of course, Chloe was shocked and outraged by the behavior of both the man and her mother. However, due to her habit of

---

27. Paine and Sandage, "More Prayer, Less Hope," 224.

28. Hall, Fujikawa, Halcrow, Hill, Delaney, "Attachment to God and Implicit Spirituality," 227.

not questioning her mother's behavior, Chloe decided that she must deserve to be treated like this.

At home, Chloe also did not feel safe, since her mother often brought home men to whom she sold snacks and alcohol (which she brewed at home). Most of the men were former soldiers in Afghanistan, and mentally quite imbalanced. One day, when she came home from school and saw men drinking at home, Chloe became indignant. One of the men in one jump reached and grabbed her by the throat, lifting her above the ground, loudly cursing and threatening her. As usual, Chloe's mother did not stand up for her daughter. On the contrary, she scolded Chloe and told her to leave.

Chloe's relationship with men has never been satisfying or safe either. Her relationship with her boyfriend, by whom Chloe had a daughter, was marked with abuse. When Chloe again complained to her mother about sexual and physical abuse by her partner, her mother said: "Well, can't you put up with it? He gives money for your mortgage!" Physical abuse from other men, even unfamiliar ones, has become a common thing for Chloe, as was emotional abuse from her mother in the form of constant intrusive interference, control, and humiliation. As a result, Chloe developed a typical chaotic attachment both to people and to God. Especially indicative was her phrase, written to me (Viktoriia) in a WhatsApp chat: "I realized that I am striving for self-destruction . . . I'm even comfortable when in pain."

Gary Sibcy and Tim Clinton write: "Children raised by insensitive parents are more likely to have behavioral problems, fewer intimate relationships with peers, and less than an intimate relationship with a future spouse. They are also more likely to turn for comfort to things – possibly resulting in addictions – rather than people or, ultimately, to God."[29] It is not surprising, therefore, that Chloe had serious drinking problems. God in her view was an impersonal force, an indifferent cosmos. She often struggled with a lack of friends, cultural, social, and especially spiritual loneliness.

As we have mentioned, people who suffer from spiritual loneliness are often overwhelmed with fear of punishment from God. They believe God has forsaken them, and are constantly concerned about how well they meet standards of holiness in order to be accepted by God. They certainly cannot live in hope, peace, and spiritual well-being.

Scripture says "we have this hope as an anchor for the soul, firm and secure" (Heb 6:19 NIV), which does not fail to help us endure in life's upheavals

---

29. Tim Clinton and Gary Sibcy, *Attachments: Why You Love, Feel and Act the Way You Do* (Brentwood: Integrity Publishers, 2002), 237.

and storms. "Those who hope in the LORD will renew their strength. They will run and not grow weary, they will walk and not be faint" (Isa 40:31 NIV). Jennifer DeSouza describes hope as a fundamental, basic, and essential part of life.[30] Hope is a prerequisite for recreation and the renewal of our strength. We just can't live without it!

A combination of a negative image of God and uncertainty in God's love and acceptance, and the false understanding that we need to earn them, has the potential for frequent mental torment, hopelessness, struggle, doubts about God, and spiritual loneliness. This constant struggle and feelings of inadequacy are completely independent of how outwardly religious we are, how often we go to church, or how much we ask God in prayers. Rather, the opposite is true. It all depends on the image of God in our minds. Accordingly, if we are convinced that, no matter what, we are accepted and loved by God in Christ, this inspires us and gives us hope to fight against sin. Scripture confirms that realization of God's kindness leads us toward repentance (Rom 2:4). The spiritual struggle of believers to comply with the moral standards of Scripture is inevitable and should be. But, in military language, our success on "the spiritual front" does not in any way affect our acceptance by God. We are referring here to the doctrine of justification by faith, not by merit. In the diagram below, we have attempted to illustrate the importance and implications of a positive and negative image of God in the mind of a Christian.

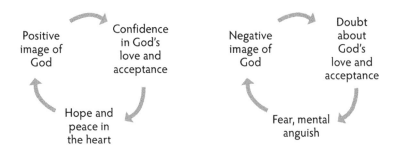

Todd Hall and his colleagues draw an interesting conclusion: Christians with insecure attachment tend to use religion to improve their emotional state, that is, they pray when things get bad so that they feel better.[31] Steven J. Sandage and Peter Jankowski call this "utilitarian use of spirituality" and "instrumental

---

30. Jennifer DeSouza, "Spirituality and Hope as Influences on Family Cohesion among African American Men" (PhD Dissertation, Walden University, 2014), 13.

31. Hall, Fujikawa, Halcrow, Hill, Delaney, "Attachment to God and Implicit Spirituality," 233.

relationship with God."[32] It is typical for Christians with chaotic and avoidant attachments.

Moreover many people with avoidant attachment are characterized by angry resentment against God. They suppress the desire to know God deep inside of them. Such people, if something goes wrong in their life, tend to blame God for it. They seem to say: "If there is a God, then he is definitely not for me, he does not care about me! I prayed, and I prayed, and there was never any answer! I don't need God!" Resentment against God then leads to leaving God, apostasy, atheism, and, as a result, sinful habits.

Conclusion to chapter 4

Before we go any further, let us quickly recap the psychological reasons for loneliness in each of the types we have identified in a graphical diagram:

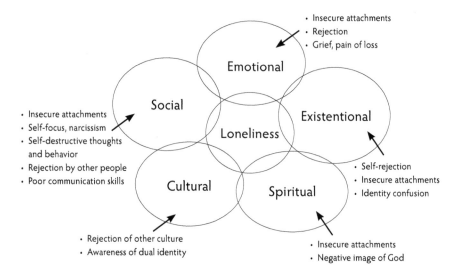

Psychological reasons for loneliness

Notice that there are common causes for almost all types of loneliness, the most common of which is an insecure attachment to people and God. At the core of every insecure attachment style is a distorted identity, deeply rooted and often unconscious, that defines how we see ourselves and the world, how we feel and act. The problem is that this style was formed in our childhood.

---

32. Sandage *et al*, "Attachment to God."

How can you influence those beliefs and those childhood experiences that result in an insecure attachment to God and other people now in adulthood? After all, the past cannot be changed. But we are convinced that spiritual loneliness, and subsequently other types of loneliness, can be overcome by directing effort to change the insecure attachment to God into a secure one. A secure attachment can be learned. Lee Kirkpatrick and Philip Shaver argue that "learning to have a secure attachment to God is possible, which has allowed some people to subsequently develop safer and more stable relationships with others."[33] We believe that qualified counseling help, and your own efforts, should be aimed primarily at changing your attachment to people and God from insecure to secure. We will further discuss below the connection between attachment and different types of loneliness, and how to change attachments to be secure in order to overcome loneliness.

---

33. Lee A. Kirkpatrick and Philip R. Shaver, "An Attachment-Theoretical Approach to Romantic Love and Religious Belief," *Personality and Social Psychology Bulletin* 18 (1992): 273, doi:10.1177/0146167292183002.

5

Effective Strategies for Overcoming Loneliness

Common advice suggests that you should just be friendlier, be more communicative, have a pet, and hope for the better, and your loneliness will pass away by itself over time. But in most cases, these tips don't work. Let us see why such advice does not always help and what does work.

We have already mentioned that different people experience loneliness differently. This happens not only because there are different types of loneliness, but also because people have different life experiences and attachment styles. They are accustomed to thinking, feeling and reacting differently. All this should be taken into account in providing help to a lonely person, which needs to be done comprehensively and in stages. This approach will greatly reduce their experience of loneliness. It is also important to determine a person's style of attachment and type of loneliness.[1] For this purpose, we have developed a questionnaire that can practically help us determine the type of loneliness or the combination (which often happens), and to what extent a person suffers from it (see the appendix).[2] The questionnaire also helps see which attachment style dominates in a particular person's relationships.

---

1. See: Enrico DiTommaso, Samantha R. Fizell, Bryn A. Robinson, "Chronic Loneliness within an Attachment Framework: Process and Interventions," in *Addressing Loneliness: Coping, Prevention and Clinical Interventions*, eds. Ami Sha'ked and Ami Rokach (NY: Routledge, 2015), 249.

2. While developing our questionnaire to determine the type of loneliness, we used parts of some well-known methodologies, with the permission of their developers. For further information about the development of the Inventory, you might be interested to read my article: Valeriia A. Chornobai, "The Development and Initial Validation of the Loneliness Inventory for Christians (LIFC)," *Skhid: Philosophical Sciences* 1, 165 (January–February 2020), http://skhid. kubg.edu.ua/article/view/197021.

We will now look at the most popular strategies for overcoming loneliness and evaluate their effectiveness.

Ami Rokach's model for overcoming loneliness consists of six strategies combined into three clusters:[3]

1. Distancing and denial;

2. Acceptance and resource development;

3. Building social bridges.

Distancing and loneliness denial strategy is about avoiding full awareness of the pain it causes. This strategy involves detaching oneself from people or situations, to reflect on and understand them. This approach, however, can only successfully block the pain of loneliness in the short term. It is not enough to deal with loneliness permanently. Moustakas noted that before loneliness can be overcome, it must be faced, accepted, and endured.[4] Distancing and denial for a long period will only aggravate loneliness, turning it into a chronic condition (like neglected gastritis). Another danger of this strategy is its passivity. It is associated with an increased risk of unhealthy behaviors such as excessive drug use, overeating, alcohol or drug abuse, self-isolation, self-delusion, and so on.

Far more effective coping strategies are those that Ami Rokach categorizes as the acceptance and resource development cluster.[5] These are the strategies

---

3. Ami Rokach, "Cultural Background and Coping with Loneliness," *The Journal of Psychology* 133, 2 (1999): 220, https://doi.org/10.1080/00223989909599735.

4. Clark E. Moustakas, *Loneliness* (Englewood Cliffs: Prentice-Hall, 1961), 103.

5. This is called cognitive-behavioral therapy. Such programs and assistance aimed at changing attitudes, ways of thinking, and, accordingly, behavior, are recognized by many scientists as the most effective in overcoming loneliness (See also: Ami Rokach, "Effective Coping with Loneliness: A Review," *Open Journal of Depression* 7, 4 (November 2018): 62, https://doi.org/10.4236/ojd.2018.74005; Cacioppo *et al*, "Loneliness," 238; Benedict T. McWhirter, John Horan, "Construct Validity of Cognitive-Behavioral Treatments for Intimate and Social Loneliness," *Current Psychology* 15, 1 (Spring 1996): 42–52, DOI: 10.1007/BF02686933; Stella Mills, "Loneliness: Do Interventions Help?" *Rural Theology* 15, 2 (2017): 118, https://doi.org/10.1080/14704994.2017.1373474; Louise C. Hawkley and John T. Cacioppo, "Loneliness Matters: A Theoretical and Empirical Review of Consequences and Mechanisms," *Ann Behav Med.* 40, 2 (Oct. 2010): 10, DOI: 10.1007/s12160-010-9210-8, https://www.ncbi.nlm.nih.gov/pmc/articles/PMC3874845/; Sean S. Seepersad, "Helping the "Poor Get Richer" – Successful Internet Loneliness Intervention Programs," in *Addressing Loneliness: Coping, Prevention and Clinical Interventions* Vol. 1, eds. Ami Sha'ked and Ami Rokach (New York: Routledge, 2015), 231–40; Вікторія А. "Гриценко, Переживання Самотності й Особливості Духовно-Емоційної та Комунікативної Сфер Життя Старших Підлітків," in *Збірник наукових праць Кам'янець-Подільського національного університету імені Івана Огієнка.* Вип. XVIII. Ред. Л. П. Мельник, В. І. Співак (Кам'янець-Подільський: Медобори-2006, 2012) [Viktoriia A. "Hrytsenko, Experiences of Loneliness and Peculiarities of the Spiritual-Emotional and

that involve changes in thinking and behavior, such as acceptance and reflection; self-development and understanding; faith, and worshiping God.[6]

Acceptance and reflection emphasizes the benefits of solitary reflection on our feelings and thoughts, as well as the awareness and recognition of our loneliness as a fact. Acceptance does not mean that we humble ourselves before the circumstances, but that we are aware of the problem of loneliness. By reflection, we mean analyzing our inner states of mind, feelings, thoughts, and experiences. Acceptance and reflection are focused on taking advantage of the opportunity to be alone to face your fears, desires, and needs as the most important means to overcome loneliness.

Understanding and resource development is aimed at a deeper understanding of oneself, self-acceptance, and intrapersonal growth. It means restoration of understanding of our identity in Christ, by "the renewal of our mind" (Rom 12:2) in line with the Scriptures, regarding who we are and what our calling is. It requires our study of God's word, the building of godly friendships, and sometimes, counseling. The process of understanding and self-development is especially effective when lonely people are active in organized groups (for example, home-groups, training, retreats, dating clubs, etc.) and are provided with professional help from counselors. This therapy can be very helpful because lonely people can have relief just by talking to another person about important issues in their life. Ami Rokach comments,

> Another benefit is that it is possible for the person seeking therapy to share strong, painful emotions without needing to censor himself or worrying about the effect it may have on his relationship with the therapist. That alone may contribute to a feeling of belonging and a connection with another caring human.[7]

In the process of overcoming loneliness, it is important to learn how to identify and change the automatic negative thoughts we have about ourselves, others, and social interactions in general, in line with the truths of God's word. Scripture teaches us: "The weapons we fight with are not the weapons of the world. On the contrary, they have divine power to demolish strongholds. We demolish arguments and every pretension that sets itself up against the

---

Communicative Spheres of Life of Older Adolescents," in Collection of Scientific Papers of the Ivan Ohienko Kamianets-Podilskyi National University. Vol. XVIII. Ed. L. P. Melnyk, V. I. Spivak (Kamyanets-Podilskyi: Medobory-2006, 2012)], 116–23, https://fkspp.at.ua/Bibl/18.pdf.

6. Ami Rokach, "Cultural Background and Coping with Loneliness," *The Journal of Psychology* 133, 2 (1999): 220. https://doi.org/10.1080/00223989909599735.

7. Rokach, "Effective Coping with Loneliness," 63.

knowledge of God, and we take captive every thought to make it obedient to Christ" (2 Cor 10:4–5 NIV). With the help of the spiritual weapons of the word of God, we can change the way we think and behave. It is in our power. It means learning to view our negative thoughts as hypotheses that need to be tested against the truth of the word, rather than facts on which to act.[8] People suffering from chronic loneliness subconsciously focus on negative things in their relationships and the behavior of others. They often expect to be excluded and rejected. To check if the way we think aggravates our loneliness, let us ask ourselves the questions: do I expect exclusion and rejection from other people? Do I think others don't want me to be around? Am I trying to avoid pain so I don't risk opening up? Did people really say something bad about me, or did I add my meaning to their words? Can I say that people are not against me, and do I risk becoming open and vulnerable again? We also need to check and analyze our behavior by asking ourselves: do I avoid the opportunity to be around others? Am I looking for excuses to decline invitations, or am I pushing others away to protect myself? Am I acting like I'm being attacked?

However, there are situations where introspection alone may not be enough. In this case, you should seek professional help from a counselor or an experienced spiritual minister.

The strategy of *faith and worshiping God* involves internal and external religious activity. At the same time, internal faith is a much more important factor for the well-being of a Christian than outward religiosity. As we have already mentioned, research shows that what has the deepest positive consequences for the psychological well-being of believers is not so much their participation in church ordinances, the number and duration of prayers or reading Scripture, but rather their personal close relationship with God, based on their positive image of God.[9] At the same time, certain internal religious beliefs, for example, insecure attachment to God, can cause concern and mental distress in the believer.[10] Internal healthy religiosity and active faith in God help us to feel connected with God and worship him, and help us to find strength, consolation, and inner peace.

---

8. Cacioppo *et al*, "Loneliness," 242.

9. Brian D. Dufton, Daniel Perlman, "Loneliness and Religiosity: in the World but Not of It," *Journal of Psychology and Theology* 14, 2 (1986):1.

10. Jolene M. Hill, "The Differential Prediction of Outcome Following Interpersonal Offenses Versus Impersonal Tragedies by Attachment to People and Attachment to God" (Thesis, Brock University, St. Catharines, August 2014), 17; Bradshaw, Ellison, and Marcum, "Attachment to God."

According to Ami Rokach, in theory and practice, the importance of any person's need for belonging is underestimated.[11] By joining religious groups and professing a common faith, we have the opportunity to connect with other Christians and thus expand our circle of friends, a sense of community and belonging.

Thus, the third cluster of strategies outlined by Ami Rokach includes expanding the social support network and increasing activity. Note here, such strategies as searching for new connections, increasing opportunities or time for communication, without first changing your way of thinking, without understanding yourself, your goals, and place in the world, are usually ineffective and may lead to even the opposite effect – exacerbating the problem of loneliness!

The *social support network expansion* strategy focuses on increasing social inclusion and interaction with others. In coping with loneliness, people who can provide us with social support are priceless! Social support can be formally defined as the interpersonal interactions and relationships that provide us with help or feelings of affection for the people we believe are caring for us.[12] As a rule, there are three types of social support:[13]

- Material support. This includes food, clothing, shelter, finances, and other material things with which we can help other people.
- Emotional support. This refers to interpersonal emotional support, including acceptance, understanding, patting on the back, and having or giving a shoulder to cry on.
- Instrumental support. This may include providing a service, practical physical assistance, information, guidance, advice, contacts such as the telephone number of a hairdresser, church pastor, landlord, etc.

Support for lonely people can be considered effective if it:

- contributes to the ordering of their worldview, restoration of hope, mobilization of initiative and internal forces;

11. Rokach, "Effective Coping with Loneliness," 68.

12. Stevan E Hobfoll, John R. Freedy, Carol Lane, and Pamela A. Geller, "Conservation of Social Resources: Social Support Resource Theory," *Journal of Social and Personal Relationships* 7, 4 (1990): 465–78, https://doi.org/10.1177/0265407590074004.

13. Joseph Walsh, Patrick R. Connelly, "Supportive Behaviors in Natural Support Networks of People with Serious Mental Illness," *Health and Social Work* 2, 4 (1996): 296–303, https://doi.org/10.1093/hsw/21.4.296.

- provides guidance and advice, confidence and emotional support in times of crisis, and a channel of communication with the social world;
- helps restore their identity;
- provides material assistance and personal support from others when needed;
- provides adequate rest and privacy.[14]

A social support network consists not only of those people who are a source of social support for us, but includes all the people with whom we interact. Relationships with those who are included in our social support network can be grouped into ten categories:

1. nuclear family;

2. extended family;

3. friends;

4. neighbors;

5. community relations;

6. school;

7. colleagues;

8. church;

9. recreational groups;

10. professional associations.

All of these people from our social network with whom we have contacted over the past two weeks have the potential to provide us with instrumental, material and / or emotional support. An example of a social support network can be seen below:[15]

14. Gerald Caplan, "Loss, stress, and mental health," *Community Men Health J.* 26, 1 (Feb 1990): 27–48, DOI: 10.1007/BF00752675. PMID: 2344725.

15. Elizabeth D. Hutchison, ed. *Dimensions of Human Behavior: Person and Environment* (Pine Forge Press, 1999), 144–45.

Social Support Network

Categories	Network member*	Types of support
Nuclear family	Mother*	Material and Emotional
	Father*	Material
	Sister*	Emotional
Extended family	Grandmother*	Emotional
Friends	John*	Emotional
Neighbors	Landlord	Instrumental
Community relations	None	–
School	Nina	Instrumental
	Academic adviser*	Instrumental
	Social worker*	Emotional
Colleagues from work	Nikolas	Instrumental
Church	None	–
Recreational groups	None	–
Professional associations	None	–
* An asterisk indicates those that the person considered members of his social network.		

Relationships with members of our social support network are not equivalent to social support because relationships can be ambivalent – both positive (source of support) and negative (source of stress). This should be taken into account by counselors, ministers, social workers, and psychologists who are helping a lonely person to cope with loneliness and the pain it causes.

It should also be taken into consideration that lonely people tend to see their social support network too narrowly (like Alex below, who named only one person), especially ignoring those whose social support they do not count on. To take the lonely peoples' "blinders" away and help them evaluate their social support networks more adequately, counselors, church ministers, psychologists, and social workers can examine the social network together with them, to see what type of social support from each member of the network they ever received or could expect to receive.

Some studies on social support suggested that to deal with stress and life challenges satisfactorily and effectively, the social support network of each person should be adequate for their needs.[16] The size of the network can vary due to individual differences in sociability and life stage. Based on this, we can assess how great a person's risk of being objectively and subjectively lonely is.

A satisfactory social support network is crucial to our mental and even physical health. "Sociability and a satisfying social support network were shown to be associated with greater resistance to developing colds when people were experimentally exposed to a cold virus."[17] Being satisfied with our social support network helps us to be kinder, more optimistic and resilient. According to Cacioppo and others, such attitudes most often attract other people, and lead to an improvement in our social network.[18] Social support also mitigated the effects of stress and depression.[19]

One should not forget about the development of a network of social contacts through communication in small groups, and friendship and sociality in general. Relationships, friends, and partners can allay some types of loneliness. However, a lonely person can find it very difficult to establish, maintain, and restore relationships. This skill needs to be learned. That's why Scripture admonishes us to "do good and to share what you have, for such sacrifices are pleasing to God" (Heb 13:16).

Increased activity as a strategy for overcoming loneliness is aimed at a commitment to working, attending, and serving in church, volunteering, and social activities. It certainly makes our lives more enjoyable, productive, and meaningful. The increased activity strategy aims to provide an active and interesting time alone or in groups, thus creating new opportunities for our mobilization and social contacts. As Olds and Schwartz pointed out, "Although increased social participation may not ultimately offer lasting, deeply personal, and intimate relationships, such participation may provide company, a sense

---

16. Elizabeth D. Hutchison, ed. *Dimensions of Human Behavior: Person and Environment* (Los Angeles: Sage Publications, 2008), 174.

17. Sheldon Cohen, William J. Doyle, Ronald Turner, Cuneyt M. Alper, David P. Skoner, "Sociability and Susceptibility to the Common Cold," *Psychological Science* 14 (2003): 389–95. See also Rokach, "Effective Coping with Loneliness."

18. John T. Cacioppo and William Patrick, *Loneliness: Human Nature and the Need for Social Connection* (New York: W. W. Norton, 2008).

19. Rokach, "Effective Coping with Loneliness," 64; David R. Brown, Jamie S. Carney, Mark S. Parrish, and John L. Klem "Assessing Spirituality: The Relationship between Spirituality and Mental Health," *Journal of Spirituality in Mental Health* 15, 2 (2013): 118, https://doi.org/10.10 80/19349637.2013.776442.

of belonging, guidance, and advice, that one gets from acquaintances and friends."[20]

Usually the efforts we make to obtain social support or to increase opportunities for social interaction are less successful in overcoming loneliness than efforts to change self-destructive attitudes and thoughts. Yet our efforts are crucial to reduce or overcome loneliness. You can ask yourself the question: "Am I looking for new acquaintances, or do I avoid them?"

Our chances of overcoming loneliness increase if the following sequence is observed. First of all, we must allow God to restore our identity in Christ to understand who we are in him, and what is our calling and purpose. Next, it is important to check and change our misconceptions and self-destructive thoughts and behavior. Only then can our efforts to establish or expand social bonds and increased activity be effective in overcoming our loneliness. And only then can the following simple practical tips be useful: call someone today, regardless of whether you feel like it or not; write to a friend you haven't spoken to for a long time; call a family member who has become estranged; invite a friend from work for coffee; go where you are usually afraid or too lazy to go, for example, to the gym or church. Even if nothing colossal and fateful comes of this, it will still help us, or those with whom we are trying to communicate, to "pump" our social muscles!

Let us remind ourselves once again that it is better to apply these listed strategies in detail and consistently. Then they are effective for mitigating or overcoming loneliness.

We will now examine effective strategies for overcoming loneliness depending on the types of loneliness.

1. Overcoming emotional loneliness

How can a person overcome loneliness if it is caused by the loss or absence of meaningful relationships due to, for example, the death of a loved one, or a breakdown in romantic relationships, rejection, or celibacy? The help given to a person who lacks trusting relationships and close emotional ties should be thorough and carried out in several directions.

One effective strategy in overcoming emotional loneliness can be a healthy religious life. Johann Zimmermann wrote in 1799 that a healthy religious life of faith can help overcome the negatives of emotional loneliness, rendering heart

---

20. Jacqueline Olds, Richard S. Schwartz, *The Lonely American: Drifting Apart in the Twenty-First Century* (Boston: Beacon Press, 2009), 1.

tranquil under the pressure of misfortunes.[21] Modern research confirms the benefits of healthy religious life in finding meaning in times of life's turmoil and crisis.[22] We define a healthy religious life as having a deep personal relationship with God based on trust and secure attachment to God, sound theology, and a positive image of God. It also presupposes one's commitment to and active participation in the social work of the local church.

According to Stella Mills, a local church can help a lonely person reduce emotional loneliness through worshiping God together and building up a deep individual relationship with God. The church has much more to offer than just social activities.[23] "When the church communicates a God who is nearer to us than our breath, it offers intimacy."[24]

Personal prayers of reflection are also helpful to reexamine life in accordance with the truth of the faithfulness and goodness of God. By the prayer of reflection here we do not mean some kind of oriental meditation practice, the purpose of which is to get rid of stressful thoughts and self-awareness. Rather, we mean deep meditation on the Scriptures, analysis of one's thoughts and reactions, combined with the proclamation of Scriptures, worship, and thankfulness to God in solitude. Here we focus on the importance of solitude for the development of such relationships with God, reducing a person's spiritual instability and emotional loneliness. This opportunity to experience the goodness of God in solitude and sincere meditation on the Scriptures helps alleviate the pain of emotional loneliness. (We will further touch on solitude as a strategy for overcoming loneliness later on.)

The church also has huge potential to help unchurched people and non-Christians cope with their chronic spiritual and emotional loneliness. It can especially provide financial and moral support to people who are experiencing loss or grief, such as widows and those having suicidal thoughts.

Let's come back to the story of Alex (from Book 2). Attacks of chronic emotional loneliness and depression were typical for Alex from time to time. However, the problem was exacerbated every time an important area of his life

---

21. Johann Georg Zimmerman, *Solitude Considered, with Respect to Its Influence upon the Mind and the Heart* (London: C. Dilly, 1799), 417.

22. Amelia J. Anderson-Mooney, Marcia Webb, Nyaradzo Mvududu, and Anna M. Charbonneau, "Dispositional Forgiveness and Meaning-Making: The Relative Contributions of Forgiveness and Adult Attachment Style to Struggling or Enduring With God," *Journal of Spirituality in Mental Health* 17, 2 (2015): 93, DOI: 10.1080/19349637.2015.985557.

23. Stella Mills, "Loneliness: Do Interventions Help?" *Rural Theology* 15, 2 (2017): 116, https://doi.org/10.1080/14704994.2017.1373474.

24. Jo Ind, *Loneliness: Accident or Injustice? Exploring Christian Responses to Loneliness in the Thames Valley* (Oxford: Diocese of Oxford, 2015), 22.

was at risk – the area of work. The chronic loneliness and depression associated with it hold the danger of suicidal thoughts and attempts.

One day Alex lost his job. As soon as I (Viktoriia) learned of this, I contacted him and found him in deep depression, fighting obsessive suicidal thoughts. After asking direct questions about how exactly he was going to take his life, I learned that Alex had a gun that he had borrowed from his father. The more specific one's plan of taking one's life, the more serious intentions are. The situation required me to act urgently, although it was complicated by my geographic distance. I could only have online communication with him.

Every day of the whole next week I was on Viber sending voice and text messages, trying to get Alex to promise me that he would not do anything to himself that day, to get him out of his bed and eat. He didn't want to initially because he could not find a reason for why he should do so. I had to persuade him. After a couple of days, to those accomplishments he added going out, and the next day a bike ride. Next, my task was to convince Alex to get to his hobby – to go out and play the piano (he plays the piano amazingly!).

When this was achieved within a week or two, it was important to encourage Alex to start looking for a job. Getting out of the acute stage of depression took a couple of months. When Alex got a good job again, his self-esteem and sense of well-being began to slowly improve. But we still had two tasks: first, preventing Alex's acute attacks of loneliness and depression by expanding and strengthening his social support network, and second, getting him back in physical shape (during that time, Alex gained an extra fifteen kilograms).

People with chronic loneliness often have the problem of being "blinkered," fixed on their experiences and pain. They think mainly of themselves, neither believing in themselves nor expecting anything good from others. Of course, this negatively affects their attempts to build romantic or any other relationships. Also, their social support network is usually very narrow. Remarkably, Alex's answer to both of my questions about who he considered as his friend and who could he turn to for help was: "No one." This was a clear overstatement. Diminishing the importance of existing (though not very close) social ties with other people is typical for lonely people. Also, it is usually combined with low self-esteem and a belief that no one can or wants to understand or help them. The efforts to expand the lonely person's "perception blinkers," build up self-esteem, and develop self-confidence and trust in others can take a long time.

It is difficult to express the relief I felt when I met Alex a year later, and he confessed that despite his pessimistic thoughts sometimes, he has returned the gun to his father, asking that he would never under any circumstances give him that gun again. A couple of months later, Alex had lost weight to the norm of seventy-five kilograms and was bragging about his constitution being in very good shape. This is not to say Alex has become an eternal optimist. But with hope and joy I watch the more confident Alex, satisfied with his work, life, as his ability to build romantic relationships is being restored.

However, it is extremely important to note that if we lack the knowledge, skills, or confidence in our ability to help people with suicidal thoughts like Alex, it is better to seek professional help.

Apart from loss, subjective or objective rejection can also lead to emotional loneliness. Guy Winch provides the following guidelines for treating the mental wounds caused by emotional loneliness due to rejection.[25]

First, it is important to identify and change our wrong attitudes and beliefs manifested in self-fulfilling prophecies and self-destructive behavior. Pessimism and negative thinking characterize lonely people, aggravating their subjective feeling of loneliness, and making them perceive the actual reactions and emotions of people distortedly, in a more negative light. This, in turn, causes in them an even greater fear of rejection and a desire to defend themselves by self-isolation, pushing other people away from them. Therefore, in the fight against emotional loneliness, it is important to fight pessimism in every possible way, being guided by the presumption of innocence concerning other people. That means we assume other people did not want to reject us, and instead we analyze and change our behavior (such as self-absorption or gloominess) which is destructive for relationships. Guy Winch lists several other behaviors not conducive to healthy relationships: finding unconvincing excuses to reject a party invitation; offensiveness; too unemotional or laconic answers, or, conversely, excessive talkativeness and interruption of others; demonstration of a lack of interest in the opinions of others; telling unfamiliar people about your shortcomings and fears.[26] Such trains of thought and behavior must be changed.

Secondly, lonely people would benefit greatly by developing their "social muscles," learning to evaluate situations from another person's perspective, restoring an emotional connection by resolving conflict situations, making new acquaintances and deepening the old ones, and also looking for opportunities for communication. Social skills such as the ability to look at things from the perspective of another person, to show empathy, and to correctly interpret the thoughts and feelings of others are poorly developed in lonely people.

---

25. Винч, *Первая Психологическая Помощь* [Winch, Emotional First Aid], 13.

26. Винч [Winch], 15.

This often causes further conflicts, including with loved ones. Therefore, it is extremely useful to develop social skills that enable us to put ourselves in the shoes of another person.[27]

Third, you can reduce the emotional distress caused by loneliness through fond memories (by viewing photos, videos, reading letters from people we love). For lonely people who have little opportunity to deepen or improve the quality of their relationship (due to geographic isolation, health problems, limited mobility, or other circumstances), buying a pet could be a solution.

Thus, for people suffering from emotional loneliness, identifying and changing self-destructive thinking and behavior can be an effective tool. It must be borne in mind that there is a risk of rumination, when we focus all our attention on our own emotional needs, leaving us blind to the feelings and needs of others. This can have a detrimental effect on our relationships with friends and family. So that the analysis aimed at detecting wrong attitudes and self-destructive behavior does not turn into "chewing a mental cud" and self-flagellation, we need to try to look at the situation through the eyes of an outside observer,[28] we need to honestly admit our mistakes, repent before God from our hearts, accept forgiveness by faith, and live on according to Scripture.

Only after that, we can proceed to the next stage – expanding the network of social connections, creating opportunities for new acquaintances, online and offline communication, and involvement in social activities. Of course, social activity alone cannot compensate for the absence of emotional or intimate relationships. At the same time, after removing obstacles in the minds of lonely people, such as misconceptions, false expectations and false perceptions, engaging in group activities can help them cope with both social and emotional loneliness, especially in the atmosphere of a Christian church that offers friendship and caring. Volunteering and ministry in the church also is a great resource. Helping others boosts our self-esteem, gives us a sense of importance and significance, helps us to give, not take, and to focus on the needs and pains of other people, not our own. Ultimately, it makes us happier, more grateful, confident, and less lonely.

Let's return to the story of the long-distance seaman Guram. Perhaps the most difficult thing for Guram in his adaptation to the ordinary life, when

---

27. On the importance of empathy, Dr. Winch put it this way: "Developing the ability to empathize helps to breathe life into any relationship. The love and attention that empathy brings create an atmosphere of benevolence and generosity that strengthens any bonds – marriage, family and friendship." Винч [Winch], 17.

28. Винч [Winch], 36.

his voyage has ended, is the realization that everyone around him is living his or her own life. "Of course, I cannot but rejoice at the fact that I am now at home, that they were waiting for me, and I missed them: my family and friends," Guram admitted.

> But when I realize that by the second week of my stay at home, the children's interest in me abruptly disappears, my wife is busy with her very important business, my friends seem to be glad to see me, but they have no time for me now, then loneliness comes.

Note here that, in contrast to the social loneliness that Guram usually experiences while on a voyage, at home, in the process of adapting to a "normal" life, he suffers more from emotional loneliness, from a lack of close emotional contact and connection with people significant to him.

> Once after the voyage, I started calling friends, informing them that I had arrived. Having called four or five friends, I heard the answer: "Wow! You're back! Great!" But only one of them agreed to meet in a cafe to drink coffee and actually showed up. I rushed to meet him, but he talked to someone on the phone all the time and in the end, he just said goodbye and left. I finished my coffee alone,

Guram recalled sadly.

What helps Guram to overcome this emotional loneliness is his awareness of it, deep relationship with Christ, and time together with other Christians in the ministry of the church. For example, Guram told me (Valeriia) that, together with his wife, he enjoys visiting a recently widowed minister of their church, and gladly participates in the ministry for non-Christian teenagers, sharing with them his testimony of how God kept him and helped him go through the difficult turns of his adolescence. Counseling sessions with a professional consultant and his wife's support help Guram cope with his self-destructive attitudes and thoughts.

Deep happy friendships soften emotional loneliness, from which even spouses are not immune. Such a relationship is not an accident, but rather the result of daily work. It is good when churches carry out special programs to restore and strengthen family relationships. Ami Rokach has some tips for couples to strengthen marital relationships and address loneliness in intimate relationships:[29]

---

29. Rokach, "Effective Coping with Loneliness," 66.

• Building relationships for the right reasons. Getting married is not a cure-all for loneliness. Much less is creating a family for fear of loneliness! If we have not solved the problem of our loneliness before marriage, then having started a family, we may find that loneliness has not disappeared, on the contrary, has worsened!

• Intimate communication and participation. Without mutual self-revealing of spouses to each other, based on trust, close relationships in marriage are impossible. It is imperative for a good and satisfying relationship for spouses to develop their ability to support, listen with interest and participation, not judge but accept their partner, even if his or her actions may not be justified.

• Interdependence. Interdependence refers to the ability to depend on the other and accept the other person's dependence on you. It involves the courage to trust each other and the risk of being vulnerable. This is typical only for relationships based on secure attachment. If one of the partners has ambivalent attachment, it makes them cling to the spouse out of fear of losing the relationship, out of lack of confidence in the partner's love. Conversely, if a spouse has an avoiding attachment style they will be emotionally insensitive to the needs, thoughts, and feelings of the other spouse. In any case, both feel empty, lonely, and unhappy. Spouses with a secure attachment can trust, be open and understand that they are, in fact, two separate personalities (and not a reflection of each other), connected as an integrated whole.

• Resolving conflicts in relationships. Conflict is normal and expected in any relationship because it allows spouses to share things that worry, upset, or annoy them. Conflicts are sometimes needed. They allow spouses to strengthen and deepen their relationship if they can resolve conflicts effectively, without any damage to their relationships. If spouses do not know how to share their feelings and resolve interpersonal conflict ineffectively, undermining trust and respect for each other over and over again, they will experience loneliness and, eventually, will drift apart from each other.

• Avoiding even the slightest neglect. In ordinary language, benign neglect is taking our partner's presence, participation, and care for granted. A grateful and caring attitude can help prevent or minimize resentment and taking a spouse for granted. In this regard, the development of the skill of putting oneself in the shoes of a partner is essential.

• Mutual growth. When in a relationship only one of the partners personally grows and the other does not, this can lead to loneliness and drifting apart from each other, because they will have fewer topics to discuss. Therefore, one of the best ways to prevent such a distance is to be interested in each other's interests, grow together and allow each other to develop (even if he attends a cooking class, and she a Bible school). Then the balance in the relationship is maintained.

• Overcoming the scars of long-term marital distress. Unresolved relationship problems or ineffectively resolved conflicts erode the spouses' trust and reduces their ability to protect the relationship from future unavoidable conflicts. It is very important here to seek help from church ministers or counselors before it is too late. We can only agree with Ami Rockach that "seeking help when problems first start is a much better and safer strategy that may succeed in not only saving the marriage but intimacy and love as well."[30]

2. Overcoming social loneliness

To illustrate one of the ways to overcome social loneliness, let's go back to my (Valeriia's) story. One day, while I was still on that long working trip in a foreign culture, the situation changed, and my social and cultural loneliness began gradually to smooth out.

They have a very lovely tradition in the church I attended there. Before each Sunday service, a worship leader would put a bouquet of fresh flowers on the altar, which would be given to whomever he or she wished, at the end of the service. The bouquet was usually given to one of the guests or church members – for instance, to a couple celebrating their marriage anniversary that week or a widow who buried her husband lately. And so, one Sunday, the worship leader announced the bouquet would go to the newest visitor in their church.

"Who joined our church during this month?" the worship leader asked. I slowly raised my hand, sure I was not alone, for at least four more Ukrainians should have been with me; but that Sunday they had decided to go to another church. I turned out to be the only newcomer. The worship leader, without thinking twice, personally walked down the entire aisle to hand the flowers over to me.

"Hi, my name is Julia," she said in English.

"Hi! I'm Valeriia," I answered in English as well.

"Valeriia?! And where are you from?" Julia immediately switched to Ukrainian. "I'm from Ukraine," she said.

"Me too!" I exclaimed with joy.

"Come over to our house tomorrow! Let's chat then," Julia suggested and handed me the flowers. It was a huge bouquet of my favorite yellow tulips.

---

30. Rokach, "Effective Coping with Loneliness," 69.

And it was March, the first Sunday after my birthday, and it was a wonderful present for my birthday!

"You are the first person," I replied, "who met with me and invited me to their home for all this time!"

As I was settling down on the university campus, I gradually began to attend lectures that I was interested in, where I met other students. I decided to cook along with other students in the kitchen, not only for myself but also for them. It didn't take long before my loneliness dissipated. I felt a lot better when my acquaintances at university began to invite me to their ladies' home group, where we shared our thoughts and feelings, stories, experiences, and prayed for each other. Since they were all from different nationalities, cultures and Christian traditions, I remember it took courage and a conscious decision to stop avoiding the people around me and decide to come to this home group. I just needed to take a step forward, start to open up, and communicate with them. At this group one sister gave me a huge chocolate heart which she had made with her own hands. Later this sister and I became good friends.

Social loneliness can be reduced by participating in group activities fitting the interests of a socially lonely person. Interactions such as attending tea and cake meetings and home group meetings help develop communication skills and increase self-esteem, as the lonely person makes new friends in a safe and pleasing atmosphere. But this method will only work if the lonely person has a desire to overcome loneliness and engage in interaction. The development of a social network and the group activity of people with common interests as strategies for overcoming loneliness are, or course, important. However, people with this type of loneliness first need to examine if their personal beliefs and behavior are the main reason for their social loneliness.

Many of the circumstances that create feelings of social loneliness are temporary. If our communication skills are strong enough, and we are confident and positive (we have a secure attachment style), then we usually make new acquaintances, and loneliness goes away on its own. But lonely people, due to some of their characteristics (introversion and low self-esteem, for instance, and especially, insecure attachment), often need help in defeating loneliness. Otherwise, their loneliness becomes chronic.

Both scientific research and the experience of the people suffering loneliness, especially for a long time, indicate that excessive social activity, when people force themselves to meet and communicate with new people, can have the opposite effect. This is especially true for people whose social loneliness is associated with a narcissistic fixation on themselves and their pain.

Changing attitudes and mindsets should be prioritized and aimed at helping the lonely person, who should be encouraged:

1. Start noticing other people not from the point of how they can solve your social or emotional needs, but from the point of how you can help them in their needs.

2. Understand your true identity and purpose of life from the perspective of the word of God;

3. Combine the purpose of your life with meeting the needs of others. This will gradually increase your self-esteem and significance for others, widen your network of acquaintances and friends, solving the problem of social loneliness.

3. Overcoming cultural loneliness

In our opinion, the most effective strategies for overcoming cultural loneliness are the following:

– The practice of temporary solitude, during which we can reassess our values, prioritize, and focus on the purpose of our life and calling.

– Generosity, a benevolent attitude, and openness towards other people manifested in an elementary smile, are also important. Interestingly, as noted by some researchers, loneliness is maintained by faulty interpretation of the social signals – such as smiles and eye contact – that are key to positive social interactions. They hypothesize lonely people have an impaired ability to smile in response to a smile.[31]

– A personal prayer of reflection should take a special place for the crystallization of the believer's identity, and the development of his sense of belonging, first of all, to Christ. The Christian's clear awareness of identity in Christ, purpose from him, belonging to him, and his acceptance and love, can neutralize the pain of cultural (as well as social and existential) loneliness that the Christian can experience while fulfilling God's calling.

Moreover, a Christian is prone to cultural loneliness not only when *living in a foreign country or culture*. It can also be experienced even when one is dedicated to God and belongs to the church in one's native culture. Almost

---

31. Emma Young, "Preliminary Evidence that Lonely People Lose the Reflex to Mimic Other People's Smiles Potentially Sustaining the Isolation," *Neuropsych* (June 23, 2019), https://bigthink.com/neuropsych/loneliness/; Tara Well, "The Link between Loneliness and Smiling," *Psychology Today* (September 26, 2019), https://www.psychologytoday.com/us/blog/the-clarity/201909/the-link-between-loneliness-and-smiling.

every new Christian who wants to follow Christ daily experiences cultural loneliness in one way or another. This is true not only for those Christians who have converted to Christ from another faith but also those who converted and devoted their lives to Christ within their culture. For them, worldly culture and values have become alien; but Christian culture (or rather, church culture) has not become theirs yet. They often lose their former friends and face misunderstandings from their family members. They feel like strangers like they're no longer part of this "world." But Christians should feel that way and not fight cultural loneliness in a relation to the worldly system.

Here the role of the church, community, and friends is clear and especially important – to make every effort so that the converted person becomes a part of the new culture of the church and community. Everyone is called to be a part of the community. If people do not feel the support of the church, they usually leave the church. The need for belonging confronts them with a choice: either to return "into the world," merging with the crowd where they were once received, by denying their new identity in Christ – renouncing themselves and their true nature; or to seek the community where they will be accepted, or to disconnect themselves from the church, as a hermit who denies his need for belonging.

Any dedicated leader or Christian seeking to fulfill their calling from God experiences cultural loneliness from time to time, often combined with emotional and social loneliness. This is because, as we described in the first part of our book, Christians dedicated to their mission do not always find understanding and support from other Christians. Sometimes, unfortunately, the opposite happens – they face criticism and resistance from those who are their own. It is not normal, but it happens sometimes. Then, cultural loneliness is inevitable. Christians dedicated to their calling and finding themselves in opposition to the mainstream can do no other than be determined to continue their ministry no matter what, and rely on the Lord's help. God will not leave nor fail to support them. Strategies that help a Christian to keep the most important things in focus and to reduce the cultural loneliness in such times are solitude, reflection on the word of God and our finiteness, and his mission.

4. Overcoming spiritual loneliness

We overcome our spiritual loneliness primarily through building or restoring our relationship with God and developing a secure attachment to God. As we wrote earlier in the first part, a broken relationship with God, as well as insecure attachment, is the root cause of spiritual loneliness. The turn from an insecure attachment to a secure one happens through reading the Scripture and renewing our minds, aimed at removing misconceptions and attitudes about an "angry, indifferent, punishing God," and creating the biblical image of God.

Earlier, we discussed how incorrect theology and a negative image of God determines an insecure attachment to God both in Christians and their children, and directly affects the likelihood of loneliness, particularly spiritual loneliness. The image we have of God and our attachment to God also determines our emotional response and behavior – what science calls religious coping.

What is religious coping, and why is *positive* religious coping effective in overcoming our loneliness while *negative* religious coping is not?

As a result of their research on the benefits and harms of different religious coping strategies, Kenneth Pargament and his colleagues determined that religious coping strategies can be both positive and negative.[32] Positive religious coping includes a steadfast faith in God's care, good intentions, and omnipotence despite our suffering.[33] Job's example is very revealing in this regard. Job said: "I know that my redeemer lives, and that in the end he will stand on the earth"[34] (Job 19:25). Negative religious coping includes feelings of disappointment or frustration with God, anger towards God, a decrease in our confidence in God's ability or desire to help us in times of suffering, and a perception of God as distant and uninterested in our well-being.[35]

This leads, respectively, to either positive consequences (our better adaptation to new life circumstances and post-traumatic growth), or negative (poor adaptation, grief, and depression). Post-traumatic growth is the process when, after suffering a very stressful or traumatic event, we still experience a positive transformation of ourselves and our worldview.[36] Yet such positive transformations do not happen automatically. When we use negative religious coping strategies – when we blame God, other people or ourselves for the situation, when we are engaged in "rumination" and perceive ourselves as a

---

32. Kenneth I. Pargament, Bruce W. Smith, Harold G. Koenig, and Lisa Perez, "Patterns of Positive and Negative Religious Coping with Major Life Stressors," *Journal for the Scientific Study of Religion* 37, 4 (1998): 710–24.

33. Anderson-Mooney *et al*, "Dispositional Forgiveness," 94.

34. "And that he shall stand" – He will stand up, as one does who undertakes the cause of another. Jerome in his translation of the Bible into Latin has rendered this as though it referred to Job "And in the last day I shall rise from the earth" – *de terra surrecturus sum* – as if it referred to the resurrection of the body.

35. Anderson-Mooney *et al*, "Dispositional Forgiveness," 93.

36. Sarah L. Moon, "Religious Coping as a Moderating Variable" (Doctor of Psychology Degree Diss., Wheaton, Illinois, October, 2013), 1.

victim of circumstances – there is no positive transformation. People react differently in times of spiritual suffering and the "Valley of Weeping" (Ps 84:6). Why is this?

It is because positive religious coping strategies are determined by our secure attachment to God, our view of the world through a positive lens, and our sense of spiritual community.[37] Examples of positive religious coping strategies include benevolent religious reappraisals of stressors, seeking spiritual support and connection, and forgiveness.[38] This can be seen when Christians evaluate their experience, describing it with such phrases: "I tried to see how God can strengthen me in this situation"; "I was looking for an even closer relationship with God amid suffering"; "I asked forgiveness for my sins," "I tried to see how in this problem I can thank God, what good can I find in it" (think of the game that Eleanor Porter's Pollyanna played).

Negative religious coping strategies are defined by insecure attachment to God, the perception of the world as a threat, and the constant struggle with feelings of insignificance.[39] For example, when faced with problems in life, people who resort to negative religious coping strategies are more likely to think that God has left them or is punishing them through this problem. Or they conclude that all the problems in their life are caused by the devil. Or they wonder if their church has forgotten them. It is not difficult to see that under the conviction that behind every difficulty in life there are the devil's schemes, there is a passive fatalistic position and an unwillingness to take responsibility for life. Negative religious coping strategies based on a negative image of God are certainly ineffective.

Extrinsic or benefit-motivated religiosity is also one of these ineffective strategies. In the book of the prophet Hosea, we read how God assessed such strategies when the people of God turned to him not sincerely, but only for some benefit: "They do not cry to me from the heart but they wail upon their beds. For grain and wine they gash themselves, they rebel against me" (Hos 7:14); "Woe to them, for they have strayed from me! Destruction to them for they have rebelled against me! I would redeem them, but they speak lies against me" (Hos 7:13). The common thread running through all of Scripture is that sincere trust and love for God is much better than formal external religiosity: "For I desire steadfast love and not sacrifice, the knowledge of God rather than burnt offerings" (Hos 6:6).

---

37. Moon, "Religious Coping," 25.

38. Moon, 25.

39. Moon, 25.

The research by Sarah Moon and her colleagues confirms that positive coping strategies reduce stress, depression, and anxiety, while negative ones do the opposite.[40] In any case, the more secure our attachment to God, the more positive our image of God, the more trust and endurance we have as we go through the "Valley of Weeping," and the faster we overcome feelings of abandonment by God and spiritual loneliness.

In their empirical study, Paine and Sandage examined how different types of prayer relate to levels of spiritual instability, hope, and attachment to God. They show that the beneficial effect of our petitionary prayer depends on the level of our spiritual stability or the security of our attachment to God.[41] Petitionary prayer does not give hope for Christians with insecure attachments. In other words, the higher level of our spiritual instability the less hopeful we are. Why is this? Spiritually unstable Christians with insecure attachments often feel disconnected from God and therefore distrustful of him. Often these Christians will interpret unanswered prayers as divine punishment or rejection. This pattern applies only to petitionary prayers: the more a spiritually unstable Christian asks from God in prayer, the less his hope is, as his doubts in God increase.[42] However, for people with insecure attachment styles, other types of prayer can be much more beneficial. Paine and Sandage argue that, for example, "Meditative or reflective prayers . . . may alleviate the distress associated with spiritual instability and promote well-being."[43] Apparently, the lower the level of our spiritual instability and the more secure our attachment to God, the more beneficial the effect of our petitionary prayer is. It has been proven that Christians with a low level of spiritual instability and a secure attachment to God are more likely to see answers to their petitionary prayers, their hope is at a higher level, and they are less lonely.[44]

Perhaps you are wondering if you can change the image of God that exists in your head when you are spiritually lonely. We are sure you can, just as you can learn secure attachment by changing negative conceptions about yourself and other people. Likewise, overcoming spiritual loneliness and changing our negative image of God is preceded by our determination to believe and base our conception about God on the word, and not on visible circumstances or our feelings, no matter how loudly they may be screaming.

---

40. Moon, 27.

41. Paine and Sandage, "More Prayer, Less Hope," 231.

42. Paine and Sandage, 231.

43. Paine and Sandage, 233.

44. Paine and Sandage, 232.

We outline the following strategies for overcoming spiritual loneliness:

1) Study Scripture to change wrong theological views, to form a biblical image of God and self. We believe that seeing ourselves the way God sees each one of us is vital for a healthy spiritual and mental life and for overcoming loneliness.

2) Concentrate on personal, thoughtful prayer, rather than on petitionary prayer, in solitude, which involves meditating on passages of the Scripture that speak of the goodness, mercy and faithfulness of God.

Some passages to meditate on:

> The Lord passed before him and proclaimed, "The LORD, the LORD, a God merciful and gracious, slow to anger, and abounding in steadfast love and faithfulness, keeping steadfast love for thousands, forgiving iniquity and transgression and sin, but who will by no means clear the guilty, visiting the iniquity of the fathers on the children and the children's children, to the third and the fourth generation" (Exod 34:6–7).

> Know therefore that the LORD your God is God, the faithful God who keeps covenant and steadfast love with those who love him and keep his commandments, to a thousand generations (Deut 7:9).

> All the paths of the LORD are steadfast love and faithfulness, for those who keep his covenant and his testimonies (Ps 25:10).

> But you, Lord, are a God merciful and gracious, slow to anger and abounding in steadfast love and faithfulness (Ps 86:15).

> The LORD is gracious and merciful, slow to anger and abounding in steadfast love. The LORD is good to all, and his mercy is over all that he has made (Ps 145:8–9).

> The steadfast love of the LORD never ceases; his mercies never come to an end; they are new every morning; great is your faithfulness. "The LORD is my portion," says my soul, "therefore I will hope in him." The LORD is good to those who wait for him, to the soul who seeks him (Lam 3:22–25).

> Who is a God like you, pardoning iniquity and passing over transgression for the remnant of his inheritance? He does not retain his anger forever, because he delights in steadfast love. He will again have compassion on us; he will tread our iniquities

underfoot. You will cast all our sins into the depths of the sea (Mic 7:18–19).

Therefore he had to be made like his brothers in every respect, so that he might become a merciful and faithful high priest in the service of God, to make propitiation for the sins of the people. For because he himself has suffered when tempted, he is able to help those who are being tempted (Heb 2:17–18).

For we do not have a high priest who is unable to sympathize with our weaknesses, but one who in every respect has been tempted as we are, yet without sin. Let us then with confidence draw near to the throne of grace, that we may receive mercy and find grace to help in time of need (Heb 4:15–16).

Of course, we understand that God's love and goodness are not his only characteristics. He is holy. He can be angry and punish. But as we have said earlier, Christians with insecure attachment have a tendency to perceive God's responses and external circumstances as evidence of God's rejection and disfavor. Therefore, they need to emphasize the love, faithfulness, and grace of God more.

Sometimes, to solve the problem of spiritual loneliness, we need reconciliation with God. And to solve the problem of existential loneliness, we need to regain the understanding of our identity in the creator's design, and to reconcile with ourselves.

5. Overcoming existential loneliness

As we wrote earlier, existential loneliness is rooted in the issue of human identity. Our identity is formed by what and with whom we identify ourselves. Part of our identity is determined by genetics (gender, skin and hair color, etc.) and family. Think about how often what we believe and think about ourselves is imposed on us by our parents?! And part of our identity is determined by our environment and past experiences – psychological factors.[45] Culture can also impose on us an identity, such as a victim, or a persecuted or despised minority. Think about how often Christians excuse themselves for the wrong behavior, allegedly inherent in all men, blond women, Ukrainians, Arabs, Caucasians,

---

45. We borrow the idea from the series of teaching "Who am I" by Duane Sheriff: https://www.youtube.com/watch?v=gPja9OQrlbs&list=PLNEz4ajKSEZ9KmBw4R2LjSWHbhhbn4zKY.

African-Americans, or whatever. What we think about ourselves, about who we truly are, determines our beliefs, feelings, behavior, purposes, relationships, and our very lives. Therefore, we need to be very careful what or who we identify ourselves with. Who do we allow to define our identity? Thomas Merton said:

> We can help one another to find the meaning of life, no doubt. But in the last analysis the individual person is responsible for living his own life and for "finding himself" If he persists in shifting his responsibility to somebody else, he fails to find out the meaning of his own existence. You cannot tell me who I am and I cannot tell you who you are. If you do not know your own identity, who is going to identify you?[46]

Jesus knew his identity through Scripture and the Holy Spirit. Jesus knew who his Father was. One day he said to his mother and his earthly father: "Why are you looking for me? Did you not know that I must be in my Father's house?" (Luke 2:49). However, Jesus Christ himself needed to grow in the wisdom and understanding of his identity: "And Jesus increased in wisdom and stature, and in favor with God and man" (Luke 2:52). Jesus read Scripture and understood that it was written about him: "Then I said, 'Behold, I have come to do your will, O God, as it is written of me in the scroll of the book'" (Heb 10:7). Surely when Jesus read the Psalms, the Holy Spirit must have been telling him: "This is about you!" Having a complete understanding of his identity, and therefore of his purpose, Jesus told the Jews: "You search the Scriptures because you think that in them you have eternal life; and it is they that bear witness about me" (John 5:39–40). "And beginning with Moses and all the Prophets, he interpreted to them in all the Scriptures the things concerning himself" (Luke 24:27).

We should also learn our identity through Scripture and the Holy Spirit. Our identity, first of all, is determined by the word of God, which tells us what we are in Christ and who Christ is in us. The apostle Paul wrote:

> I became a minister according to the stewardship from God that was given to me for you, to make the word of God fully known, the mystery hidden for ages and generations but now revealed to his saints. To them God chose to make known how great among the Gentiles are the riches of the glory of this mystery, which is Christ in you, the hope of glory. (Col 1:25–27)

---

46. Merton, *No Man is an Island*, 16.

Christians' knowledge of their identity enables them to know their calling as well. Paul wrote about his calling: "But when he who had set me apart before I was born, and who called me by his grace, was pleased to reveal his Son to me, in order that I might preach him among the Gentiles, I did not immediately consult with anyone" (Gal 1:15–16). In fact, neither other people nor even we ourselves should define who we really are, but only Scripture!

Knowing that doubts about identity make people incapable of recognizing and fulfilling their vocations, the devil does his best to make people confused about their identity. He tried to make Jesus doubt his identity too, asking: "If you are the Son of God . . ." He tried to make Jesus worship something or someone other than God: "Again, the devil took him to a very high mountain and showed him all the kingdoms of the world and their glory. And he said to him, 'All these I will give you, if you will fall down and worship me'" (Matt 4:8–9). And he tries to do the same with all people. He tries to distort our identity, what we believe about ourselves, and make us worship creation instead of the creator. How many Christians today think they are what they feel?! They say: "I know what God says in the Scriptures, but I just don't feel that way!" They worship their feelings instead of the creator. How many Christians allow the kingdoms of this world and the secular value system to define their identity and significance?

Remember the story of our Daniel? Daniel found his identity in God: "Only union with Christ makes me whole, relieves of my loneliness," he says. Daniel is often involved in volunteer projects. But that alone is not a solution to Daniel's existential loneliness. According to him, in the moments of existential crisis, when his identity as a Christian is under attack, his ministry and activities seem like dust to him. "There are times when everyone admires me, but inside I feel unworthy, unclean." At such moments Daniel returns to the "cornerstone" of his self-worth and significance – the Scriptures. Because Daniel understands unless a person in an existential crisis sees himself in Christ through the prism of Scripture, through the eyes of God, his ministry is only a temporary help, as an attempt of self-realization and confirmation of his significance. "This requires constant analysis of what in me, in my feelings, thoughts, attitudes does not correspond to Christ and what needs to be got rid of, and what is mine, unique and not sinful," continues Daniel.

The positive aspect of existential loneliness, as Daniel notes, is that the awareness of one's uniqueness helps a person to better concentrate on his mission, to understand his purpose. "My loneliness helps me better understand the purpose for which I live as if it creates a higher meaning."

So, in the process of overcoming existential loneliness, Christians have at least two advantages. First, they can allow God to determine who they are in Christ, trusting Scripture, not their own ideas and feelings, as the truth. And second, if Christians find their meaning of life in the eternal God, in knowing him, and their purpose in serving him, then they find that their life has eternal meaning as well. It is independent of the changing trends of the world or life cataclysms such as a crisis in relationship with someone or even the death of a loved one.

"Now I enjoy being alone," says Daniel. Let us note here that the awareness and acceptance of one's uniqueness subsequently allows a person not to be afraid of solitude, to better endure and more effectively use the time alone, and even to desire it. Thomas Merton put it this way:

> The man who fears to be alone will never be anything but lonely, no matter how much he may surround himself with people. But the man, who learns, in solitude and recollection, to be at peace with his own loneliness, and to prefer its reality to the illusion of merely natural companionship, comes to know the invisible companionship of God. Such a one is alone with God in all places, and he alone truly enjoys the companionship of other men, because he loves them in God, in whom their presence is not tiresome, and because of whom his own love for them can never know satiety.[47]

As Rae Andre also states: "Only when we learn to live alone and even to love alone – when we face our alienation, our vulnerability, our creativity, our uniqueness, our humanity, and our desires – will the problems of finding others and finding community become less urgent."[48]

It is clear that sometimes people devote their whole life to finding answers to the questions about identity and purpose; this is not a matter of one day. It is a long and sometimes painful process of hearing God, of analyzing ourselves and deciding what or which norms we will comply with, what truth about our "real self" we will choose to believe: the one the world around us dictates, our thoughts and feelings, or what the Scripture says? There is no victory over existential loneliness without awareness, without understanding our true identity, which we find in Christ.

---

47. Merton, *No Man Is an Island*, 128.

48. Rae Andre, *Positive Solitude: A Practical Program for Mastering Loneliness and Achieving Self-Fulfillment* (New York: Harper Collins, 1991), 19.

We have summarized the strategies discussed for overcoming each of the five types of loneliness in this table:

Strategies for overcoming loneliness (summary)

Loneliness type	Strategies
Emotional	- worshiping God and developing a deep relationship with him based on secure attachment; a personal prayer of reflection; - identifying and changing wrong attitudes and self-destructive behavior; - developing the ability to look at things from another person's perspective and build an emotional connection for making new acquaintances and deepening old ones, as well as to create opportunities for communication; - building friendship and social support network expansion; - healthy religious and volunteer activities; - reducing emotional pain by feeding on pleasant memories (viewing photos, videos, reading letters from people we love) or purchasing a pet; - special programs/seminars/small groups for widows, single people; - counseling to restore broken relationships due to conflict.
Social	- identifying and changing wrong attitudes and self-destructive behavior; - group activity of people with common interests; - maintaining existing relationships with family, friends, community, church; - communication skills development; - social support network expansion; - counseling to restore broken relationships due to conflict.
Spiritual	- an emphasis on personal prayer of reflection, rather than a prayer of begging, reflection on Scriptures; - accurate biblical theology and the formation of the correct image of God and self; - solitude.

Cultural	- personal prayer of reflection for a better understanding of one's identity; - focusing on the purpose of life, on the fulfillment of the calling from God; - joining religious groups and professing a common faith to develop a sense of belonging; - values reassessment and prioritization; - solitude; - smile, generosity.
Existential	- personal prayer of reflection for a better understanding of one's identity to answer the question: "Who am I?" "Why am I here?" to identify and change wrong attitudes and self-destructive behavior; - solitude; - healthy religious and volunteer activities.

Conclusion to chapter 5

We are convinced that loneliness of any type is, in general, evil because it brings suffering and pain. But despite this, you can see some positive aspects in each type of loneliness. It's like a toothache. The toothache itself is bad. But many of us in our right mind would never go to the dentist to have our bad tooth treated, if not for the unbearable pain it brings! So it is with loneliness: a constant, unstoppable feeling of loneliness is there to draw our attention to the fact that there is a problem in our relationship with ourselves, God, or other people.

Loneliness is so widespread, that some of us perceive it as a natural, integral part of our lives. And therefore, many people do not consider it possible or correct to fight it. And yet, by nature, humans were not created for loneliness, but unity and community with themselves, God, and other people. Therefore, the absence of such unity brings torment, pain. Pain, which can and should be treated. Thus we tried to describe the methods which deal not only with the symptoms but also with the causes of the "illness" of loneliness, and which are most effective in overcoming it.

The reader may notice that the following three strategies are repetitive in overcoming all five types of loneliness: solitude, personal prayer of reflection and meditation on Scripture, and identification and change of our misconceptions and self-destructive behaviors. We believe these are prerequisites for successfully overcoming loneliness.

In our opinion, the value and significance of solitude as a recreational resource can hardly be overestimated for overcoming loneliness and for better self-knowledge. The Scriptures command us to watch our "life and doctrine closely" (1 Tim 4:16), which time in solitude provides us with. As our research shows, it includes an encounter with loneliness and requires our willingness to experience fear, anger, agony, and/or frustration.

Solitude can be effective in dealing with the pain of loneliness as it stops our attempts to deny loneliness. As we learn to enjoy our own company, we are more able to understand the causes of our loneliness and cope with it. Then can we understand ourselves as a person in Christ, be aware of our inner strength and resources, despite the longing of loneliness we may experience from time to time.

An important condition for overcoming our loneliness is identifying and changing our misconceptions and self-destructive behavior. It is the essence of a Christian's independent work of the renewal of one's mind through the truths of Scripture, and the essence of the help for Christians suffering from loneliness. In essence, this "renewal of the mind" is aimed at restoring the Christian's identity in Christ. We are convinced, the way we answer the question "Who are we" is key. It defines our purpose, way of thinking, feelings, and behavior. We cannot achieve our goals unless we know who we are. And the devil knows that too. That is why he tries so hard to pervert our identity. Jesus identified with us in our humanity so that we can identify with him in his divinity.

Too many Christians do not know who they are in Christ, what they have, and what they are called to in him. For the creation with hope awaits the revelation of the sons of God (Rom 8:19). The more all Christians and the church of Christ as a whole understand their identity, the less loneliness fallen humanity is going to face. Christian identity restored in line with Scripture, in Christ, undoubtedly leads to a healthier view of ourselves and others, safer attachments, and healthier relationships. Thus, it brings us closer to solving the problem of our loneliness.

Part 3

Loneliness and Singleness: Slavic Christian Context

One of the main reasons why I (Valeriia) decided to write this book was that I had quite a lot of Christian friends struggling with singleness. Among these single Christians, there were also rare "specimens" satisfied with their status – I, for one. Of course, I expected to get married one day, someday, but I was busy serving the Lord, taken up with ministry all the time. To be honest, until the age of twenty-five, I didn't think about marriage at all; and I was not particularly worried about getting married. But this was rather an exception. One way or another, many of my Christian friends suffered from their singleness and were desperate to get married, yet for various reasons, it didn't work out. So I wanted to figure out why and how I could help them.

Although many good books have been written by Christians on marriage and singleness, there are still many blind spots requiring a modern reader to seek answers. Is singleness a gift of God to be used or a curse that needs to be broken? What does the Bible say about this? Is it more spiritual to be single than married? Why was singleness so popular in the Christian church in the early centuries AD, and why is it gaining popularity now? How can a Christian know if God is calling him or her to celibacy or marriage? Single living or living in a family – which is better for an adult Christian? If marriage is the will of God, why are there so many Christians who suffer because they are not married? Is the problem with them, with society or with God? Or is it not a problem at all, leaving them free to live for themselves and be glad that they are not bound by any marriage? Is singleness related to loneliness in any way? How? Is marriage the solution to loneliness? And in general, does faith (or religiosity) help single Christians solve their problem of loneliness, or does it hinder them? What is the role of a church community in this?

Our Christian friends of different denominations, nationalities, and cultures have asked us these questions. It is too early to regard these topics as comprehensively studied, especially since different Christian traditions sometimes come to opposite conclusions on these questions. In attempting to answer them, we tried to remain as objective and faithful to Scripture as possible. We hope that this part of the book will shed some light on these important aspects of life.

6

Singleness in Scripture

1. Definitions of key terms

First of all, since in our review we will touch on the works of authors of different cultures and traditions, we will look at the meaning of some basic terms and their translation into Russian. In particular, speaking of an unmarried person, modern evangelical English-speaking authors use the term "single." This word conveys the idea of something one-of-a-kind, unique or exclusive. But in Russian "single" is usually translated by the word "lonely, loner" from which the term "loneliness" is derived. Another Russian word translated as "bachelor, bachelorette" is no better either. In Russian, it carries the idea of something blank, idle, empty, and wasted, as if implying that an unmarried person wastes away his or her life for nothing, in vain. And although this is exactly how people who have not been married for a long time may feel, this does not mean that their life is empty. These semantic meanings seem to reflect a certain negative attitude towards single people in Slavic culture, which, of course, cannot but put pressure on them.

The terms "single" and "lonely" are not equal in meaning and therefore are not interchangeable either. A single person might live alone and not be lonely at all; and a person can be married yet feel alienated from their spouse, thus feeling lonely. Moreover, these concepts have changed their semantic load over time. "Single" used to mean someone who has never been married. Nowadays, this term is much broader. It also includes single parents with children; those who once were married or had a partner but are not currently in an exclusive relationship; and divorced or widowed persons.[1]

---

1. Cited from Jill Reynolds, Margie Wetherell, and Stephanie Taylor, "Choice and Chance," *Sociological Review* 55, 2 (2007), 331.

About a hundred years ago, singleness by default assumed abstinence from sex outside of marriage. Singleness was almost equal to virginity. Now, given modern social trends such as the separation of sexual life from any commitments or ethical standards, increase in cohabitations, divorces, single parenthood rates, and legalization of same-sex relationships in certain Western countries, the meaning of singleness has also changed. We cannot take it for granted that the modern young person understands that any unmarried (single) Christian, who wishes to live up to biblical standards, is expected to abstain from any sexual relations outside of marriage.

Further, "singleness" and "celibacy" are used almost as synonyms in English literature. "Caelibatus" simply means "an unmarried person" in Latin, the same as "bachelor, bachelorette" today. However, for a modern Russian-speaking person, celibacy is associated exclusively with the vow of life-long abstinence from any sexual relations given by priests, monks, and nuns. Singleness is not associated with abstinence nowadays.

Regardless of our age, marital status, or position in the church, the New Testament encourages us to chastity. According to the apostles, chastity is based on God's grace given to a believer to deny ungodliness and worldly passions (Tit 2:6, 12; 1 Tim 3:2), and to abstain from fleshly lusts, which war against the soul (1 Pet 2:10). Chastity, therefore, is integrity of behavior and character, the purity of driving motives and thoughts, the ability to control your desires, and in a narrower sense, abstinence from illicit sexual actions or thoughts. The opposite of chastity is passionate lust and sexual immorality (see 1 Thess 4:3–5; Eph 4:17–19; Col 3:5; Rom 13:13).

Studying writings of the church fathers, we will hardly find the concept of singleness in the modern sense of the word as a definition of the person without a partner. Instead, they use the word "virginity," just as we would say "chaste singleness." For them, virginity is not just the physical state before the first sexual act, but internal integrity, which includes physical abstinence from sex before marriage, and purity in thoughts and motives.

So, here we will talk about people who, for various reasons, are not married and do not have stable romantic relationships, for which we will use the term "person without a partner" or "single person" in its broadest sense. Let's consider what Scripture tells us about singleness.

2. The Old Testament view of singleness and virginity

According to the Torah, virginity was a necessary virtue for marriage, while its absence before marriage has always been considered a shameful sin, and evidence of immorality. From Deuteronomy 22, we conclude that female virginity in ancient Israel was identified not only with personal or even family dignity but also with the innocence of the whole nation. The loss of virginity before marriage is called an "outrageous thing, evil, promiscuous" and a sin against the whole society, which was punished by death (see Deut 22:21, 24 NIV). The Law of Moses also protected the rights of girls, obliging a man who seduced a virgin not pledged to be married, to marry her alone without the right to divorce (Exod 22:16–17; Deut 22:28–29).

The Jewish tradition treated singleness negatively, identifying it with infertility, as something shameful. Abraham's wife Sarah and Samuel's mother Hannah, in the Old Testament, and Elizabeth the wife of Zechariah in the New Testament (Gen 30:23; 1 Sam 1; Luke 1:25) are examples. Singleness was considered a sign of a curse so much so that, as the Jewish Encyclopedia tells us, one rabbi taught that "a Jew who does not have a wife cannot be called a fully human being."[2] In the Talmud, we find an even more radical statement: "He who does not participate in the reproduction of the human race is equal to those shedding human blood."[3]

Within the framework of the Jewish tradition, the well-known passage of Scripture from Genesis 1:28 "be fruitful and multiply" was interpreted as God's commandment, obligatory for all. Thus, intimate relationships are encouraged by the Torah and limited only by the bonds of official marriage, ritual purity laws, and the requirements of endogamy. Priests were, therefore, expected to marry since their rank, according to the Law, could only be inherited by their children (see: Exod 29:9; 40:13–15; Lev 21:7–14).

Along with this basic negative attitude towards singleness, however, there were also special cases of voluntary refusal to marry in the Old Testament times. In particular, God commanded the prophet Jeremiah to refrain from starting a family, at least, "in this place" (in Israel) and for some time (Jer 16:2). Considering the context in which the prophet lived and served, we believe the meaning of this refusal was to use this symbolic action to announce the inevitability of God's punishment to Israel for their apostasy. Also, by not

---

2. Лев Каценельсон, Давид Г. Гинцбург, Еврейская энциклопедия, ред. Т.4. (СПб.: Тип. акц. общ. Брокгауз - Ефрон, 1906–1913) [Lev Katsenelson, David G. Gintsburg, Jewish Encyclopedia, eds. T.4 (St. Petersburg: Brockhaus-Efron Publishing, 1906–1913)], 24.

3. Epstein, *Babilonian Talmud: Yebamot* 63b, general ed. transl. W. Slotki (London: Soncino Press, 1938), 426. Quoted in: Пітер Браун, *Тіло і Суспільство. Чоловіки, Жінки і Сексуальне Зречення в Ранньому Християнстві*, transl. В. Т. Тимофійчука (К.: Мегатайп, 2003) [Peter Brown, Body and Society. Men, Women and Sexual Renunciation in Early Christianity, Ukrainian transl. V. T. Timofiichuk (K.: Megatype, 2003)], 76.

marrying, Jeremiah was able to avoid much worry for his own family, due to the country's future economic and political crisis (Jer 16:9–13).

There are other biblical examples of voluntary singleness – for example, the eighty-four-year-old widow Anna. Since the Bible specifically mentions that she had lived with her husband from virginity for only seven years, and then served the Lord in the temple "day and night with fasting and prayer" (Luke 2:37), it can be concluded that she voluntarily refused remarriage after her husband's death. For her, this meant giving up the social and economic stability and security that a second marriage would have given her.

The ascetic, celibate, and short life of John the Baptist also had a high goal. He was fully dedicated to his mission – to prepare the hearts of the people for the coming of the Messiah (John 3:29). Of course we also have the example of the Messiah himself – Jesus Christ. The Christian tradition fully agrees that the Lord was not bound by any bonds of marriage. He called himself the bridegroom, betrothed not to a specific person, but to the whole church (Mark 2:19; Matt 25:1–13; Rev 21:2, etc.).

We come across marriage as an allegory of the union between God and his people for the first time in the Old Testament, where the virginity and chastity of the people are identified with faithfulness in the marriage covenant. Jeremiah, Ezekiel, and Hosea describe the chosen people that became unfaithful to the Lord and violated the covenant using language of sexual relations (Jer 3; Ezek 16; Hos 2). The nation of Israel backslid from God and therefore was conquered by her enemies. Nevertheless, the prophets mourn the loss of her integrity repeatedly calling her "a virgin" who will turn to the Lord from her heart (Amos 5:2; Isa 37:22; Jer 14:17; Lam 1:15; 2:13).

Speaking about the restoration of love and faithfulness in the relationship between God and his people and the return of sovereignty to Israel, the prophet again uses the same word – "virgin": "I have loved you with an everlasting love; therefore I have continued my faithfulness to you. Again I will build you, and you shall be built, O virgin Israel" (Jer 31:3–4). This last metaphor, emphasizing the close bond and love between God and Israel, suggests first that God is taking the initiative in restoring relations with his people, and second that integrity can be regained.

Theologically speaking, our virginity as people was "lost" due to being born with a sinful nature. This is what is called "original sin," and during a person's life, it begins to manifest itself in full force, expressed in various sinful actions, feelings, and thoughts. But at the moment of turning to Christ, a person is born again and given the virginity of Christ, along with the forgiveness of all sins and justification. Moreover, the person is given a new divine nature and the grace to live this life in integrity henceforth!

In the same way, the idea of virginity, not as something to be lost, but rather something to be sought, found, and developed independently of past sexual experience, was also understood by some church fathers.[4] Origen (second–third century AD) goes as far as to call Rahab the prostitute "a pure virgin" who is now "united to Christ."[5]

This truth, that real integrity is found only in Christ, is firstly humbling, pointing out to those who have kept themselves from extramarital affairs that there is a spiritual integrity they can only gain when they are born again. And those who are born again understand that only the grace and power of God helped them keep themselves from sexually illicit relationships. For those who have had an unholy sexual experience and therefore considered themselves defiled, unclean, or even worthless, this truth gives hope that their integrity in the eyes of God can be regained and their value is preserved in Christ.

3. Singleness and virginity in the New Testament

For the New Testament writers, the "virgin of Israel" is identified with the church. There we find the concept of the union of Christ and the church in a heavenly marriage. A marriage between a man and a woman is just an earthly symbol, a prototype of that union. This is especially clear in the theology of the apostle Paul, in which Christ is more than once compared with the bridegroom, who "loved his church and gave himself up for her" (Eph 5:25). Paul also betrothed the church to Christ to present her "as a pure virgin" (2 Cor 11:2).

Below is a brief review of several key passages from the New Testament that speak directly of virginity and singleness.

In 1 Corinthians 7 the apostle Paul seems to be answering the church in Corinth about the principles of marriage and singleness.[6] According to Heinrich Meyer, the reason for this chapter is that, given the case of immorality in the Corinthian church (which is discussed in the previous chapter of the epistle) "there must have been opponents of marriage at Corinth," which

---

4. See Kathryn Wehr, "Virginity, Singleness and Celibacy: Late Fourth-Century and Recent Evangelical Visions of Unmarried Christians," *Theology & Sexuality* 17, 1 (2011): 75, 78, https:// doi:10.1558/tse.v17i1.

5. Origen, *Homilies on Joshua*, trans. by Barbara J. Bruce, ed. by Cynthia White (Washington: The Catholic University of America Press, 2002), 73.

6. Archibald Robertson and Alfred Plummer, *The International Critical Commentary: 1 Corinthians* (Edinburgh: T&T Clark, 1957), 138.

additionally led to divisions in this community into different parties.[7] Either way, here Paul states, "Now concerning the things of which you wrote to me: it is good for a man not to have sexual relations with a woman" (1 Cor 7:1). According to American bibliologist of Greek origin, Spiros Zodhiates, the phrase "not to have sexual relations" literally translated from Greek means "not to be connected or have anything in common."[8]

Here, of course, Paul was not referring to the general renunciation of sexual relations even in marriage, and did not dissolve the marriage, as some might think. Thus, in verse 2 he says, "But because of the *temptation to sexual immorality*, each man should have his own wife and each woman her own husband" (1 Cor 7:2); and in the same chapter, Paul states:

> But if you do marry, you have not sinned; and if a virgin marries, she has not sinned . . . If anyone is worried that he might not be acting honorably toward the virgin he is engaged to, and if his passions are too strong and he feels he ought to marry, *he should do as he wants*. He is not sinning. They should get married . . . A woman is bound to her husband as long as he lives. But if her husband dies, she is *free* to marry anyone she *wishes*, but he *must belong to the Lord* (1 Cor 7:28, 36, 39 NIV, author's emphasis).[9]

Note here that Paul suggests marriage as a measure against sexual immorality, and it is not sinful, provided one marries (or remarries) a person who believes in Christ. The apostle as well recommends practicing temporary abstinence for spouses, provided it is reciprocal, brief, and devoted to prayer for the couple's spiritual growth.[10]

However, the apostle Paul still gives preference to singleness, although he gives his opinion on marriage or abstaining from it as advice, not a command (see 1 Cor 7:6, 25 and 40). In verse 9 he continues: "But if they cannot control themselves, they should marry, for it is better to marry than to burn with passion." As scholars Canon Spence and Joseph Exell note in their commentary

---

7. Heinrich August Wilhelm Meyer, ed. *Critical and Exegetical Hand-Book: to the Epistles to the Corinthians* (New York: Funk & Wagnalls Publishers, 1884), 149.

8. Spiros Zodgiates, ed. *Hebrew–Greek Key Word Study Bible* (Chattanooga: ANG International, 2008), 2111. This is a common idiom for temporal abstinence from sexual relations, as in Exod 19:15 or 1 Sam 21:4.

9. The phrase (Greek: ὑπέρακμος) can be translated as either "the best time, the most suitable time, or marriageable age (of a woman)" or "passions are too strong" (of a man).

10. Robertson and Plummer, eds. *The International Critical Commentary. 1 Corinthians*, 134. Temporary abstinence for a spiritual purpose is also recommended in the Old Testament (for example, Eccl 3:5; Joel 2:16).

on 1 Corinthians, "The original tenses give greater force and beauty to this obvious rule of Christian common sense and morality. The verb 'marry' is in the aorist – 'to marry once for all' and live in holy married union; the verb 'burn' is in the present – 'to be on fire with concupiscence' Marriage once for all is better than continuous lust."[11]

Laura Smit believes that "being aflame with passion must mean a sexual desire that is beyond self-control, something along the lines of sexual addiction."[12] If it was the case, this would mean that Paul recommended marriage only for sexually addicted people, and this theory seems unlikely. Rather, in a society as full of temptations as the city of Corinth, he advises marriage for Christians not as the lesser of two evils, but as a blessing and necessary protection from sin for those who do not have the "gift of singleness" and thus, find it hard to control their sexual desires.

Further, in 1 Corinthians 7, we also find the rationale for Paul's understanding of the single lifestyle as a spiritual gift: "I wish that all were as I myself am. But each has his own gift from God, one of one kind and one of another" (1 Cor 7:7 NIV). Here Paul uses the Greek word *charisma* "gift of grace," which is generally used concerning the gifts of the Holy Spirit. Accordingly, singleness is a gift of God, a particular grace for the individual to remain single. In other letters Paul states that spiritual gifts are given by God, to equip the saints for the work of ministry, for building up the body of Christ (Eph 4:12), and to each is given the manifestation of the Spirit for the common good (1 Cor 12:7). We conclude that, like any other spiritual gift, singleness is given to a Christian by God for maximum efficiency and benefit in serving the Lord.

In addition, Paul gives several arguments in support of a single lifestyle. He writes:

> I think that in view of the *present distress* it is good for a person to remain as he is. Are you bound to a wife? Do not seek to be free. Are you free from a wife? Do not seek a wife. But if you do marry, you have not sinned, and if a betrothed woman marries, she has not sinned. Yet those who marry *will have worldly troubles*, and I would spare you that . . . I want you to be free from anxieties. The unmarried man is anxious about the things of the Lord, how

---

11. Canon H. D. M. Spence, Joseph S. Exell, ed. *The Pulpit Commentary: 1 Corinthians* (New York and Toronto: Funk & Wagnalls Company, 189), 225.

12. Laura A. Smit, *Loves Me, Loves Me Not: The Ethics of Unrequited Love* (Grand Rapids : Baker Academic, 2005), 75.

to please the Lord. But the *married man is anxious about worldly things*, how to please his wife. (1 Cor 7:26–28, 32–33, author's emphasis)

One of the main questions when examining this passage is whether these counsels of the apostle Paul have a universal character or not. Are they relevant to all Christians at all times, or did they apply exclusively to the Corinthian community of that period? The latter point of view is based on a literal reading of the Greek text, in which the expression translated as "present distress" means "imminent necessity, present danger." Perhaps here Paul is referring to the persecution of Christians by the Roman authorities or their oppression by the Jews, which undoubtedly was a greater threat to married Christians than to unmarried.

> It is easier for many to suffer themselves than to see their dear ones suffer . . . Shall I see my wife and children exposed to nameless insult and hideous cruelty, or forswear the faith? This was the dread alternative set before many married men in the days of Paul.[13]

In any case, as Spence and Exell aptly sum up, one should not enter into marriage recklessly, without taking into account the circumstances of the time and one's own limitations.

On the other hand, Paul says that the gift of singleness is important because: "time is very short" and "the present form of this world is passing away," contrasting secular concerns with the importance of doing one's service to the Lord. Here we see that Paul's readiness to serve the Lord entirely, without being bound by family responsibilities, seems to him especially important at a time when at any moment earthly history can end with the second coming of Christ. If this is so, then the words of the apostle should not weaken, but acquire even greater relevance for the church of the third millennium. It is obvious that for us modern Christians that the moment of Christ's return to earth is even closer than for the first Christians. And therefore, for every Christian, regardless of social status – rich or poor, married or not – it is important to concentrate on fulfilling our ministry with "undivided devotion" to the Lord (1 Cor 7:35).

Further, in this chapter, the apostle Paul continues his train of thought:

---

13. See: Spence and Exell, *1 Corinthians*, 244.

But whoever is *firmly established in his heart, being under no necessity but having his desire under control,* and has *determined* this in his heart, to keep her as his betrothed, he will do well. So then he who marries his betrothed does well, and he who refrains from marriage will do even better. (1 Cor 7:37–38, author's emphasis)

Here the apostle states that marriage is a good thing and that the one who marries of his own free will does not sin, yet Paul offers singleness as the best alternative.

Jesus Christ also taught about singleness as a spiritual gift when his disciples asked him about a man's responsibility in marriage.

The disciples said to him, "If such is the case of a man with his wife, it is better not to marry" But he said to them, "Not everyone can receive this saying, but only those to whom *it is given.* For there are eunuchs who have been so *from birth,* and there are eunuchs who have been *made eunuchs by men,* and there are eunuchs who have *made themselves eunuchs* for the sake of the kingdom of heaven. Let the one who is able to receive this receive it." (Matt 19:10–12, author's emphasis)

Jesus distinguishes here three categories of eunuchs. The first are not capable of sexual life due to some physical problem; the second were made eunuchs by others (it is known that castration was quite common in the Middle East in ancient times).[14] In the third category, the Christian tradition primarily understood not as much those who physically castrated themselves (although such examples are known in church history), as those who voluntarily renounced marriage, family, and intimacy for the sake of the kingdom of God to focus on higher goals and mission, as Christ himself did. Moreover, we note that Jesus says here that this is not given to everyone. Accordingly, for those people to whom this gift is not given, it would be a violation of God's will and order to shirk marital responsibility.

Based on the fact that a single lifestyle is a spiritual gift, we conclude that marriage is a gift from God as well, which is given to a believer to enable him to serve the Lord most efficiently. As the apostle Peter said: "As each has received a gift, use it to serve one another, as good stewards of God's varied grace . . . so that in everything God may be glorified through Jesus Christ" (1 Pet 4:10–11).

---

14. See: Piotr O. Scholz, *Eunuchs and Castrati,* trans. John A. Broadwin and Shelley L. Frisch (Princeton: Markus Wiener Publishers, 1999), 74.

Conclusion to chapter 6

Summarizing the biblical teaching about a single lifestyle, we can point out the following criteria by which believers can identify whether it is God's will for them to marry, or whether they should remain single. These are the signs that God is calling you to singleness and that you possess the gift of singleness:

1. If *you understand marriage would be an obstacle in the way of your serving the Lord* due to some circumstances. For instance, if you know that right now you need to focus on missionary work in one of the countries where Christianity is being persecuted, and you would be especially vulnerable had you a family – it would be more of a burden for you than a help, and an additional source of worries. If that is the case, most likely God is calling you to singleness, at least at this stage of your life.

At the same time, if you have a sense of urgency about the mission entrusted to you as the apostle Paul had, considering the time to be "very short," do not misinterpret his words. Paul wrote "From now on, let those who have wives live as though they had none . . . and those who deal with the world as though they had no dealings with it. For the present form of this world is passing away" (1 Cor 7:29, 31). Paul is *not* calling Christians to leave their families for mission. There were many fanatical Christians in the early church who, in reckless religious zeal, did just that – they left their wives, husbands, and children for the sake of a mission – and it was a clear misinterpretation. Here Paul emphasizes that whether we are married or not, the main goal of every Christian should be to fulfill our calling for the glory of God. For some Christians, it is easier to stay single because they do not need to be additionally distracted by caring for their family and children.

But for the Christians not called by God to a life of singleness, it is important to consider their family a part of their mission and service to the Lord, which cannot be neglected. Therefore, the key motivation for marriage should be the desire to glorify the Lord as much as possible. As Mark Ballenger aptly points out, "You can be a single person and waste your life on worldly concerns or be a married person and use your life for kingdom purposes."[15]

2. The second sign that God is calling you to a life of singleness is that you have *special grace or the ability to control your sexual desires without much problem.* In most cases, this does not mean that God completely takes away

---

15. Mark Ballenger, *The Ultimate Guide to Christian Singleness* (CreateSpace Independent Publishing Platform, November 3, 2017), 149.

your sexual desires.[16] Rather you receive from God the ability to cope with the pressure of the flesh quite easily, "being under no necessity" in the words of the apostle Paul. You have no urgent need for sexual relations. The apostle Paul in his other epistle to the Corinthians spoke about himself experiencing the same temptations (inwardly burning) as any other person (2 Cor 11:29). Paul, however, received a special grace from God to be faithful to him (remain single) and overcome these temptations. If the struggle for sexual purity is too intense for someone, if Satan tempts him into promiscuity, then Paul gives practical advice to such a Christian to marry, saying that "it is better to marry than to burn with passion" (1 Cor 7:9).

3. The third criterion by which one can know if God calls him or her to a life of singleness is a *strong desire and firm determination to devote oneself entirely to the service of the Lord* (1 Cor 7:37). Both in marriage and singleness, the personal desire of a person is taken into account.

However, if you do not want to get married because you are afraid to trust and love or you are afraid of being hurt in a relationship (as you previously were), or you don't want to have anything to do with the opposite sex at all because you have a lot of complexes and a low opinion about yourself, – those are not biblical signs that God has given you the gift of singleness. Rather, they are signs of your need for emotional healing.[17] Also, if the very thought that "God forbid, I have this gift of singleness!" or "I will never create my own family" scares you to death, most likely you do not have this gift. The Bible says "it is God who works in you, both to will and to work for his good pleasure" (Phil 2:13). So relax, because people with the gift of singleness are quite happy about not having romantic relationships in their lives, they do not suffer from temptations in the sexual sphere too much, and their decision not to marry is motivated not by the desire to live an unburdened life, but to serve the Lord without distraction.

And lastly, you can determine if you have the spiritual gift of singleness, so to speak, "empirically." We mean there are questionnaires that can help you see whether you have the gift of singleness or not, even if this gift is hidden and you are not aware of it. One of the best methods, in our opinion,

---

16. Here we disagree with Ballenger, who seems to think that God completely takes away the desire to have sexual relations in the case of a gift of singleness. See: Ballenger, *The Ultimate Guide to Christian Singleness*, 21.

17. See good teaching on this subject by Mark Ballenger "5 Things That Mean God Is Preparing You to Find True Love Soon," https://youtu.be/uiCvRNIMTBM.

is the Christian A. Schwarz's test on spiritual gifts.[18] This test consists of 180 statements, and you get a complete picture of all the spiritual gifts you have. It is very useful to know in which ministry you can be as effective to the Lord as possible. Understand that to discover that you do not have some kind of gift is also a good reason for joy. This allows you to focus on the very things God has called you to and equipped you for.

If you find yourself scoring high in the spiritual gift of singleness, you may find the following tips helpful for developing this gift:

- Keep using the gift to the glory of God and for the development of his church.
- Don't allow other Christians to persuade you into marriage, because "everybody should do so."
- Remember that you who have the gift of singleness are still subject to sexual temptations. Therefore, do not overestimate your strength too much. Learn from Christians who have this gift how they have learned to handle it.[19]

Let us conclude: marriage must be respected as the universal will of God; in it a person can realize God's command to multiply and have dominion on earth, as well as satisfy sexual needs in a safe, legal and sanctified way. Singleness, however, is the best choice for Christians determined to serve God without being distracted by family responsibilities. A person with the gift of singleness has more opportunities for using other gifts more effectively. This gift will be especially helpful for those planting new churches or going on a mission to another country since this kind of work requires special mobility and the ability to adapt, which family people often do not have.

In the next chapter, we will try to answer the question of why the single lifestyle was such a popular and widespread practice in the history of the Christian church, as well as trace its connection with loneliness in the life of modern Christians.

---

18. The full test can be found here: Christian A. Schwarz, *The 3 Colors of Ministry: A Trinitarian Approach to Identifying and Developing Your Spiritual Gifts* (St. Charles: ChurchSmart Resources, 2001), 64–84.

19. The tips are borrowed from Schwarz's book, *The 3 Colors of Ministry*, 150–51.

7

Singleness of Christians in The History of The Church

1. Genesis of the tradition

If you make an excursion into church history, you find that at the dawn of the Christian era a single lifestyle among Christians was very popular, to the point that it was difficult to find a church father who did not write at least something in defense of singleness: an apology, a treatise, or a sermon. Exploring this topic gives us the impression that the church fathers wrote in defense of singleness and celibacy more than family.[1] One of the earliest works is *Two circular letters on virginity or to virgins* traditionally attributed to Clement of Rome (died AD 99), in which the author promotes virginity (singleness) in every possible way, calling it a true life of faith and identifying it with holiness.[2]

In the writings of Ignatius of Antioch (died AD 107) we see that as early as the first century the church supported not only widows but also virgins, who were equated in status with them. In his letter to the church community in Smyrna, he specifically welcomes "virgins who are called widows."[3] The church fathers viewed virginity (chaste singleness) as a complete, immaculate

---

1. Reasons why the church fathers wrote so little in defense of family may be that in accordance with Jewish tradition, the institution of marriage as such was never disputed in the church of the apostles' time, and since it was part of civil law, theologians did not consider it necessary to specifically discuss it. But virginity for life and celibacy were quite rare phenomena in late antiquity and therefore required a special apology.

2. See Clement of Rome, *Two Epistles Concerning Virginity*, transl. B. P. Pratten, ed. Alexander Roberts and James Donaldson (Edinburgh: T&T Clark, 1867).

3. Ignatius of Antioch, "Letter to the Smyrnaeans," Chapter 8, in *Patristics.info*, ed. Luke Wilson (06 Jul 2022), https://patristics.info/ignatius-of-antioch-letter-to-the-smyrnaeans.html.

way of life, accessible and appropriate for everyone who seeks to be a follower of the Lord.

Obviously, their sermons had their influence. Peter Brown, a researcher of late antiquity, argues that the singleness of Christian women and men became so widespread that the churches perceived it as a standard and a common practice.[4] According to Justin Martyr (AD 100–65), there were

> many, both men and women, who have been Christ's disciples from childhood, remain pure at the age of sixty or seventy years; and I boast that I could produce such from every race of men. For what shall I say, too, of the countless multitudes of those who have reformed intemperate habits, and learned these things?[5]

Gradually, the practice of renunciation of sexual life and marriage became so popular among Christians that it resulted in general criticism from their pagan contemporaries. In fact, the craze for singleness among Christians in the culture of the Roman Empire of that era was perceived not only as something strange and even obscene for a Roman citizen, but also as a dangerous practice, for it undermined the very foundations of society and threatened the demographic and political stability of the state.[6] Dmitry Valentei reports that one of the attempts to counteract this "pernicious trend to singleness" and promote fertility by political measures was the law of the emperor Augustus Octavian with later amendments by the consuls Marcus Papius Mutilus and Quintus Poppaeus Secundus (AD 9). Among other things, this law obliged all noblemen aged 25–60 and all women of 20–50 years of age to marry and have children, and also introduced a number of restrictions on the right to inherit for bachelors and the childless, along with severe penalties for adultery. Especially merciless pressure in the performance of this reproductive public duty was exerted on young women: to be not considered childless or deprived

---

4. He writes, "Many Christians already took for granted habits of rigorous sexual abstinence and had long practiced rites of baptismal initiation that linked the beginning of the true life of Christian with the perpetual renunciation of sexual activity. Behind even the most extreme statements of many of the leaders of the second and third centuries – highly articulate men, for the most part – we can usually sense the mute assent of whole churches, even of whole Christian regions." See Peter Brown, *The Body and Society: Men, Women and Sexual Renunciation in Early Christianity* (New York, Guildford, Surrey: Columbia University Press, 1988), 88.

5. Justin Martyr, *First Apology*, Chapter 15, in Patristics.info, ed. Luke Wilson (06 Jul 2022), https://patristics.info/justin-martyr-first-apology.html.

6. Дмитрий И. Валентей, ред., *Демографический Энциклопедический Словарь* (М.: Советская энциклопедия, 1985) [Dmitry I. Valentey, ed., Demographic Encyclopedic Dictionary (Moscaw: Soviet Encyclopedia, 1985)], 135.

of the privileges mentioned, women under this law had to give birth to at least three children.[7]

Given the above-mentioned restrictions, we can now only guess what socio-economic and psychological pressure those single Christians of the Roman Empire were under. They were subjected to ridicule and mockery from the pagans. Theologians of the first four centuries had to defend the ideas of a celibate lifestyle; the fourth century was especially rich in apologies for celibacy. They include the epistolary heritage of Augustine Aurelius, Ambrose of Milan, Athanasius the Great, Basil of Caesarea, Gregory the Theologian (Gregory of Nazianzen), Gregory of Nyssa, John Chrysostom, Jerome of Stridon and many more.[8]

Among the works of Gregory the Theologian (AD 325–39) devoted to this topic, the main one is a poem called "In Praise of Virginity." In line with all other ancient authors, St. Gregory uses the term "virginity" in a sense of chaste singleness. Marriage, according to Gregory, helps to overcome loneliness and is a manifestation of love for another person and God. However, Gregory sees the goal of singleness as the complete dedication of all thoughts and desires to Christ. Comparing marriage and virginity, Gregory traditionally puts the latter above the former. He considers singleness more perfect and divine, but more difficult and dangerous. However, unlike most of his theologian contemporaries, Gregory expresses the idea, quite progressive for his era, that

---

7. Those who were not married, according to this law, did not receive anything at all by will, and those who were married and had no children could receive only half of the inheritance. See: Иосиф А. Покровский, *История Римского Права*, пер. с лат., науч. ред. и комм. А. Д. Рудокваса (СПб: изд.-торг. дом «Летний сад», 1999) [Joseph A. Pokrovsky, History of Roman Law, trans. from Latin, scientific ed. and comm. A. D. Rudokvas (St. Petersburg: Publishing house "Letniy Sad", 1999)], 455.

8. See, for example: St. Basil, "An Ascetical Discourse and Exhortation on the Renunciation of the World and Spiritual Perfection," in *Ascetical Works*, ed. Monica Wagner (Washington: The Catholic University of America Press, 1999), muse.jhu.edu/book/20872; St. Basil of Caesarea, "Letter 199," in *Nicene and Post-Nicene Fathers*, Second Series, Vol. 8, transl. Blomfield Jackson, eds. Philip Schaff and Henry Wace (Buffalo: Christian Literature Publishing Co., 1895), 236, http://www.newadvent.org/fathers/3202199.htm; Gregory of Nyssa, "On Virginity," in *Nicene and Post-Nicene Fathers*, Second Series, Vol. 5, transl. William Moore and Henry Austin Wilson, eds. Philip Schaff and Henry Wace (Buffalo: Christian Literature Publishing Co., 1893), http://www.newadvent.org/ fathers/2907.htm; John Chrysostom, "Homily 62 on Matthew," in *Nicene and Post-Nicene Fathers*, First Series, Vol. 10, transl. George Prevost and rev. M.B . Riddle, ed. Philip Schaff (Buffalo: Christian Literature Publishing Co., 1888), http://www.newadvent.org/ fathers/200162.htm; St. Jerome, "Letter 22, To Eustochium," in *Nicene and Post-Nicene Fathers*, Second Series, Vol. 6, transl. W.H . Fremantle, G. Lewis and W.G. Martley, eds. Philip Schaff and Henry Wace (Buffalo: Christian Literature Publishing Co., 1893), http://www.newadvent. org/fathers/3001022.htm; Augustine of Hippo, "On Holy Virginity," in *Nicene and Post-Nicene Fathers*, First Series, Vol. 3, transl. C. L. Cornish, ed. Philip Schaff (Buffalo: Christian Literature Publishing Co., 1887), http://www.newadvent.org/fathers/1310.htm, etc.

the meaning of marriage is not limited to childbearing: its essence is in the mutual love of spouses, growing into love for God.[9]

Note that in the Hellenistic era, and even more so in the era of Christianity, singleness and abstinence from sexual relations were considered interrelated, and childbearing was encouraged only within the bonds of legal marriage. At the same time, singleness was not limited to abstinence from sexual relations only, but was all about one's growth of love for God and union with Christ. So, both in marriage and singleness, Gregory encouraged communion with God. Ambrose of Milan (AD 340–397), in his treatise "On Virginity and Marriage," even calls celibacy a "sacrament" and "best of marriages."[10] Speaking of celibacy as a sacrament was quite unusual for the Christian church, but was in line with the spirit of that time.

It is known that by the time of the recognition of Christianity as the legitimate religion of the Roman Empire (fourth century AD), there was a whole class of people called "virgins," both men and women, who devoted themselves to celibacy and were highly respected in the church. Ambrose even mentions separate monasteries for virgins (*ad monasterium virginale*) in his voluminous treatises on virginity and singleness.[11] John Chrysostom (347–407 AD) also tells us about 3,000 widows and single virgins in the maintenance of the Antiochian church, in addition to prisoners, the sick, and strangers.[12]

Similar to the practice of widowhood when people refused remarriage "for the sake of the Lord's body" (devoting the rest of their life to the service in church), singleness gradually acquired the characteristics of a lifestyle generally recognized and accepted by the church. Also, thanks to the works of such theologians as Gregory of Nazianzen and Augustine, the practice of "spiritual marriage" was popularized – a phenomenon when Christian spouses,

9. Saint Gregory of Nazianzus, "In Praise of Virginity," in *On God and Man: the Theological Poetry of St. Gregory of Nazianzus*, transl. Peter Gilbert (Crestwood: St. Vladimir's Seminary Press 2001), 98–99, https://archive.org/details/ongodmantheologi0000greg/page/98/mode/2up?q=88&view=theater.

10. Ambrose of Milan, "Concerning Virginity," Book I, chapter 6, in *Nicene and Post-Nicene Fathers*, Second Series, Vol. 10, transl. H. de Romestin, E. de Romestin, and H. T. F. Duckworth, eds. Philip Schaff and Henry Wace (Buffalo: Christian Literature Publishing Co., 1896), https://www.newadvent.org/fathers/34071.htm.

11. Ambrose of Milan, "Concerning Virginity," Book I, chapter 11, 16.

12. John Chrysostom, "Homily 58 on Matthew," in *Nicene and Post-Nicene Fathers*, First Series, Vol. 10, transl. George Prevost, rev. M. B. Riddle, ed. Philip Schaff (Buffalo: Christian Literature Publishing Co., 1888), 407.

being legally married, lived together, but voluntarily abstained from intimate relationships throughout their lives.[13]

However, as early as the second century some church fathers were alarmed by the penetration of the obligatory celibacy heresy in the church. In particular, Irenaeus, Bishop of Lyon (130–202 AD), warns of the heresy of the so-called "Encratites" (abstainers) who preached celibacy for life and declared marriage "a corruption and fornication."[14] We find a similar warning by Tertullian (160–220 AD) in a letter to his wife that Christ did not come to separate the spouses and destroy the marriage union as if with his coming every marriage became lawless.

> This is a charge they (heretics) must be prepared to answer who, among other perversions of doctrine, teach their followers to divide those who are "two in one flesh," opposing the will of him who first subtracted woman from man and then . . . added two together again who had originally been substantially one. Finally, we do not read anywhere at all that marriage is forbidden.[15]

Clement of Alexandria (150–215 AD) also warned about the danger of neglecting marriage and excessive enthusiasm for asceticism. The soundness of his arguments is impressive:

> So no one should ever think that marriage under the rule of the Logos is a sin, if he does not find it bitter to bring up children; indeed, for many people, childlessness is the most grievous experience of all. At the same time, if he does not regard the

---

13. Августин Аврелий, "О Супружестве и Похоти," in *Трактаты о Любви: Сборник Текстов*, ред. Ольга Зубец (М.: Российская Академия Наук, 1994) [Augustine Aurelius, "On Marriage and Lust," in Treatises on Love: A Collection of Texts, eds. Olga Zubets (Moscow: Russian Academy of Sciences, 1994)], 18. See also: Григорий Богослов, "К Монахам," in *Творения: Песнопения Таинственные*, Т. 2 (СПб.: Издательство П. П. Сойкина, 1912) [Gregory the Theologian, "To the Monks," in Creations: Mysterious Chants, Vol. 2 (St. Petersburg: P. P. Soikin Publishing House, 1912)], 169–72.

14. Ириней Лионский, *Против Ересей. Доказательство Апостольской Проповеди*, пер. прот. П. Преображенского, Н.И. Сагарды, (СПб.: Издательство Олега Абышко, 2008) [Irenaeus of Lyons, Against Heresies. The Demonstration of the Apostolic Preaching, rus. trans. arch. P. Preobrazhensky, N.I. Sagarda (St. Petersburg: Oleg Abyshko Publishing House, 2008)], 94.

15. Tertullian, "To His Wife," transl. William P. Le Saint, in *Writers: The Works of The Fathers in Translation*, Ed. Johannes Quasten, Joseph C. Plumpe (Westminster:The Newman Press, 1956) 11, 12. Interestingly, in another treatise on "The Exhortation to Chastity," Tertullian seems to contradict himself when he claims that marriage "consists of concupiscence which is the essence of fornication." See Tertullian, *On Exhortation to Chastity*, Chapter IX, https://ccel.org/ccel/s/schaff/anf04.xml.

production of children as bitter because it drags him away from the things of God, for which there is necessarily no time, but does not look favourably upon life as a bachelor, then he can look forward to marriage, since there is no harm in disciplined pleasure, and each of us is in a position to make a decision over the engendering of children. I realize that there are some people who have used the excuse of marriage to abstain from it without following the principles of sacred knowledge and have fallen into hatred of humankind so that the spirit of Christian love has vanished from them.[16]

The very existence of such a motivating marriage argument in the writings of the church fathers indicates that single ascetic life was the choice of many Christians and a phenomenon so popular that it bordered on heresy at an early stage of the Christian church.

Despite all the warnings, "spiritual marriage" was becoming quite common even among the lay people, as evidenced by the series of rules adopted at the Synod of Gangra (340 AD) against those who, by practicing abstinence, avoided intimate relationships in marriage. In particular, canons 9 and 10 warn a Christian against abstaining from married life and maintaining virginity: "If any one shall remain virgin, or observe continence, abstaining from marriage because he abhors it, and not on account of the beauty and holiness of virginity itself, let him be anathema."[17]

These rules prove that the attitude towards marriage was ambiguous, and the idealization of virginity was widespread in early Christianity. But there is a question still: why was the idea of singleness and abstinence from marriage so popular among early Christians? Where did such a unanimous passion for singleness come from for almost all the church fathers? And most importantly, how relevant and applicable are these concepts for us – Christians of the twenty-first century?

---

16. Clement of Alexandria, "Stromateis," Book Three, transl. John Ferguson, in *The Fathers of the Church, A New Translation*, Ed. Director Thomas R. Halton (Washington: The Catholic University of America Press, 1991), 297.

17. "The Council of Gangra" (Canon 9, 10), in *Corpus Juris Canonici, Gratian's Decretum, Synodical Letter and Canons*, Pars I., Dist. XXX, c. V, 104.

2. Reasons for the popularity of singleness among early Christians

According to Orthodox Bishop Augustine (Gulyanitsky), there were a number of reasons for the widespread popularity of the single lifestyle among Christians in the first four centuries of the new era. First of all, it was the desire of true Christians in their chastity to point out to the morally decaying Roman Empire the source of such spirituality.[18] In the same train of thought, Peter Brown argues that the driving motive of the first Christians in refusing marriage was their witness to the world that its seemingly unshakable order could be changed. More and more Christian men and women "used their bodies" to mock the worldly way of life through a rather drastic measure – singleness for life, proclaiming the coming of a new reality – the kingdom of God.[19]

Also, the metaphor of singleness as spiritual marriage to Christ the heavenly bridegroom was one of the most popular among the early Christians, which helped spread singleness. For the first Christians, this image of Christ as the bridegroom probably had practical significance, emphasizing the hope for guidance, protection, and new close relationships with him. Gradually, a whole doctrine of betrothal to Christ took shape, which subsequently became officially fixed in the canons of the Catholic Church and singled those who remained chaste all their lives out into a separate class. They were endowed with high status and the right to be called *sponsae Christi* (brides of Christ), *Christo dicatae* (dedicated to Christ), *Christo maritatae* (wives of Christ), or *Deo nuptae* (brides of God).[20]

However, the image of Christ the bridegroom was not the only one. The fathers of the church often compared a chaste and celibate lifestyle with an angelic life that began already on earth. For instance, Ambrose of Milan admonished his sister Marceline, who devoted herself to singleness, to remain faithful, comparing her celibacy with heavenly life started on earth.[21] This

---

18. See: Предисловие Епископа Августина Гуляницкого к "Двум Окружным Посланиям св. Климента Римского о Девстве, или к Девственникам и Девственницам," [Preface by Bishop Augustine Gulyanitsky to the "Two Epistles of St. Clement of Rome on Virginity"] https://acathist.ru/en/literatura/item/ep-avgustin-gulyanitskij-dva-okruzhnykh-poslaniya-sv-klimenta-rimskogo-o-devstve-ili-k-devstvennikam-i-devstvennitsam.

19. See: Peter Brown, *The Body and Society*, 64.

20. This doctrine was most developed in the Catholic Church, where even now there is a separate order – "Ordo virginum" (Order of Maidens). More about it: https://consecratedvirgins. org/whoarewe; João Braz de Aviz, José Rodríguez Carballo, "Instruction 'Ecclesiae Sponsae Imago' on 'Ordo Virginum,'" *Bolletino Sala Stampa Della Santa Sede*, 04.07.2018, http://press. vatican.va/content/salastampa/en/bollettino/pubblico/2018/07/ 04/ 180704d.pdf.

21. See: Saint Ambrose, "Concerning Virginity," Book I, 52, https://www.newadvent.org/ fathers/34071.htm. See also: Gregory Nazianzen, "Oration 43. Funeral Oration on the Great S. Basil, Bishop of Cæsarea in Cappadocia," in *Nicene and Post-Nicene Fathers*, Second Series, Vol.

idea comes from the words of Jesus about the resurrection, recorded in the Gospel of Luke: "Jesus replied, "The people of this age marry and are given in marriage. But those who are considered worthy of taking part in the age to come and in the resurrection from the dead will neither marry nor be given in marriage" (Luke 20:34–35 NIV). From this we conclude that marriage is God's institution for earthly life, and in heaven everyone will be single, abiding in spiritual union and unity with God.

The church fathers also pointed out the following practical advantages of celibacy. Summing up the patristic wisdom, provided the person is living a chaste life, it saves a woman from the pains of childbirth, the anxieties of motherhood and then widowhood, and her children, of orphanhood. It relieves her from the stress of maintaining external beauty, and from the unfair, selfish or cruel attitude of earthly husbands. The first Christians were largely driven by the expectation of the imminent second coming of Christ, in the light of which marriage and all earthly pleasures and hardships associated with it fade away.

Another motive of the first Christians for preferring celibacy was persecution, both by political and religious authorities of the second and third centuries. Although they were limited in time and selective, they nevertheless contributed to the spread of celibacy.

An analysis of some church fathers' lives allows us to conclude that in many respects their personal experience contributed to such an idealization of celibacy. Augustine, Tertullian, and Origen were influenced by the philosophical ideas of Gnosticism and Stoicism which saw sexual attraction and marriage as expressions of sinful, vicious, vile human nature. Celibacy, they believed, was an integral component of "true," perfect Christianity.[22] Thus, by their writings, sermons, and personal example, they made an impact on popularizing the ascetic life and celibacy in particular. As Christianity spread, the church gained power and influence, and with it, its moral foundations weakened, prompting many zealous Christians to seek fellowship with God in solitude and ascetic monastic celibate life.

7, trans. Charles Gordon Browne and James Edward Swallow, ed. Philip Schaff and Henry Wace (Buffalo: Christian Literature Publishing Co., 1894), http://www.newadvent.org/fathers/310243. htm.

22. Perhaps, such rigor was Augustine's extreme response to his promiscuity in his young years before conversion to Christianity. In his "Confessions," Augustine admits that by the age of 18 he already had a son out of wedlock. For more detailed information, see: Augustine, *Confessions*, transl., ed. Albert C. Outler (1955), 78, https://faculty.georgetown.edu/jod/augustine/conf.pdf.

Another reason for the popularity of celibacy among church communities of the third to sixth centuries could have been financial benefit. Because both abortion and the infanticide of unwanted children were prohibited by state laws at that time and condemned by the church, some parents could "consecrate" an unwanted child, especially a girl, to the Lord and put her in the care of the church. In this "godly way" they could avoid expenses for her maintenance and dowry.[23] Indeed, in one of his letters, Bishop Basil of Caesarea confirms this:

> Many girls are brought forward by their parents and brothers, and other kinsfolk, before they are of full age, and have no inner impulse towards a celibate life. The object of the friends is simply to provide for themselves. Such women as these must not be readily received before we have made public investigation of their own sentiments.[24]

It seems that at that time, it was not taken into account whether a person had a gift of singleness or not, and the financial difficulties of families contributed to the spread of monasticism and celibacy.

Gradually, the celibacy of the higher clergy acquired almost a sacred essence and became a "must-have" both in the Catholic and Orthodox Churches.[25] Protestant theology, however, reflects the right of both the laity and clergy to marry. This concept is rooted, first of all, in their conviction that neither Christ himself nor the apostles ever preached compulsory celibacy for the followers of Christ, emphasizing the eclectic nature of this gift, which "not everyone can receive . . . but only those to whom it is given" (Matt 19:11–12). Holy Scripture repeatedly mentions married ministers (Mark 1:30; 1 Cor 9:5; Acts 18:2–26; 21:5). The first church had many married bishops. For example, Clement of Alexandria had a wife, and not only that, he was convinced that all the apostles, including even the apostle Paul, were married. In the *Stromateis*, in support of his thought, he argues that

---

23. John Boswell, "Eastburn, Expositio and Oblatio: The Abandonment of Children and the Ancient and Medieval Family," *The American Historical Review* 1, Vol. 89 (Feb. 1984): 20.

24. Here, based on the context, by the "full age" St. Basil means 16–17-year-olds. Basil the Great, *Second Canonical Epistle*, Rule 18, https://people.ucalgary.ca/~vandersp/Courses/texts/cappadoc/basilcep.html#CXCIX.

25. In practice, celibacy became mandatory for all Catholic priests only during the reign of Pope Gregory VII in the 11th century. In the Orthodox Church, in accordance with the rules in force since 1869, a priest can marry, but subsequently cannot be ordained to the rank of bishop or higher. See: Максим Козлов, "О Практике Целибата в Русской Церкви" [Maxim Kozlov, "On the Practice of Celibacy in the Russian Church"] http://www.taday.ru/text/814342.html.

In one of his letters Paul has no hesitation in addressing his "yokefellow"! He did not take her around with him for the convenience of his ministry. But the apostles in conformity with their ministry concentrated on undistracted preaching, and took their wives around as Christian sisters . . . through whom the Lord's teaching penetrated into the women's quarters without scandal.[26]

In addition, from a Protestant point of view, the obligatory vow of celibacy, both for bishops and for ministers of a lower rank, is considered a gross violation of the norms of the Bible:

Therefore an overseer [bishop] must be above reproach, the husband of one wife . . . He must manage his own household well, with all dignity keeping his children submissive, for if someone does not know how to manage his own household, how will he care for God's church? (1 Tim 3:2, 4–5)

Based on this, marriage and having a godly family is perceived as one of the conditions for a "blameless" priesthood for all ranks. Therefore, almost all Protestant denominations prefer that their clergy be married.

Protestants also perceive the requirement of celibacy for priests as one of the clear apostasy signs, which characterize the end of times. "The Spirit expressly says that in later times some will depart from the faith by devoting themselves to deceitful spirits and teachings of demons, through the insincerity of liars . . . who forbid marriage" (1 Tim 4:1, 3). According to Martin Luther, this requirement of obligatory celibacy for priests is a violation of the sixth commandment, because "If it were true . . . that a pastor cannot serve God if he has a wife of his own, then this sixth commandment would have to be entirely abolished and would not apply generally to persons of all kinds, and permit them to have their own wives." He calls obligatory celibacy a devilish suggestion that led to many temptations, sins, strife, and, ultimately, to the decision of the Eastern Church to separate.[27]

Obligatory celibacy and ascetic single living as the best way of restraining the flesh regardless of the gift of singleness always seemed very doubtful to Protestants. Biblical commentator William Barclay urges: "Examine yourself . . .

---

26. Clement of Alexandria, *Stromateis*, 289. Here, probably, Clement means the verse from Phil 4:3, where the phrase: "true companion" (γνήσιε σύζυγε) he interprets, in line with the translation common at that time as "a faithful and lawful companion, wife" (Aeschylus, Euripides).

27. Schism is meant here. See: Martin Luther, *Works of Martin Luther*, Volume IV (Philadelphia: A. J. Holman Company and the Castle Press, 1931), 362.

and choose that way of life in which you can best live the Christian life, and don't attempt an unnatural standard which is impossible and even wrong for you being such as you are."[28]

Conclusion to chapter 7

Having briefly highlighted the development of celibacy in Christianity, we see that throughout its history the Christian church has gone through extremes. Celibacy of Christians was either suppressed by political and economic means and ridiculed by secular people, or it was erected on a pedestal of "true holiness" under the influence of the heretical ancient philosophies in the church itself. Scripture unambiguously says both singleness and marriage are God-given gifts to Christians to serve God most effectively. Therefore, finding out if one has or has not the gift of singleness is quite important.

Let's now look at how this applies to the modern Christian and what it means to be single in Slavic culture today.

---

28. Barclay's Daily Study Bible, 1 Corinthians 7, in *Bible Commentaries*, https://www. studylight.org/commentaries/eng/dsb/1-corinthians-7.html.

8

Singleness in the Life of Modern Christians

1. Causes of singleness

Singleness can be a result of one's conscious choice to refuse to create a family. Yet often single people want to create a family and have close relationships, but for various reasons they fail to do it. Such singleness can feel enforced.

First, there may be objective factors for one's singleness: for instance, some physical bodily defects severely limiting the ability to communicate or meet new people; inability to have sex due to physical or mental illness; or a gift of singleness that is rarely mentioned or recognized, especially in Protestant circles.

Also, life crises, such as a recent divorce, broken romantic relationships, or the death of one of the spouses may be the cause. All this usually emotionally traumatizes a person, making him or her psychologically unprepared to build new romantic relationships.

Economic reasons (like coming from a poor family; no accommodation, low incomes; social environment issues; alcohol abusive or sick parents), can also influence marriage prospects, especially when there is still a strong economic and/or psychological dependence on the parental family, which is common for Slavic families. A career, a long path of self-realization, or even a church ministry can be an obstacle to creating a family for some.

The reason for singleness can also be a homosexual orientation. In a Slavic cultural context, where same-sex relationships are condemned according to traditional biblical values and same-sex "marriages" are illegal, marrying someone of the opposite sex just to ward off suspicion for such a person would simply be dishonest. Of course, this is a huge topic that cannot be covered entirely within the framework of this book. We would just like to say that in our opinion a person cannot be a fully consistent Christian and remain a practicing homosexual at the same time. We are aware that there is controversy over what leads people to be attracted to the same sex. We are convinced that homosexual attraction is not innate but acquired, at the core of which is a distorted personal identity. Whatever people's views on that may be it is undeniable that such attraction can be the cause of acute inner struggle and loneliness for those committed to living in accordance with teachings of Jesus. People with these desires need the renewal of their mind, restoration of their identity in Christ, and support of a loving community who will encourage and help them to live out lives that show the true freedom which walking in the path of obedience, faithful to Christ's calling, brings. All this is possible in Christ and through his changing grace only.

Next, the objective lack of a suitable partner and a narrow social circle may be one of the reasons why a Christian, in spite of the desire to have a family, remains single: "I have not yet met the one," say unmarried men. "My biggest problem is to find someone single, of suitable age and level. They seem to have died out . . . there is not a 'normal' single brother in our church," say unmarried women. Of course, everyone has their own standards for "normal"; nevertheless, it may really be the case that there is not a single suitable person for a romantic relationship in somebody's environment.

Deficiencies in social or communication skills such as lack of self-confidence, taciturnity, shyness, withdrawal, and distrust also prevent many from forming and maintaining healthy close relationships. Flaws in one's appearance, usually imaginary (too fat/thin, too short/tall, having a too-long nose, crooked, oblique, and so on) are also quite common reasons for not being able to build close relationships with the opposite sex. Such rejection of oneself and an inferiority complex and low self-esteem are especially typical for women who grew up without their father, because it is the father whose approval, unconditional love, and acceptance form self-confidence in girls.

Internal psychological problems may be an equally common cause of involuntary singleness as they can prevent close relationships. Examples are fear of intimacy due to traumatic previous experiences, a negative model of a parental family, unhealthy emotional dependence on parents, psychological unpreparedness for married life, and fear of taking responsibility or care of another person. Such a person would like to start a family, yet understands that marriage is a big responsibility, and is not yet ready for it. Such people tend to have requirements too high for themselves and a future partner. Another psychological problem that creates barriers to building strong, healthy romantic relationships can be an insecure attachment style in interpersonal relationships. Let's illustrate with a story.

When I (Valeriia) first met Alexandra, a twenty-five-year-old woman, she told me her story. She grew up in a loving Christian family with both parents caring for her. They always attended church together. But the sudden death of her father affected the entire family. Her mother developed some mental problems, which negatively influenced Alexandra. Then she experienced multiple sexual abuses in her late teen years. Alexandra was eventually diagnosed with complex post-traumatic stress disorder (CPTSD) with dissociative tendencies. In recent years, she attended therapy sessions with a psychotherapist, which helped her recall and deal with the emotional wounds of sexual abuse which happened when she was a child. This fact, deeply buried in her memory, now surfaced.

It may seem strange that such an experience as rape can be forgotten; but in fact, we are created in such a way that our consciousness does not "forget" extremely traumatic events but suppresses them. This is how our psyche's protective mechanism works, that we honestly do not remember events too unpleasant or painful, but which, nevertheless, continue to influence our reactions and behaviour. It is not surprising that such traumatic events defined Alexandra's chaotic attachment style, which currently overshadows her relationships – with her mother, God, and her romantic partner.

Her relationship with her mother was always complicated. When Alexandra's father was alive, she had a warm and trusting relationship with her mother. The father was a support and the "wall" the whole family could safely lean on. But when he died suddenly, their mother went into a protracted deep depression, emotionally detached herself from everyone, and was unable to function normally as a mother. So from her early years, Alexandra had to take responsibility and play the role of a parent for her mother emotionally. Building healthy boundaries in the relationship with her mother is still a problem for her.

All these difficult events could not but influence Alexandra's relationship with God. She lacks trust:

> When I experienced strong emotions such as anger, grief, and sadness, I always prayed that God would let me stop feeling them. But when I still felt them, in this I saw proof that God had left me or did not hear me. My relationship with God was complicated and unstable. On the one hand, I love him very much. On the other hand, I find it difficult to trust him. I am extremely afraid of death and the prospect of eternal life with God does not delight me at all.

From our point of view, such an inconsistent relationship with God, that is close at one time and distant at another, is a characteristic of people with a chaotic attachment style. The problem gets even worse when a person subconsciously projects such an insecure attachment style onto his or her romantic relationships, which, of course, complicates them.

After these traumatic experiences, Alexandra finds it difficult to start new relationships or maintain old ones. From adolescence until recently, she had unstable and sometimes even unhealthy relationships with men, which is typical for people with chaotic attachment. She always wanted to have a serious romantic relationship, but when this happened, in her words, she sabotaged her own life and provoked her partner to break up. "When I started to feel good about achieving something in life, I would call the person who, as I knew, would 'break' this goodness." Also, sabotage could take on the guise of starting a conversation with her boyfriend on a challenging topic when Alexandra was too tired to communicate calmly and constructively. People with chaotic attachment seem to think, "It is easier to destroy it yourself, having a sense of control, than having to trust others that they would not break your heart again in a thousand pieces," says Alexandra.

Alexandra's emotional instability is one of the symptoms of her chaotic attachment. Some weeks things may go well. She may feel she can have healthy boundaries with the people around her, can manage her emotions, and be kind to herself. However, things may change quickly, which is very discouraging and tiring for her. In such moments she always feels frustrated, discouraged, and overwhelmed with thoughts.

The good news is that any insecure attachment can be changed to a secure one. This change does not happen by itself, however. It takes meticulous work to identify your self-destructive thoughts and emotions and get them in line with the truth of the word of God. In Alexandra's case, she also needed additional professional therapy to learn how to deal with self-sabotaging tendencies more effectively.

Her experience is that now she "bounces back to normal" faster in this healing process. She made a list of the things that make her more vulnerable to emotional failures: having little physical exercise, eating too many sweets, not getting enough sleep, etc. At my request, Alexandra also wrote down some of the things that help her cope with negative thoughts and emotions: walking, journaling, praying, taking necessary vitamins or medicines, showering, doing art or a hobby, communicating with friends, sleeping, and being kind to herself.

She has been in a stable and good relationship with a Christian boyfriend for almost a year and now they are engaged. Initially, her chaotic attachment and low self-esteem made Alexandra afraid that she would become a burden in the relationship. It is still hard for her to believe that she deserves and can expect something good from life. But she tries to work on it every day. The realization of the self-sabotaging tendency played a decisive role in her healing. She also understands that communication and openness are key in any relationship, but they are even more significant if one of the partners survived trauma. Alexandra tries to tell her boyfriend what she needs when she feels triggered – preferably before she gets triggered. In Alexandra's case, her boyfriend usually hugs her to help her calm down.

> I don't share with him all the details of what happened and I may never do so. But I think it's important that he knows how my past affects me now and how he can help me. I think our backgrounds made it more urgent for us to communicate, and that made our relationship stronger.

We have presented this story of Alexandra to illustrate the point that internal personality problems such as insecure attachment can be the reason why a Christian may have difficulties in romantic relationships. With that said, let's briefly consider another sensitive topic: is singleness a sign of a curse or a punishment from God due to a person's sin?

To navigate this topic properly we need to understand what the Bible says about curses and blessings. In the book of Proverbs we find that "houses and wealth are inherited from fathers, but a prudent wife is from the LORD" (Prov 19:14). And "He who finds a wife finds a good thing and obtains favor from the LORD" (Prov 18:22). We may safely conclude then that a good, reasonable, and prudent wife is a blessing from the Lord.

Yet Christians who have not been able to create a family for a long time, start to have a suspicion that maybe God is not blessing them by not giving them this "good thing." In extreme cases, some Christians even begin to wonder if some kind of curse is at work in their lives. This is especially typical for Christians in Eastern European and African cultures.

We do encounter the word "curse" in several ways in the Scriptures: as God's punishment for sin or violation of his commandments (Deut 11:28; 28:15–18) and as a negative prophecy or wish spoken by a person against another person (Ps 109:7–18), an entire nation (Num 22:12, 17) or oneself (Gen 27:13).[1] There

---

1. The Hebrew language has at least five verbs with a similar meaning, "to curse." One of the most common verbs is *arar*, which means, in fact, "to bind with a curse, spell; surround with obstacles" (Gen 3:14; 4:11; Num 22:6, etc.). Another frequently encountered verb is *kelal*, which means "to wish and speak badly or disparagingly about someone, to slander." It is opposite in

are also several biblical examples when curses pronounced against somebody came true in those people's lives (Judg 9:20; 56–57, as one). However, Scripture states that "an undeserved curse has no effect" (Prov 26:2 TLB). The question is, what is an "undeserved curse" and how can it be deserved?

On the one hand, every living person has sinned at least once. Scripture states there is none righteous, not even one (Rom 3:10, 12). So for our sinful deeds, according to God's justice, we are all worthy of punishment and fall under God's curse, for "it is written, 'cursed be everyone who does not abide by all things written in the Book of the Law, and do them'" (Gal 3:10).

On the other hand, Scripture also says that Christ redeemed us from the curse of the law by becoming "a curse" for us (Gal 3:13). Now we can draw the following conclusions:

1) In the lives of people who are not God's children (those who are not in Christ), any curse can be effective (including passed down from generation to generation (see Exod 20:5; Deut 28:18; Lam 5:7) or pronounced on them by other people) because they are deserved. Non-Christians are already under God's condemnation (1 Sam 2:30; Mark 16:16; John 3:18).

2) At the same time, any curse pronounced against the children of God is powerless. God turns it into a blessing (Deut 23:5; Neh 13:2). No one can curse what God has blessed. Those who are in Christ cannot be cursed by either God or man, because in Christ we are already blessed by God not according to our merits, but according to his grace (Eph 1:3; 2:7). Now, if in the Old Testament God's people could not be cursed by a sorcerer Balaam (Num 22:12, 18) because God loved his people and blessed them, much less the children of God in Christ Jesus can be cursed.

3) For Christians to believe in the force of a curse pronounced by someone against them or their family, to believe in all kinds of superstitions, or if they are afraid they will be fulfilled in his life, is a sin because this is unbelief in being blessed by God in Christ. In this case, if Christians believe that some kind of a curse, spell or evil eye is operating in their life, with power over their family, then by this sin of unbelief in God and fear they give the right to the devil to interfere in their life and bring curses. A biblical example: after all of the disasters that happened to him Job notes, "For the thing that I fear comes upon me, and what I dread befalls me" (Job 3:25). The principle given by Christ operating here is "according to your faith be it done to you" (Matt 9:29). Therefore, believers do not need to be afraid of any curse even actually

---

meaning to the verb "to bless" (Deut 11:28; 28:15, etc.). See Zodgiates, ed. *Hebrew–Greek Key Word Study Bible*, 1811, 2013.

uttered by someone in their life. Instead, they need to accept by faith the atoning sacrifice of Christ and live in blessing, just as they once received the remission of their sins by faith.

4) However, personal sin can indeed be the barrier that prevents a person from creating a God-blessed family. From the story of Samson, we understand that his promiscuity with dubious women, the repeated violations of his Nazarite vows, and self-indulgence, resulted in his disability to have a happy God-blessed marriage, and ultimately in Samson's premature death (see Judg 14:1; 16:1, 4). Likewise, someone who had an "intense" sex life before marriage should not be surprised if it would not be possible to suddenly build a good, blessed marriage on a bad foundation. That person will need to make a lot of effort even though now a Christian.

Marriage is associated in the Bible with God's favor. Isaiah the prophet declares: "You shall no more be termed Forsaken, and your land shall no more be termed Desolate, but you shall be called My Delight is in Her, and your land Married; for the LORD delights in you, and your land shall be married" (Isa 62:4). God loves godly marriages and he blesses them, but God does not favor the sinner (Jer 14:10).

In Deuteronomy 7:9–15, God promises to bless his people, multiply them, give offspring and provide for them if his people will obey and keep his laws. But there is a condition of God's blessing: love for God expressed in obedience to his word and trust in him. Although we are Christians and live in the New Testament, and God loves us unconditionally and has already blessed us in Christ, yet we believe this condition applies to us as well. If we are obedient to God and try to live according to his word, cooperating with his laws and not resisting them, then we make ourselves able to receive blessings from him.

God may hesitate to bless us with a family if he knows that the future husband or wife can become an idol for us. According to the Bible, an idol is anything a person turns to for salvation other than God. The prophet Ezekiel states: "Son of man, these men have taken their idols into their hearts, and set the stumbling block of their iniquity before their faces. Should I indeed let myself be consulted by them?" (Ezek 14:3). Hosea adds: "with their silver and gold they made idols for their own destruction" (Hos 8:4). Interestingly, the Old Testament eloquently calls our idols – our search for satisfaction outside of God – "lovers" (Jer 3:1; Ezek 23:20; Hos 2:13). God uses overtly sexual language because for many people, intimacy is the strongest and highest transcendental experience they have had on earth.

Many single Christians idealize marriage, expecting it to bring them complete satisfaction, and solve all their problems, believing that a husband or wife will meet all their needs. But this is self-deception and sin. Sin is putting anything ahead of God, anything we want more than God. Such idealization is akin to idolatry. As Mark Ballenger says, "Idolatry in marriage, or allowing your desire to find a spouse to override your desire to love God, is sinful. Put God first . . . Instead of putting God first *in order to* find a spouse, you need to strive to put God first '*in*' your search for a spouse."[2]

Ultimately, humans cannot meet *all* our needs; they were not created for this. Only God is capable of this. He wants to be the source of our enjoyment and the supplier of our needs. God promises "Delight (literally, enjoy, take pleasure) yourself in the LORD, and he will give you the desires of your heart. Commit your way to the LORD; trust in him, and he will act" (Ps 37:4, 5).

This does not mean, however, that the absence of a husband or wife is a sign of God's displeasure, punishment or, moreover, a curse. Neither does it mean that a single Christian must necessarily look for sin to repent so that God's blessing to start a family may come. Perhaps this period of unwanted singleness is needed to help this Christian get ready for a family life. Perhaps he or she is simply not ready for a serious relationship (the person usually is sure that he or she is absolutely ready!). The mere fact that your friend, having barely reached the age of adulthood, got married is not evidence of God's special favor or confirmation of her spirituality or success. Sometimes God postpones his answers to test our trust in him. Or maybe he has already blessed us, and we just need to learn how to accept this blessing by faith.

We should prayerfully ask God why we might not be ready for marriage. What prevents blessing from coming into our lives? Are there any qualities of ours that would destroy our relationships in marriage? God will tell us.

Now let us look at the difficulties that non-family Christians most often face.

2. Challenges single Christians face and the biblical response

It is difficult to rank the top "problem" areas for single Christians, since this is an individual matter, and will differ depending on gender, age, economic status, and even culture. But if we sum up what causes the greatest difficulties for Christian women and men in connection with their singleness, then these will be the following challenges:

---

2. Mark Ballenger, *The Ultimate Guide to Christian Singleness*, 36, 176.

Emotional loneliness

We know that on average, the level of emotional, social, cultural, and existential loneliness among single Christians is significantly higher than among married Christians.[3] Yet single Christians suffer from emotional loneliness in a special way.

We already mentioned that the period of singleness can be a temporary gift (before marriage) or for life. But it can only be a gift when it is voluntarily accepted as a gift. Otherwise, it will be associated with loneliness. This is how one woman comments on her loneliness:

> The most difficult thing is when there is no one to share life with. I know that my family and friends love me, but . . . when I come home from work, I have no one to talk to, no one to take care of, no one to take care of me, and no one to share dinner with. Sometimes women just want to be hugged. Having a man who I can love and who will love me back is what I really want.[4]

This unfulfilled need for intimacy, acceptance, and care causes a strong sense of emotional loneliness. Loneliness is especially acute for not married adults who have mainly married friends. The unexpected death of a spouse or the "death" of the relationship itself – a divorce – can also be a reason for such loneliness. Moreover, the pain of loss in such cases is often intensified by the feeling of betrayal. To experience the death of a relationship in which five, ten, or twenty years of love and trust have been invested, is an appalling shock. But we are still sure that healing from emotional loneliness is possible.

The previous section of the book is all about strategies for coping with all types of loneliness, including emotional. Therefore, here we will briefly list the main steps of overcoming this type of loneliness in singles.

First of all, deal with self-destructive attitudes, the negative expectations, scepticism, sarcasm, and pessimism typical for single people. When neglected, this negativism tends to accumulate and complicate relationships with other people. Negativism develops when a person has lost the expectation of something good to come. This is nothing other than unbelief. Negativism is

---

3. The data is based on a survey conducted among Christians in Ukraine in 2019. The same category of "single" included those respondents who at the time of the survey did not have close romantic relationships, or who were widowed or divorced. See: Чорнобай, "Богословське Осмислення Феномена Самотності" [Chornobai, "Theological Reflections on the Phenomenon of Loneliness"], 193.

4. Derived from the comments to the video: Mark Ballenger, "How to Deal with the Hardest Parts of Singleness: Loneliness, Confusion, Anger towards God," https://www.youtube.com/watch?v=YX5-py23vLk.

usually a trait of those people who have gradually lost gratitude not only for the little things in life but also for big ones, like family, friends, or church. Negativism, if not dealt with in time, develops into a habit that leads to depression, constant fears, doubts, anxiety, and apathy. It makes the person fail to love unconditionally. Such a person expects gratitude for love and, when not received, is disappointed. Also, this inability to look forward with hope and confidence is a sign of ageing, soul ageing.

How can we deal with negative self-destructive thoughts and attitudes? To defeat negativism, you first need to recognize it, honestly admit it to yourself and repent. Then, as the Scripture teaches, one must literally "take captive" – stop – every thought that rebels against the truth of the word (2 Cor 10:4–5). In practice, this means forcing ourselves to think about what God says about us in the Bible instead of thinking about what we feel, think, or fear. Next, stop speaking words of negativism, sarcasm about yourself and your future (such as: "I will never get married! As always, they will betray me and leave me," etc.). Instead, speak words of truth and faith. And, finally, it is important to pay attention and remind ourselves of all those blessings with which God has already blessed us, and which we are accustomed to take for granted, and thank God for them. In my personal experience, I (Valeriia) have found these tips useful in warding off negativism.

The second important step in overcoming emotional loneliness is a healthy religious life, which includes a close trusting relationship with God, secure attachment and a positive image of God in the mind of the believer. At this stage, it is also critically important for believers to understand their identity in Christ: that they are a child of God, loved by him, unconditionally accepted and important. They have a mission to accomplish and a role to play. In this regard, of course, believers have an advantage over unbelievers because in close communion with God, the feeling of loneliness is reduced.

Friends also help to cope with loneliness. Quality and not quantity plays the decisive role. It is better for you to have one real, close friend who will listen and support with a kind word and deed than a thousand so-called "friends" on social networks. Of course, developing close friendships takes time and effort. At the same time, it is important to respect the boundaries in these relationships, from being overly obsessed with one person, even if it is your best friend. Therefore, one should strive to expand the circle of one's fellowship with other believers of both sexes and different ages.

The last step that will help in overcoming emotional loneliness is volunteering, serving in a church or mission. Take up any activity that demonstrates your concern for those who need our help: the elderly, the children of your friends or children without parents, etc. Such concern is usually returned a hundredfold in reciprocal love. This will help the lonely person shift the focus from their emotional needs to the needs of others, give them the feeling that they are not living in vain, and make them more attractive to others.

Sexual frustration

Next but not a less serious challenge for singles is sexual frustration. Unfulfilled sexual desires and the need for love and intimacy all exacerbate feelings of loneliness. One woman writes about it this way: "I am thirty-five and by the grace of God I am still a virgin. And it's hard! I am human and God created me with a sexual desire that I cannot yet righteously satisfy. How discouraging to think that I could never have that kind of life experience if I never got married!" And for those singles that had experienced intimate relationships before becoming a Christian and now are living a chaste life, this intense desire is even more amplified and is a source of constant inner pain, struggle, and disappointment. Such singleness often feels like a forced one, when a person has no gift nor inclination to singleness, and in fact has a desire to start a family, but for various reasons, cannot. Such people may suffer particularly from emotional loneliness or even sexual disorientation.

In the struggle for sexual purity, Mark Ballenger gives single Christians some practical advice:

1. feed on God before you fight lust;

2. starve your sinful nature;

3. do it all by grace and by faith.[5]

This means we need to draw closer to God, and focus on the grace that we have in Christ to successfully overcome the temptation. Understanding that we are sanctified in Christ, and we have already been given freedom and victory over sin, makes us successful in the fight against it. The Bible does not absolutize sex. Intimacy in an earthly context is only a guiding thread, only an image and a faint reflection of the happiness and pleasure that awaits believers in heaven. True freedom from inner frustration is rooted in the conviction that God is the source of all happiness, of everything that has ever captivated our heart. For,

---

5. See: Mark Ballenger, "3 Strategies to Win the War on Lust in 2022," https://www.youtube.com/watch?v=Amdu9vMWBrk.

as Dallas Willard put it, "he is the most joyous being in the universe."[6] Psalm 36:8 confirms this idea: "They feast on the abundance of your house, and you give them drink from the river of your delights." The source of all goodness and pleasure, which we partly tasted on earth, we can experience in fellowship with him, but even more awaits us when we meet him in eternity.

The second piece of advice involves not just not feeding your carnal desires, but also deliberately avoiding sexual temptations. This means consciously avoiding places or situations where you know you can be tempted physically or emotionally in your imagination. It helps control your sexual desires, thoughts, and fantasies. That is the responsibility of every Christian. The Christian's abstinence is a promise to remain faithful to Christ, which, among other things, means keeping oneself from all sexual relations and thoughts outside of marriage. That is why it is important to avoid situations that can provoke sexual desire and lead us to sin (such as watching movies, melodramas containing explicit scenes, watching pornography, and masturbation). Instead, we should fill our thoughts with the word of God. "So flee youthful passions and pursue righteousness, faith, love, and peace, along with those who call on the Lord from a pure heart" (2 Tim 2:22). Temperance helps develop the fruit of the Spirit that is self-control. This spiritual skill will be useful in a future marriage as well.

Understanding that sexual temptations are not eternal also helps. We do not mean that they will weaken with age (although this is also true), but that God does not "let you be tempted beyond your ability, but with the temptation he will also provide the way of escape, that you may be able to endure it" (1 Cor 10:13).

Absence of children and the fear of being left alone

Also, the absence of children and the fear of being completely alone in old age takes third place in our ranking of the most "problematic challenges" for single Christians. At a certain age, almost every person has a desire to have children. It is natural. And therefore, the very idea that they will never become a mom or dad, they will not have a legacy that could be left behind, they will never have an amazing experience of conception and the birth of a new life – the very thought terrifies and depresses many single Christians.

---

6. Dallas Willard, *The Divine Conspiracy. Rediscovering Our Hidden Life in God*, EPub Edition (Harper Collins ebook, 2009), ISBN: 9780061972775, https://oceanofpdf.com/please-wait-for-few-moments-6.

In this line of thought, Barry Danylak assures that the chaste life of celibate Christians reflects the idea of the resurrection Jesus mentioned in the Gospel of Luke 20:34–35. Realizing that "the true and final satisfaction of all human needs, in the final analysis, will be only in the coming age of the kingdom of God," Christians, by their chaste life in celibacy, already now testify to this future resurrection.[7]

This idea, of course, is bright and beautiful. On the other hand, it is not only the need to ensure the continuation of the family line and leave behind a legacy that drives people in their desire to have children. This is a natural innate desire and need of every person from God, which, by the way, can also contribute to the spread of the kingdom of God, if children are brought up in gospel truth. The concept of the single chaste life of Christians as an image of the resurrection since ancient times caused a lot of criticism from the pagans, saying that the natural "procreation, and not the chilling doctrine introduced by Saint Paul, was the only way to ensure a 'resurrection of the dead.'"[8]

On the other hand, unmarried Christians without biological children of their own may find comfort in having spiritual children. If you look at the situation from the perspective of eternity, then indeed, "not sexual intercourse, but the preaching of the gospel brings true procreation"[9] – and the marital status of a person does not affect preaching of the gospel in any way. Colón and Field express a similar thought: unlike the Old Testament realities, "We no longer have to search for a kinsman redeemer to provide a physical heir to keep the family line intact. Instead, we are called to make disciples of others, creating spiritual heirs that will allow for the continuation of the church."[10]

The pressure of relatives, inner circle and often, unfortunately, brothers and sisters from the church is a major source of irritation for many single Christians. This pressure comes in two ways. On the one hand, single Christians often fall under the suspicion and condemnation of their relatives and church fellows for their singleness. Many married people in churches wonder why so many adult singles, being, as they say, sane and rather nice, having a desire to start a family, nevertheless, still do not marry. Then these "caring" relatives or Christians, not seeing any external obstacles that would prevent single people

---

7. See Barry Danylak, *Redeeming Singleness: How the Storyline of Scripture Affirms the Single Life* (Wheaton: Crossway, 2010), 208.

8. Peter Brown, *The Body and Society*, 7.

9. Peter Brown, *The Body and Society*, 7.

10. Christine A. Colón and Bonnie E. Field, *Singled Out: Why Celibacy must be Reinvented in Today's Church* (Grand Rapids: Brazos Press, 2009), 163.

from marrying, come to the conclusion that these single Christians are simply too demanding or picky. "They are too picky: this one is not the one, and that one will not work," they say reproachfully out of the "best of intentions," of course, sometimes shamelessly interfering in the private lives of single people, and sometimes even trying to "match them up" with somebody. One sister from the church told me (Valeriia) that her "compassionate" mother tried so hard to give her in marriage that she published an ad in the local newspaper on behalf of her daughter saying: "I am looking for a partner for a serious relationship," and gave her daughter's phone number. She did this without the daughter's consent!

Perhaps some singles appreciate this "care" in their life (although I have not met such people). Mostly, it irritates and depresses them, and makes singles feel inadequate and strange, like a commodity that is "past its sell-by date" and urgently needs to be sold at a discount before it goes bad. All this is because there is no balanced theological position or teaching regarding singleness in the evangelical community. Rather than being seen as a wonderful opportunity to serve God without distractions, as the apostle Paul advises, "celibacy is seen repeatedly not only as second best but also as a guarantee of an unfulfilled, miserable life," Colón and Field note.[11]

Such a negative or suspicious attitude of evangelicals toward singleness only reinforces the loneliness of single Christians. A famous verse from the book of Genesis that "it is not good that the man should be alone" (Gen 2:18) is often quoted in churches in support of marriage. And families are truly important. But if we consider this biblical truth in a broader spectrum, and not only as an argument in favour of marriage, we see that the role of the inclusive Christian community as a family of God is very important. The church must create an atmosphere of family, acceptance, and integration of each person regardless of his or her marital status. Even the church fathers, such as Basil the Great, recommended in their rules for monastic life that monks would not live and work alone but constantly be in communion and community.[12]

---

11. Colón and Field, *Singled Out*, 139.

12. According to St. Basil, the cenobite is better than the anchorite for the following reasons. (i) None of us is self-sufficient in the matter of providing for our bodily needs. (ii) Solitude is antagonistic to the law of love, since the solitary is bound to serve his own interests. (iii) It is harmful to the soul, when we have no one to rebuke us for our faults. (iv) Certain specific Christian duties, such as feeding the hungry and clothing the naked, are impossible for the true solitary. (v) We are all members one of another and Christ is our Head. How can we keep our relation to Christ intact if we separate from our brethren? (vi) We have different spiritual gifts. In a community each shares in the gifts of the brethren. (vii) Most important of all, the solitary is in danger of self-pleasing, and thinking he has already attained perfection, he

Also, in the light of Jesus's words that "whoever does the will of God" is truly his brother and sister and mother (Mark 3:35), our understanding of the family is expanding. This means that everyone who fulfils the will of God by believing in him, regardless of their sex, race, ethnicity, social or marital status, can equally be part of the family of Christ, have a personal relationship with him, and serve him. So the church family, where everyone is called to care for and love each other, acquires a special meaning and in a sense substitutes as family for those who do not have it. In every church community, not only should the traditional nuclear family feel accepted and valued but equally, single Christians.

On the other hand, some "spiritual" Christians try to impose guilt on single believers for their desire to marry by saying something along the lines: "Isn't Christ enough for you?" Interestingly, this phrase often comes from a person who is married. Yet there are physical expressions of love (hugs, kisses, touches, caresses) that simply cannot be experienced but with other people. Usually, God does not come down from heaven to embrace us but shows his love for us through another person, in marriage, for instance. None of this is a bad thing if expressed in marriage. But single people often are deprived of these intimate manifestations of love. So the strong desire to get married one day most Christians have is a good desire.

As we know, Jesus often directly asked people, "What do you want?" (Matt 20:21; Mark 10:51) – in other words, "What are your true desires?" Christ expected a direct and sincere answer to his questions. Also, while tempted in the wilderness, Jesus is known to be hungry. It is his natural reaction that legitimizes our thirst as well, which should be recognized and not shamed. Therefore, Christians who are not married but want to be should not feel guilty about their desire, as if a relationship with God is not enough for them. As Mark Ballenger put it in his excellent book, "desire to have a spouse is not an expression of your lack of joy in Christ."[13] After all, as mentioned in the first part of the book, God created Eve for Adam before their fall, as well as their need to have close relationships. This desire must be recognized, accepted and entrusted to God, "who works in you, both to will and to work for his good pleasure" (Phil 2:13). So we think if a Christian has a strong desire to get married one day to glorify God in his or her marriage, it is a good sign that this Christian has no gift of singleness and it is the will of God for them to get

---

cannot practice humility, pity or long-suffering. See William Kemp Lowther Clarke, *St. Basil the Great: a Study in Monasticism* (Cambridge: Cambridge University Press, 1913), 85–86.

13. Mark Ballenger, *The Ultimate Guide to Christian Singleness*, 39.

married, therefore such a Christian should pursue marriage, believing God will work it out according to his good pleasure.

Hopelessness

Probably one of the hardest things about being single is to keep hope alive. Many believers, especially if their period of singleness has gone on much longer than they expected, tend to fall into one of two extremes. One is constantly chasing romantic relationships as soon as the previous ones are over. For them, the experience of loneliness due to their singleness develops into a "neurosis of singleness," in which the desire to find a husband or wife becomes a super-goal, an obsessive painful condition. Few people are aware that it is their obsession with the idea of marriage that repels potential partners from them.

Others say goodbye to any hope of ever starting a family. They gave up on themselves, concluding that family was not for them. Others passively wait for a fabulously charming princess or prince. And some, both women and men, seek comfort and compensation for the absence of real relationships in fantasies, movies, or pornography. Because "hope deferred makes the heart sick" (Prov 13:12), some people prefer to bury hope altogether or stay as far away from their true desires as possible. This is a logical and tragic, but false way out. The tragedy of such a decision becomes even worse by the fact that, in the words of John Eldredge, this "suicide of soul" is committed under conviction that this is precisely what Christianity teaches.[14]

How can we keep our hearts alive and have good desires without losing heart if they don't come true the way we thought?

It is crucial not to give up on your destiny, and not lose hope, because that hope as a guiding thread can bring us to the desired goal. In Hebrew, the word "hope" sometimes is translated as "thread, rope."[15] Hope is always directed to the future. Scripture states, "For in this hope we were saved. Now hope that is seen is not hope. For who hopes for what he sees?" (Rom 8:24). Of course, this hope in Romans 8 refers specifically to the hope of the new creation and becoming fully like Christ. And this is indeed our prime hope. But it also reveals the principle of how hope works. Hope gives us the ability to see the

---

14. John Eldredge, *The Heart: Desire/Waking the Dead* (Nashville: Thomas Nelson, 2007), 34.

15. For example, this word (*tikvah*) meaning "rope" is used in Joshua 2:18, when Rahab the prostitute having let the Jewish spies go unharmed, urged them to save her and her entire family from destruction. And the sign by which they should have recognized her house was a red rope tied to her window. For her, this red rope meant the hope of salvation.

unseen and is based on our imagination. Just as before the construction of any building there is a preliminary plan, so the dreams in our imagination are the basis for hope. However, our dreams are at risk of being only empty fantasies, and our hopes at risk of being shattered, unless they are based on the promises in the word of God. By receiving a revelation of God's promises in hope and applying them by faith to our situation, we receive the promised, if we do not give up (Gal 6:9). About Abraham Scripture says that "In hope he believed against hope, that he should become the father of many nations, as he had been told, 'So shall your offspring be'" (Rom 4:18). And, as you know, Abraham received the promised heir at an unthinkable age (when he was 100 years old!), although he had to wait on this for about twenty-five years. In the context of our topic, this means that a life partner may appear at any, even a very mature age, for the person who has longed for marriage for a long time, and perhaps who has humanly speaking given up all hope, but longs to trust Christ more fully in whatever situation they find themselves.

Low self-esteem

Those who are divorced or have never been married often doubt whether they deserve to be loved and whether anybody can like them. And therefore especially "women will often settle for much less than what they're worth."[16] We have noticed that both men and women with low self-esteem tend to look for the reasons for their singleness in themselves, in their internal shortcomings and complexes. Such people fall into a vicious circle: their complexes prevent them from finding a life partner and the absence of a family feeds these and new complexes. Therefore, many who suffer in their singleness do not even try to look for solutions and only fix their attention on one problem, which, in their opinion, is the main obstacle to marriage. As a result, such people are difficult to communicate with, difficult to establish relationships with, they are very tense and uneasy, and outwardly they are of little interest. On the other hand, people with too much self-esteem often see the reasons for their singleness only in external circumstances. They often tend to blame other people and God. In communication, they are suspicious and arrogant, often believing they need no relationships at all.

What is adequate self-esteem? Self-esteem is always formed by a person in comparison with the norm adopted in a significant community. But the truth is that the norm in society is constantly changing under the influence of culture,

---

16. Barbara Sroka, *One is a Whole Number* (Victor Books, 1978), 70.

fashion, and simply sinful human nature. Therefore, what was considered something wild, unacceptable and even unnatural fifty years ago, can be considered normal now. In this regard, Christians again have an advantage: their self-esteem is based on eternal unshakable standards – on the word of God. For Christians, that is the norm. This means that Christians should not let the world's value system, the social environment, and even other people determine their worth, but only God by his word. And God has valued every person very highly – at the price of the blood of his own Son. When Christians understand the truth that God values and loves them unconditionally, it allows their self-esteem to rise.

On the other hand, Scripture affirms that God is holy himself and requires the same holiness from us (Lev 11:44; Matt 5:48). If we are honest, we will acknowledge our shortcomings in comparison to these high ethical standards of God's holiness. We need God's grace and mercy which God has already given us in Christ. God looks at the Christian through the lens of the sacrifice of his Son. He does not impute to the believer his sins, but instead gives him forgiveness and the righteousness of Christ, "who saved us and called us to a holy calling, not because of our works but because of his own purpose and grace, which he gave us in Christ Jesus" (2 Tim 1:9). When we understand our identity in Christ and our need for God's grace and goodness, it humbles us making our self-esteem to be adequate.

Financial problems

Financial problems are last in our ranking of the top problems single people face, but not the least. Perhaps, for Christians from prosperous countries with stable economies, the financial issue is not a problem, but for the Slavic ones it is a problem, especially for young women, as well as church workers in full-time ministry. Speaking about the most difficult aspects of her single life, one young lady from Ukraine (twenty-three years old) shared with me: "You feel like a dray horse – you constantly have to think about where to earn money just for a living. I have to constantly take responsibility for all domestic issues: tighten a leaking tap, change a wheel, and fix a gas water heater. I feel like a semi-male. I also want to look attractive . . . but there is simply no time to think about it!" Such financial insecurity is exhausting and depressing for women.

In this regard, the biblical story of Ruth has always been a great encouragement for me personally. She was a widow and refugee in a foreign country who happened to be in a rather horrible financial situation. But she did not lose faith in the living God. And, therefore, she was able not only to overcome all her material difficulties but also to get married very successfully and give birth to a child who became Christ's ancestor! God blesses the faithful (2 Chr 16:9).

Now let us look at solo-living and its connection with loneliness.

3. Solo-living and the connection between singleness and loneliness

As we have stated in the first part of the book, all normal people need some time and space for themselves – we all need solitude. Given current social trends, however, it is necessary to note the existence of so-called "institutionalized solitude." This state-recognized and legally enshrined human right to privacy and personal space is called "solo-living," living alone. At the heart of both solitude and solo-living is freedom of choice, which leads to greater satisfaction with one's life than if these conditions were imposed on a person without consent or were the result of a combination of circumstances. Let us now note the reasons and motives for solo-living and solitude.

Surprisingly, solo-living is the most common type of household in Western Europe and North America. It is chosen by more than fifty percent of the adult population,[17] and its popularity is on the rise, which is a cause for concern as the number of marriages annually declines and divorces rise, both in Western Europe and North America.[18] Almost all modern Western European trends in marriage and demographic spheres also take place in Slavic societies: for example, an increase in the age of first marriage.[19] Also, every year there is a decrease in the number of marriages against an increase in the share of divorces and cohabitation (the so-called "civil marriage") in Ukraine.[20]

---

17. According to the State Statistics Service of Ukraine for 2018, about 20% of adult citizens in Ukraine live in single-person households. See: *Держстат України*, 2009–2019. "Шлюби та розірвання шлюбів." ["Marriages and Divorces," State Statistics Service of Ukraine, 2009–2019.] Accessed January 18, 2023, http://db.ukrcensus.gov.ua/mult/dialog/statfile_c_files/shlub.html.

18. Aarno Laihonen, "Trends in Households in the European Union: 1995–2025," *Statistics in Focus*, Theme 3, 24 (2003): 3, https://core.ac.uk/ download/pdf/148911875.pdf.

19. Although this indicator in Ukraine is still lower than in most European countries, nevertheless, as of 2018, the average age of registration of first marriage for women is 25 years, and for men almost 28 years (compared to 21 and 24 in 1990 respectively). Also, the number of marriages before the age of 18 is decreasing (1% of marriages compared to just fewer than 10% in the mid-1990s). See: *Держстат України*, 2009–2019. "Шлюби та розірвання шлюбів." ["Marriages and Divorces," State Statistics Service of Ukraine, 2009–2019.] Accessed January 18, 2023, http://db.ukrcensus.gov.ua/mult/dialog/statfile_c_files/shlub.html.

20. The information is given according to the State Statistics Committee of Ukraine. Although the number of divorces in Ukraine in 2017 decreased compared to 1990, but in percentage terms in 2017, 55.6% of marriages ended in divorce, while in 1990 this percentage

Let us try to analyse the benefits and challenges associated with living solo, to get a better understanding of the reasons why this lifestyle is so popular in modern society. The researchers Bella DePaulo and Eric Klinenberg highlight the following: greater freedom in choosing the circle of communication and times of solitude; greater mobility and independence in decision-making; absence of responsibilities and duties associated with caring and providing for the family; more opportunities for self-realization, professional growth, self-development and participation in social activities; and greater opportunities for establishing communication with friends, parents, and relatives.[21] The fact that married people spend less time with friends and parents than when they were single, in our opinion, is explained by the fact that married people, especially in the first five years of their married life, tend to narrow their social circle and focus more on relationships with each other.

Eric Klinenberg, in a somewhat optimistic light, notes that:

> young and middle-age singletons have helped to revitalize the public life of cities, because they are more likely than those who live with others to spend time with friends and neighbours, to frequent bars, cafes, and restaurants, and to participate in informal social activities as well as in civic groups . . . Cultural acceptance of living alone has helped to liberate women from bad marriages and oppressive families.[22]

Sociologist Roona Simpson comes to a similar conclusion in her recent study of women who never married. She notes that "for some participants, singleness was thus represented as a positive aspect of identity. Several depicted the experience of singleness as personally empowering" based on their ability to manage their households on their own, without the help of men. This, of course, challenges the idea of traditional gender roles and the complementarity of women and men.[23]

---

was 40%. See: *Держстат України*, 2009–2019. "Шлюби та розірвання шлюбів." ["Marriages and Divorces"].

21. Bella De Paulo, "Single in a Society Preoccupied with Couples," in *The Handbook of Solitude: Psychological Perspectives on Social Isolation, Social Withdrawal, and Being Alone*, edited by Robert J. Coplan, Julie C. Bowker (Hoboken: Wiley Blackwell, 2014), 302; Eric Klinenberg, *Going Solo: The Extraordinary Rise and Surprising Appeal of Living Alone* (New York: Penguin, 2012), 102.

22. Klinenberg, *Going Solo*, 230–31.

23. See: Simpson, "Singleness and Self-identity: The Significance of Partnership Status in the Narratives of Never-Married Women," *Journal of Social and Personal Relationships* 33.3 (2016): 395, https://doi.org/10.1177/ 0265407515611884.

However, despite all these advantages of solo-living, it also is potentially connected with certain challenges. Numerous studies state that people who live without a partner and alone are at greater risk of suffering from social isolation and loneliness.[24] Moreover, solo-living requires singles to have a certain economic stability and independence. That is why states encourage young people to live separately – it is economically beneficial for the state. After all, each person living separately needs a separate stove, refrigerator, washing machine, car, etc. For the sake of their comfort, they would rather buy their own than share it all, as they would if they lived in a family. This means in societies where most people live separately and value their comfort, there will always be a demand for these things.

Marriage, however, is a more financially advantageous social status, since it usually provides more secure financial support for family members. After all, suppose that a solo-living person fell ill or, even worse, lost the ability to work. Who will take care of him or her then? For many middle-aged and older single women and widows, caring for a household becomes a burden because they usually have fewer sources of income than married women and are therefore in less stable economic conditions.[25]

The increase of solo-living and the divorce rate are worrying signs of self-centeredness and decreasing attachment to others. After all, a person who lives alone for a long time gets used to predominantly respecting his or her own desires and interests, and the main motive in staying that way may be living for one's own pleasure and comfort.[26] This is pure selfishness.

---

24. For example, see: Нелли Романова, "Социальный Статус Одиноких Женщин в Современном Российском Обществе: Теоретико-Методологический Анализ на Материалах Забайкалья" (Дисс. док. социол. наук, Бурятский Государственный Университет, Улан-Удэ, 2006) [Nelli Romanova, "The Social Status of Single Women in Modern Russian Society: Theoretical and Methodological Analysis on the Materials of Transbaikalia" (Diss. Doctor of Sociology, Buryat State University, Ulan-Ude, 2006)], 26; Жанна Пузанова, "Социологическое Измерение Одиночества" (Автореф. дисс. док. социол. наук. Москва, 2009) [Zhanna Puzanova, "The Sociological Dimension of Loneliness" (Abstract of diss. doc. sociology. Moscow, 2009)], 11; Béatrice D'Hombres, Sylke Schnepf, Martina Barjaková, and Francisco Teixeira Mendonça, "Loneliness – an Unequally Shared Burden in Europe," *Science for Policy Briefs: European Union* 4 (2018): 3–4, https://ec.europa.eu/jrc/en/ research/crosscutting-activities/fairness; Roona Simpson, "Singleness and Self-Identity," 396.

25. See: Karen T. Seccombe and Rebeca L. Warner, *Marriages and Families: Relationships in Social Context* (Belmont: Thomson/Wadsworth, 2004), 292; Leslie A. Morgan, *After Marriage Ends: Economic Consequences for Midlife Women* (London: Sage, 1991), 29.

26. Roona Simpson, "The Intimate Relationships of Contemporary Spinsters," *Sociological Research Online* 11, 3, http://www.socresonline.org.uk/11/3/simpson.html.

According to Eric Klinenberg, one such motive that encourages people to stay single or even break off relationships is their inner loneliness, feelings of emptiness and inability to live together with other people. He writes:

> For no matter how socially active, professionally successful, or adept at going solo one makes oneself, there is something uniquely powerful about the intimate connection forged through sharing one's home with another person. Then again, there is also something uniquely painful about sharing one's home with someone who has squandered or abused this intimacy and trust . . . One reason so many people separate is that they are lonely with each other.[27]

Due to the prevalence of solo-living, the idea of mutual commitment in relationships and belonging, which is the norm for married life, is also under threat. After all, married life still involves a greater degree of commitment, intimacy and mutual knowledge than any other type of relationships.

Note, that the Bible uses the phrase "one body" to denote such closeness in interpersonal relationships only concerning spouses (Gen 2:24; Matt 19:6) and believers who collectively represent the body of Christ (Rom 12:5; 1 Cor 6:15–16; Eph 3:6; 4:4).[28] Just as in marriage, so the church is an image of unity, commitment, and wholeness in Christ. Therefore, the church community, in particular, is essential for the normal development of a person and for overcoming loneliness.

Conclusion to chapter 8

We have already pointed out that the unsatisfied need for affection and intimacy is one of the problems associated with singleness and solo-living. From the Christian moral point of view, sexual relations should always be accompanied by trust, devotion, and care in a legal marriage. But for non-Christians living single, sex and commitment are separate things from each other. Nowadays, Christians who for religious reasons choose to remain chaste until marriage are often misunderstood and criticized by their contemporaries. They are considered strange, old-fashioned, and narrow-minded. As a result, they feel culturally lonely. In modern secular culture, sexual activity is often seen as the

---

27. Klinenberg, *Going Solo*, 84.

28. In this regard, 1 Cor 6:15–16 is especially interesting as it parallels physical unity in one "flesh" (*sarx*) of husband and wife in marriage and the spiritual union in one "body" (*soma*) of believers in Christ.

basis of human identity – what it means to be a real man or woman. However, a Christian's conscious choice in favour of chastity is a step toward a better understanding of the believer's true identity based not on his sexuality, marital status, or role, but on belonging to Christ.

As we have already said, unlike the celibacy of the times of the first church, the modern phenomenon of solo-living does not pursue the goal of exercising believers in some kind of spiritual practices, but is an expression of individualistic ideals of freedom and comfort. Although living solo is more convenient as bringing more moral satisfaction with life, however, it can exacerbate social loneliness and isolation.

This popularity of the solitary lifestyle may be one of the signs of the end times that the biblical authors warn about. See what the apostle Paul writes in 2 Timothy: "This know also, that in the last days perilous times shall come. For men shall be lovers of their own selves . . . without natural affection, trucebreakers . . . traitors" (2 Tim 3:1–4 KJV). The Greek term for "without natural affection" depicts a person devoid of kinship or friendship affections, any feelings of love and closeness. So Scripture warns that in the last times people will become especially unable to get along together. It looks like the current situation. We, as the people of God, must be aware of this danger and counter these modern social trends by building and maintaining strong Christian families and communities to confront loneliness and isolation. We should understand that the devil does hate strong traditional families, especially Christian ones as much as he hates church. And he will do whatever he can to ruin them or prevent them from forming. Therefore, let there be family and let there be church.

Summary

This book which consists of three independent parts aims to convey one idea that we were not created to be lonely. There is an innate desire in every one of us to belong and be accepted in God's design. And, as the Scripture puts it, two are better than one. Yet, in this broken world, we often suffer from loneliness of many types. We have discovered that there are at least five distinctive types of loneliness – social, emotional, cultural, existential, and spiritual. Bible stories, however, give us an insight into how each of these types of loneliness occurs and what we can do to deal with them.

Further, we attempted to illustrate all five types of loneliness through the true stories of real people we know and interviewed to analyze the most significant causes of loneliness and the most efficient ways to overcome it.

We believe that a root of the problem of almost every type of loneliness lies in identity confusion. So, restoration of our true identity as Christians is the main goal in overcoming our loneliness. In this process the main strategies that help in overcoming loneliness successfully are solitude, personal prayer of reflection and meditation on Scripture, identification and change of our self-destructive thoughts and behaviors.

Finally, we wrote the last part of the book, specifically with Christian singles in mind. We made a lengthy study of the place singleness and solo living have been taking in the history of the Christian church and how they contribute to loneliness. All this was done to help those Christian singles with a gift of singleness detect and embrace their gift and serve the Lord most efficiently. And those Christians who are not happy with their single state, who know that marriage is the will of God for their lives, hopefully, could find here some valuable ideas of how to overcome loneliness while waiting for fulfillment of God's will for them in marriage.

We believe that just as making the correct diagnosis is crucial for the successful treatment of any illness, it is also necessary to discern what type of loneliness we suffer from before attempting to treat it. We also showed how our loneliness is connected to our attachment style. For this purpose, at the end of the book we provided a unique questionnaire to help the reader find it all out.

Appendix

The Loneliness Inventory for Christians (LIFC)

Instructions: You can fill in this questionnaire to find out what type and level of loneliness you have. You can also find out if you can make the best of your time in solitude or not. Please read the statements below carefully and express your agreement or disagreement with them, recalling what reaction you personally experienced in such a situation. It is better to give the answer that first came to your mind as honestly as you can. If the situation below does not apply to you, please tick the answer "Strongly disagree." Write the number in the space provided, using the following rating scale: Strongly disagree = 0, Rather disagree = 1, Rather agree = 2, and Strongly agree = 3. NOTE that items marked with (R) are reverse scored! (Strongly disagree = 3, Rather disagree = 2, Rather agree = 1, and Strongly agree = 0)

№	Statement	Strongly disagree	Rather disagree	Rather agree	Strongly agree
		0 (R - 3)	1 (R - 2)	2 (R - 1)	3 (R - 0)
1	I have close people with whom I share my most intimate thoughts and feelings (R)[29]				
2	I can depend upon my friends for help (R)				
3	I lack intimacy and emotional warmth in my relationship				

---

29. Items 1, 2, 7, 15 and 33 were borrowed from the SELSA, however, we have changed the initial phrase "romantic or marital partner" to "close people" as it better serves our research. For the reference, see: Enrico DiTommaso, Barry Spinner, "The Development and Initial Validation of the Social and Emotional Loneliness Scale for Adults 'SELSA,'" *Personality and Individual Differences* 14 (1993): 127–134.

№	Statement	Strongly disagree	Rather disagree	Rather agree	Strongly agree
		0 (R - 3)	1 (R - 2)	2 (R - 1)	3 (R - 0)
4	I trust God's guidance in my life, although I do not always understand it (R)				
5	When I am alone by myself, I experience significant discomfort[30]				
6	I have a hobby, business, or ministry that I enjoy doing in my church or community (R)				
7	I feel close to my family (R)				
8	I miss close, trustful relationships based on mutual love and affection				
9	I have friends with whom I communicate regularly and with pleasure (R)				
10	God seems indifferent and distant to me[31]				
11	I do not feel genuine love and support from my husband / wife / partner in close relationships at the moment				
12	A person needs to be alone to understand or feel some important things (R)				
13	No one in the community where I live seems to care much about me[32]				
14	I feel like I don't belong when I'm with others[33]				

30. Items 5, 12, 16, 39, 40, and 41 were derived from the LACA Scale. For references, see: Alfons, Marcoen, Luc Goossens, and Paul Caes, "Loneliness in Pre through Late Adolescence: Exploring the Contributions of a Multidimensional Approach," *Journal of Youth and Adolescence* 16 (1987): 561–577.

31. Items 10 and 23 were derived from the Spiritual Well-Being Scale. See: Craig W. Ellison, "Spiritual Well-Being: Conceptualization and Measurement," *Journal of Psychology and Theology* 11, 4 (1983): 330–338.

32. Items 13, 34 and were derived from the Differential Loneliness Scale – short student version. For further reference, see: Nancy Schmidt, Vello Sermat, "Measuring Loneliness in Different Relationships," *Journal of Personality and Social Psychology* 44 (1983): 1038–1047.

33. The ideas of items 14, 29 and 39 were borrowed from the Motivation for Solitude Scale – Short Form (MSS-SF). See: Virginia Thomas, Margarita Azmitia, "Motivation Matters: Development and Validation of the Motivation for Solitude Scale – Short Form (MSS-SF),"

№	Statement	Strongly disagree 0 (R - 3)	Rather disagree 1 (R - 2)	Rather agree 2 (R - 1)	Strongly agree 3 (R - 0)
15	I have close people who give me the support and encouragement I need (R)				
16	I like being on my own (R)				
17	The society I live in evolves feelings of rejection and disgust in me				
18	My experiences with God are very intimate and emotional (R)[34]				
19	There are no friends in my life who understand me and share my beliefs				
20	Few people from my environment share my principles, ideals and values				
21	In fact, nothing in life depends on me				
22	I prefer not to depend too much on God				
23	I think God loves me unconditionally and helps me (R)				
24	My inner circle of people supports me in my hobbies and vocation (R)				
25	It seems to me that God is not always fair				
26	Sometimes I get the feeling that I belong to a different country or culture				
27	Life seems pretty boring and pointless to me				
28	It seems to me that people think I'm not quite adequate (I'm strange)				
29	I'm looking for opportunities to be alone so I can engage in activities that really interest me (R)				

Journal of Adolescence 70 (2019): 33–42.

34. Items 18, 22, 32, and 43 are borrowed from AGI (Attachment to God Inventory). See: Richard Beck, Angie McDonald, "The Attachment to God Inventory, Tests of Working Model Correspondence, and an Exploration of Faith Group Differences," *Journal of Psychology and Theology* 32, 2 (2004): 92–103. https://doi.org/10.1177/009164710403200202.

№	Statement	Strongly disagree 0 (R - 3)	Rather disagree 1 (R - 2)	Rather agree 2 (R - 1)	Strongly agree 3 (R - 0)
30	I feel like a "black sheep" – a person who is very different from others				
31	I'm quite happy with the way I have lived my life (R)[35]				
32	I just don't feel a deep need to be close to God				
33	I don't have a single person from my family on whose support I could count				
34	At this moment, I have a relationship that gives me mutual emotional pleasure and satisfaction (R)				
35	There is a purpose to my life (R)				
36	I feel like no one truly understands my feelings				
37	I am confident that God is ready to hear me whenever I call on him (R)				
38	No matter how hard I try, nothing can be changed in life				
39	Solitude helps me to reflect and understand myself better (R)				
40	The possibility of staying single for the rest of my life scares me				
41	When I'm alone, thoughts of loneliness weigh me down				
42	My life is filled with deep meaning (R)				
43	I often worry about whether God is pleased with me				

35. Items 31 and 35 were borrowed from ELQ (Existential Loneliness Questionnaire): Aviva M. Mayers et al., "The Existential Loneliness Questionnaire: Background, Development, and Preliminary Findings," *Journal of Clinical Psychology* 58 (September 9, 2002): 1183–1193.

Scoring:
Emotional loneliness = sum of items: 1, 3, 8, 11, 15, 34
Social loneliness = sum of items: 2, 6, 7, 9, 13, 14, 19, 33
Cultural loneliness = sum of items: 17, 20, 24, 26, 28, 30, 36
Existential loneliness = sum of items: 21, 27, 31, 35, 38, 42
Spiritual loneliness = sum of items: 4, 10, 18, 22, 23, 25, 32, 37, 43
Aversion to solitude = sum of items: 5, 12, 16, 29, 39, 40, 41

Loneliness type	Level — Low level of loneliness, sum of items	Average level of loneliness, sum of items	High level of loneliness, sum of items
Emotional	0–5	6–11	12–18
Social	0–7	8–15	16–24
Cultural	0–6	7–13	14–21
Existential	0–5	6–11	12–18
Spiritual	0–8	9–17	18–27
Aversion to solitude	0–6	7–13	14–21

Interpretation of the results

Below you can find the interpretation of the results according to each type and level of loneliness.

1. Emotional loneliness:

1.1. Low level of emotional loneliness: You have no problem forming reliable deep relationships with your loved ones. It's easy for you to show emotional attachment in relationships, both new and existing. Other people usually find it easy to get emotionally close to you and obtain great pleasure from their relationship with you. You have a lot of self-confidence, and you don't waste time worrying about the success or failure of your relationship. This attitude helps you be much calmer in interpersonal relationships, resulting in their prosperity and stability.

1.2. Average level of emotional loneliness: Although you can devote yourself emotionally to close relationships, sometimes you find it hard to form reliable deep relationships with loved ones based on mutual trust. Be careful not to let lack of trust ruin your relationship, as this can cause people to shun you. So, if you try not to fear rejection, open up more in your existing relationships with loved ones and enjoy them more, you will have stable development of the relationships and success in them.

1.3. High level of emotional loneliness: Your test results show that you have a relatively high level of emotional loneliness. Emotional loneliness occurs in the absence of secure emotional attachment in a relationship, when there is no sense of deep understanding, belonging, unity, and acceptance from a significant other. Perhaps this means that other people also find it difficult to get emotionally close to you and do not get much satisfaction from their relationship with you. Making an effort to get rid of negative thoughts and expectations of defeat or rejection, to open yourself up to more trusting relationships, as well as your self-confidence, can help you have better emotional stability, enjoy your relationships with loved ones more and to create new deep and trusting relationships.

2. Social loneliness:

2.1. Low level of social loneliness: Social loneliness means a feeling of dissatisfaction with the number of your social relationships. It develops when a person is deprived of the possibility of meaningful communication and understanding with other people. However, the results of this test indicate you have no social loneliness at the moment. We congratulate you on good communication, understanding, and connection with other significant people in your life!

2.2. Average level of social loneliness: Your test results indicate that you have an average experience of the loneliness. Social loneliness means dissatisfaction with the number of social relationships due to a lack of meaningful communication and understanding with other people. This type of loneliness often develops due to a person's poor social skills, on a long-term business trip to an unknown place, or after moving abroad or joining a new group. It's usually nothing serious to worry about, as everyone sometimes can feel lonely. However, it can become a problem if these feelings are long-lasting and consistent even if you are surrounded by friends or family.

2.3. High levels of social loneliness: Your answers to this test show you suffer from extreme and severe social loneliness. A certain temporary feeling of loneliness is a normal part of life for most people. But when your loneliness prevails and lingers longer than usual – like now – it can be a sign that the social connections with other people in your life are not quite balanced. Maybe trying to be more open on your part to form new friendships with people, or to communicate with members of your family, whom you trust, will require some effort and time, but they will be worth it. After all, such steps help many people to get rid of the feeling of social loneliness.

3. Cultural loneliness:

3.1. Low level of cultural loneliness: Your results indicate that you have no cultural loneliness. This may mean that you feel like an integral part of the society you belong to and that you are quite satisfied with the cultural norms that dominate it.

3.2. Average level of cultural loneliness: You experience moderate cultural loneliness, which is evident when a person regards the culture generally accepted in society as unacceptable. People often experience this type of loneliness, for instance, in societies that socially and culturally rapidly change, which can contribute to the generation gap and social inequality. Sometimes you feel you cannot comply with the norms of the society you live in.

3.3. High level of cultural loneliness: The high level of cultural or prophetic loneliness observed in you indicates a prominent detachment from the current cultural environment and your rejection of social norms and values generally accepted in a certain community. For many devoted to God Christians, such loneliness is often a natural consequence of their fulfilment of God's will: the more a person realizes his calling from God, the more "alien" the surrounding world seems to him. This type of loneliness was also a characteristic of outstanding people in history whose progressive ideas were far ahead of their time. Almost all the prophets mentioned on the pages of the Bible felt a similar loneliness: Moses, Elijah, Jeremiah, the apostle Paul, and Jesus himself. Maybe you are one such person!

4. Existential loneliness:

4.1. Low level of existential loneliness: The results of this test show that you have very little or almost no existential loneliness. This may mean that you are a person who is in complete harmony and unity with yourself, having understanding of the meaning of your life and purpose, a clear awareness of your uniqueness, and your place in the universe. Keep up in the same way!

4.2. Average level of existential loneliness: Your results correspond to an average level of existential loneliness, which may indicate that you are in the quest for meaning and purpose in life. Oddly enough, such existential loneliness is often the result of certain painful circumstances or suffering in a person's life. However, such experiences usually result in inner growth and a greater awareness of a person's fundamental uniqueness, his place and purpose in the universe, his "Self" if the person doesn't quit this pursuit.

4.3. High level of existential loneliness: The results of this test indicate that you experience acute existential loneliness. Such existential loneliness comes when a person loses harmony and unity with himself. It's felt like a certain self-estrangement, and disappointment in life and it is often expressed in the quest for meaning in life. Accordingly, such loneliness is overcome by a person's awareness of his fundamental uniqueness, by an understanding of his place in life, purpose, and identity.

5. Spiritual loneliness:

5.1. Low level of spiritual loneliness: Your test results show that you hardly experience any spiritual loneliness. This means that your relationship with God seems to be based on a secure attachment to him and trust. You enjoy personal communication with him, despite the incomprehensible or even sad events that sometimes happen in your life.

5.2. Average level of spiritual loneliness: Your test results indicate your average level of spiritual loneliness. This may mean that you have personal relationships with God, but they lack trust, emotional closeness, and reliability at the moment. As a rule, you are sure of God's faithfulness and love for you personally, but sometimes, perhaps, under the influence of certain life circumstances, you begin to doubt this.

5.3. High level of spiritual loneliness: Your test results show that you have a relatively high level of spiritual loneliness. Spiritual loneliness is the experience of a gap or lack of connection and trust in a person's relationship with God. This type of loneliness is a characteristic of people who have either never had the experience of a personal, trust-based relationship with God or those believers who, due to certain life circumstances, feel that God has abandoned them or even betrayed them. Spiritual loneliness is often felt like being abandoned by God. We believe this type of loneliness was experienced by Jesus on the cross when he turned to his God and Father: "My God, my God, why have you forsaken me?" (Mark 15:34). This is precisely the feeling of spiritual alienation from God that Jesus Christ endured facing death on the cross to destroy human alienation, separation from God, overcome the eternal spiritual loneliness of all people and bring them closer to the Heavenly Father. So now we may draw closer to God with confidence!

6. Aversion to solitude:

6.1. Low level of aversion to solitude: You have a rather positive attitude towards solitude. Most likely, you enjoy the time spent alone even if it was not planned. You know how to use the time of solitude effectively. You even purposefully look for it because excessive communication with people exhausts you. Such a positive attitude to solitude and ability to spend time efficiently can help against loneliness.

6.2. Average level of aversion to solitude: An average level of aversion to solitude means that you are usually quite good at using the time spent alone to your advantage and for self-realization. However, sometimes your solitude is tinged with loneliness at this stage of life. Your continuing to escape or fear of being alone might contribute to your loneliness. However, solitude is a good time for rest, restoring emotional balance, self-realization, and understanding your identity.

6.3. High level of aversion to solitude: The test results confirm that you have a high level of aversion to solitude. Solitude is mainly associated with unpleasant feelings for you. The fact is that such an aversion to solitude can increase your vulnerability to loneliness when you are alone. And a person's positive attitude towards solitude can, on the contrary, protect against loneliness when a person is alone. Therefore, it is important to learn not to be afraid to be alone, because this is an opportunity to think about your path, your role, and your place in life, to rethink it; learn to use the time of solitude for self-realization, creativity, or helping others. Such steps of yours will bring good results in your life over time because loneliness can only be overcome by someone who can endure solitude.

The Relationships Questionnaire (RQ)[36]

This is a 4-item questionnaire designed to measure your attachment style. Following are four general relationship styles that people often report. Place a checkmark next to the letter corresponding to the style that best describes you or is closest to the way you are.

_____ A. It is easy for me to become emotionally close to others. I am comfortable depending on them and having them depend on me. I don't worry about being alone or having others not accept me.

_____ B. I am uncomfortable getting close to others. I want emotionally close relationships, but I find it difficult to trust others completely, or to depend on them. I worry that I will be hurt if I allow myself to become too close to others.

_____ C. I want to be completely emotionally intimate with others, but I often find that others are reluctant to get as close as I would like. I am uncomfortable being without close relationships, but I sometimes worry that others don't value me as much as I value them.

_____ D. I am comfortable without close emotional relationships. It is very important to me to feel independent and self-sufficient, and I prefer not to depend on others or have others depend on me.

Keys:
The letters correspond to secure (A), chaotic or disorganized (B), ambivalent-anxious or dependent (C), and avoidant (D) attachment styles.

---

36. Kim Bartholomew, Leonard M. Horowitz, "Attachment Styles Among Young Adults: A Test of a Fourcategory Model," *Journal of Personality and Social Psychology* 61 (1991): 226–244.

Bibliography

Ambrose of Milan. "Concerning Virginity." Pages 363–87 in vol. 10 of *Nicene and Post-Nicene Fathers*, Second Series. Translated by H. de Romestin, E. de Romestin, and H. T. F. Duckworth, eds. Philip Schaff and Henry Wace. Buffalo: Christian Literature Publishing Co., 1896. https://www.newadvent.org/fathers/34071.htm.

Anderson-Mooney, Amelia J., Marcia Webb, Nyaradzo Mvududu, and Anna M. Charbonneau. "Dispositional Forgiveness and Meaning-Making: The Relative Contributions of Forgiveness and Adult Attachment Style to Struggling or Enduring with God." *Journal of Spirituality in Mental Health* 17.2 (2015): 93, DOI: 10.1080/19349637.2015.985557.

Andre, Rae. *Positive Solitude: A Practical Program for Mastering Loneliness and Achieving Self-Fulfillment*. New York: Harper Collins, 1991.

Aristotle. "Politics." Pages 1986–2129 in vol. 2 of *The Complete Works of Aristotle*, ed. Jonathan Barnes. Princeton: Princeton University Press, 1995.

Augustine of Hippo. "Homily 4 on the First Epistle of John." Pages 481–87 in vol. 7 of *Nicene and Post-Nicene Fathers*, First Series. Translated by H. Browne, edited by Philip Schaff. Buffalo: Christian Literature Publishing Co., 1888. http://www.newadvent.org/fathers/170204.htm>.

Augustine of Hippo. "On Holy Virginity." Pages 417–38 in vol. 3 of *Nicene and Post-Nicene Fathers*, First Series. Translated by C.L . Cornish, edited by Philip Schaff. Buffalo: Christian Literature Publishing Co., 1887. http://www.newadvent.org/fathers/1310.htm.

Augustine of Hippo. *Confessions*. Newly translated and edited by Albert C. Outler, 1955. https://faculty.georgetown.edu/jod/augustine/conf.pdf.

Ballenger, Mark. "3 Strategies to Win the War on Lust in 2022." Accessed December 20, 2022. https://www.youtube.com/watch?v=Amdu9vMWBrk.

Ballenger, Mark. "How to Deal with the Hardest Parts of Singleness: Loneliness, Confusion, Anger towards God." Accessed December 20, 2022. https://www.youtube.com/watch?v=YX5-py23vLk.

Ballenger, Mark. "The Ultimate Guide to Christian Singleness." CreateSpace Independent Publishing Platform. Accessed November 3, 2017.

Ballenger, Mark. "5 Things That Mean God Is Preparing You to Find True Love Soon." Accessed January 16, 2022. https://youtu.be/uiCvRNIMTBM.

Barclay's Daily Study Bible. "1 Corinthians 7." In *Bible Commentaries*. Accessed December 20, 2022. https://www.studylight.org/commentaries/eng/dsb/1-corinthians-7.html.

Barth, Karl. *Church Dogmatics. The Doctrine of Creation.* In vol. 3 of *The Work of Creation*, Part 1. Translated by J. W. Edwards, O. Bussey, H. Knight, edited by G. W. Bromiley, T. F. Torrance. London: T&T Clark International, 1958.

Bartholomew, Kim, and Leonard M. Horowitz. "Attachment Styles among Young Adults: A Test of a Four Category Model." *Journal of Personality and Social Psychology* 61 (1991): 226–44.

Basil of Caesarea. "An Ascetical Discourse and Exhortation on the Renunciation of the World and Spiritual Perfection." In *Ascetical Works*, edited by M. Monica Wagner. Washington: The Catholic University of America Press, 1999. muse.jhu.edu/book/20872.

Basil of Caesarea. "Letter 199. To Amphilochius, concerning the Canons." Pages 236–40 in vol. 8 of *Nicene and Post-Nicene Fathers*, Second Series. Translated by Blomfield Jackson, edited by Philip Schaff and Henry Wace. Buffalo: Christian Literature Publishing Co., 1895. http://www.newadvent.org/fathers/3202199.htm.

Basil the Great. "Second Canonical Epistle." Rule 18. Accessed December 20, 2022. https://people.ucalgary.ca/~vandersp/Courses/texts/cappadoc/basilcep.html#CXCIX.

Baumeister, Roy F., and Mark R. Leary. "The Need to Belong: Desire for Interpersonal Attachments as a Fundamental Human Motivation." *Psychological Bulletin* 117.3 (1995): 497–529. https://doi:10.1037/0033-2909.117.3.497.

Beck, Richard, and Angie McDonald. "The Attachment to God Inventory, Tests of Working Model Correspondence, and an Exploration of Faith Group Differences." *Journal of Psychology and Theology* 32.2 (2004): 92–103. https://doi:10.1177/009164710403200202.

Blue Letter Bible. "Psalm 78. Probable Occasion when Each Psalm was Composed." Accessed December 5, 2022. https://www.blueletterbible.org/study/parallel/paral18.cfm.

Boswell, John. "Eastburn, Expositio and Oblatio: The Abandonment of Children and the Ancient and Medieval Family." *The American Historical Review* 1.89 (February, 1984): 10–33.

Bowlby, John. *Attachment and Loss: Attachment.* Second Edition, vol. 1. Tavistock Institute of Human Relations: Basic Books, 1982.

Bowlby, John. *Attachment and Loss: Loss*, vol. 3. New York: Basic Books, 1980.

Bowlby, John. *Attachment and Loss: Separation*, vol. 2. New York: Basic Books, 1973.

Bradshaw, Matt, Christopher G. Ellison, and Jack P. Marcum. "Attachment to God, Images of God, and Psychological Distress in a Nationwide Sample of Presbyterians." *The International Journal for the Psychology of Religion* 20.2 (2010): 130–147. DOI: 10.1080/10508611003608049.

Braz de Aviz, João, José Rodríguez Carballo. "Instruction 'Ecclesiae Sponsae Imago' on the 'Ordo virginum.'" *Bolletino Sala Stampa Della Santa Sede* (04 July, 2018). http://press.vatican.va/content/salastampa/en/bollettino/pubblico/ 2018/07/04/180704d.pdf.

Brown, David R., Jamie S. Carney, Mark S. Parrish, and John L. Klem. "Assessing Spirituality: the Relationship between Spirituality and Mental Health." *Journal of Spirituality in Mental Health* 15.2 (2013): 118–224. https://doi.org/10.1080/193 49637.2013.776442.

Brown, Peter. *The Body and Society: Men, Women and Sexual Renunciation in Early Christianity.* New York, Guildford, Surrey: Columbia University Press, 1988.

Cacioppo, John, and William Patrick. *Loneliness: Human Nature and the Need for Social Connection.* New York. London: W. W. Norton and Company, 2008.

Cacioppo, Stephanie, Angela J. Grippo, Sarah London, Luc Goossens, and John T. Cacioppo. "Loneliness: Clinical Import and Interventions." *Psychological Science* 10.2 (2015): 238–249. DOI: 10.1177/1745691615570616.

Calvin, John. *Institutes of the Christian Religion.* Translated by Ford Lewis, edited by John T. McNeill. Battles. Louisville: Westminster John Knox Press, 2001.

Cambridge Bible for Schools and Colleges. "Genesis." Accessed September 01, 2019. https://biblehub.com/commentaries/genesis/4-12.htm.

Caplan, Gerald. "Loss, Stress, and Mental Health." *Community Men Health J.* 26.1 (February 1990): 27–48. DOI: 10.1007/BF00752675.

Chornobai, Valeriia A. "The Development and Initial Validation of the Loneliness Inventory for Christians (LIFC)." *Skhid: Philosophical Sciences* 1.165 (January–February 2020). http://skhid.kubg.edu.ua/article/view/197021.

Chornobai, Valeriia. "Attachment to God as a Deterrent against Loneliness." *Modern Science – Moderní věda* 1 (2018): 79–85.

Chrysostom, John. "Homily 58 on Matthew." Pages 358–63 in vol. 10 of *Nicene and Post-Nicene Fathers*, First Series. Translated by George Prevost and revised by M. B. Riddle, edited by Philip Schaff. Buffalo: Christian Literature Publishing Co., 1888.

Chrysostom, John. "Homily 62 on Matthew." Pages 381–86 in vol. 10 of *Nicene and Post-Nicene Fathers*, First Series. Translated by George Prevost and revised by M.B . Riddle, edited by Philip Schaff. Buffalo Christian Literature Publishing Co., 1888. http://www.newadvent.org/fathers/200162.htm.

Cigna 2018 U.S. "Loneliness Index. Gen Z (Adults Ages 18–22) is the Loneliest Generation." Accessed May, 18 2023. https://www.cigna.com/static/www-cigna-com/docs/about-us/newsroom/studies-and-reports/combatting-loneliness/loneliness-survey-2018-full-report.pdf.

Clarke, William Kemp Lowther. *St. Basil the Great: A Study in Monasticism.* Cambridge: Cambridge University Press, 1913.

Clement of Alexandria. "Stromateis." Book Three. In *The Fathers of the Church. A New Translation.* Translated by John Ferguson, edited by Thomas R. Halton. Washington: The Catholic University of America Press, 1991.

Clement of Rome. *Two Epistles Concerning Virginity.* Translated by B. P. Pratten, edited by Alexander Roberts and James Donaldson. Edinburgh: T&T Clark, 1867.

Clinton, Tim, and Gary Sibcy. *Attachments: Why You Love, Feel and Act the Way You Do.* Brentwood: Integrity Publishers, 2002.

Cohen, Sheldon, William J. Doyle, Ronald Turner, Cuneyt M. Alper, and David P. Skoner. "Sociability and Susceptibility to the Common Cold." *Psychological Science* 14 (2003): 389–95.

Colón, Christine A., and Bonnie E. Field. *Singled Out: Why Celibacy Must be Reinvented in Today's Church*. Grand Rapids: Brazos Press, 2009.

Consecrated virgins. "Who are consecrated virgins?" Accessed January 14, 2023. https://consecratedvirgins.org/whoarewe.

Counted, Victor. "God as an Attachment Figure: a Case Study of the God Attachment Language and God Concepts of Anxiously Attached Christian Youths in South Africa." *Journal of Spirituality in Mental Health* 18.4 (2016): 316–46. https://doi.org/10.1080/19349637.2016.1176757.

Danylak, Barry. *Redeeming Singleness: How the Storyline of Scripture Affirms the Single Life*. Wheaton: Crossway, 2010.

De Paulo, Bella. "Single in a Society Preoccupied with Couples." In *The Handbook of Solitude: Psychological Perspectives on Social Isolation, Social Withdrawal, and Being Alone*, edited by Robert J. Coplan and Julie C. Bowker, 302–16. Hoboken: Wiley Blackwell, 2014.

DeSouza, Jennifer. "Spirituality and Hope as Influences on Family Cohesion among African American Men." PhD Diss., Walden University, 2014.

D'Hombres, Béatrice, Sylke Schnepf, Martina Barjaková, and Francisco Teixeira Mendonça. "Loneliness – an Unequally Shared Burden in Europe." Science for Policy *Briefs: European Union* 4 (2018). https://ec.europa.eu/jrc/en/ research/crosscutting-activities/fairness.

DiTomasso, E., S. R. Fizzel, and B. A. Robinson. "Chronic Loneliness within an Attachment Framework: Process and Interventions." In *Addressing Loneliness: Coping, Prevention and Clinical Interventions*, eds. A. Sha'ked and A. Rokach. NY: Routledge, 2015.

DiTommaso, E., and B. Spinner. "The Development and Initial Validation of the Social and Emotional Loneliness Scale for Adults 'SELSA.'" In *Personality and Individual Differences* 14 (1993): 127–34.

Dufton, Brian D., and Daniel Perlman. "Loneliness and Religiosity: in the World but Not of It." *Journal of Psychology and Theology* 14. 2 (1986): 135–45. https://doi.org/10.1177/009164718601400205.

Eldredge, John. *The Heart: Desire/Waking the Dead*. Nashville: Thomas Nelson, 2007.

Ellison, Craig W. *Loneliness: The Search for Intimacy*. NY: Christian Herald Books, 1980.

Ellison, Craig W. *Saying Good-bye to Loneliness and Finding Intimacy*. San Francisco: Harper and Row Publishers, 1983.

Ellison, Craig W. "Spiritual Well-Being: Conceptualization and Measurement." *Journal of Psychology and Theology* 11.4 (1983): 330–38.

Encyclopaedia Britannica. "Transcendentalism." Accessed May 27, 2020. https://www.britannica.com/event/Transcendentalism-American-movement.

Encyclopaedia Judaica. "Pesikta Rabbati." Encyclopedia.com. Accessed December 22, 2022. https://www.encyclopedia.com/religion/encyclopedias-almanacs-transcripts-and-maps/pesikta-rabbati.

Epstein, *Babilonian Talmud: Yebamot 63b*, edited, translated by W. Slotki. London: Soncino Press, 1938.

Granqvist, Pehr. "Mental Health and Religion from an Attachment Viewpoint: Overview with Implications for Future Research." *Mental Health, Religion and Culture* 17.8 (2014): 777–93. https://doi.org/10.1080/13674676.2014.908513.

Gregory Nazianzen. "Oration 43. Funeral Oration on the Great S. Basil, Bishop of Cæsarea in Cappadocia." In *Nicene and Post-Nicene Fathers*, Second Series, vol. 7, translated by Charles Gordon Browne and James Edward Swallow, edited by Philip Schaff and Henry Wace. Buffalo: Christian Literature Publishing Co., 1894. http://www.newadvent.org/fathers/310243.htm.

Gregory of Nazianzus. "In Praise of Virginity." In *On God and Man: The Theological Poetry of St. Gregory of Nazianzus*. Translated and introduced by Peter Gilbert, 98–99. Crestwood: St. Vladimir's Seminary Press, 2001. https://archive.org/details/ongodmantheologi0000greg/page/98/mode/2up?q=88andview=theater.

Gregory of Nyssa. "On Virginity." Pages 343–71 in vol. 5 of *Nicene and Post-Nicene Fathers*, Second Series. Translated by William Moore and Henry Austin Wilson, edited by Philip Schaff and Henry Wace. Buffalo: Christian Literature Publishing Co., 1893. http://www.newadvent.org/ fathers/2907.htm.

Grenz, Stanley J. *The Social God and the Relational Self. A Trinitarian Theology on the Imago Dei*. London: Westminster John Knox Press, 2001.

Hall, Todd W., Annie Fujikawa, Sarah R. Halcrow, Peter C. Hill, and Harold Delaney. "Attachment to God and Implicit Spirituality: Clarifying Correspondence and Compensation Models." *Journal of Psychology and Theology* 37.4 (2009): 227–44. doi:10.1177/009164710903700401.

Hans Urs von Balthasar. *Mysteriurn Paschale: The Mystery of Easter.* San Francisco: Ignatius, 2000.

Harman, Robert. *Foundations of Faith: Understanding the Doctrines of Salvation, Baptism, and Eternal Judgment.* Global Vision Ministries: Antikva, 2003.

———. *One Sure Thing: The Power of a Life Grounded in Assurance.* Williamsburg : Wellhouse Publishers, 2016.

Hawkley, Louise, and John T. Cacioppo. "Loneliness Matters: a Theoretical and Empirical Review of Consequences and Mechanisms." *Annals of Behavioral Medicine* 2.40 (October, 2010): 218–27. https://doi: 10.1007/s12160-010-9210-8.

Hegg, Tim. "Studies in the Biblical Text: Psalm 22:16." Accessed January 17, 2021, https://torahresource.com/psalm-2216-like-lion-pierced/.

Hengstenberg, Ernst Wilhelm. *Commentary on Ecclesiastes with Other Treatises.* New York: Sheldon and Company, 1890.

Hill, Jolene M. "The Differential Prediction of Outcome Following Interpersonal Offenses versus Impersonal Tragedies by Attachment to People and Attachment to God." Thesis, Brock University, St. Catharines, August 2014.

Hobfoll, Stevan E., John R. Freedy, Carol Lane, and Pamela A. Geller. "Conservation of Social Resources: Social Support Resource Theory." *Journal of Social and Personal Relationships* 7.4 (1990): 465–78. https://doi.org/10.1177/0265407590074004.

Hughes, Philip Edgcumbe. *A Commentary on the Epistle to the Hebrews*. Grand Rapids: Eerdmans, 1977.

Hume, David. *Enquiries Concerning Human Understanding and Concerning Principles of Morals*. Oxford: Clarendon Press, 1975.

Hutchison, Elizabeth D., edited *Dimensions of Human Behavior. Person and Environment*. Pine Forge Press, 1999.

Ignatius of Antioch. "Letter to the Smyrnaeans." Chapter 8. In *Patristics.info*, edited by Luke Wilson (06 Jul 2022). https://patristics.info/ignatius-of-antioch-letter-to-the-smyrnaeans.html.

Ind, Jo. *Loneliness: Accident or injustice? Exploring Christian responses to loneliness in the Thames Valley*. Oxford: Diocese of Oxford, 2015.

Jacqueline Olds, and Richard S. Schwartz. *The Lonely American: Drifting Apart in the Twenty-First Century*. Boston: Beacon Press, 2009.

Jerome of Stridon. "Letter 22, To Eustochium." Pages 22–41 in vol. 6 of *Nicene and Post-Nicene Fathers*, Second Series. Translated by W. H. Fremantle, G. Lewis, and W. G. Martley, edited by Philip Schaff and Henry Wace. Buffalo Christian Literature Publishing Co., 1893. http://www.newadvent.org/fathers/3001022.htm.

John Gill's Exposition of the Bible. "Jeremiah." Accessed February 27, 2020. https://www.biblestudytools.com/commentaries/gills-exposition-of-the-bible/jeremiah-20-7.html.

Justin Martyr. "First Apology." Chapter 15. In *Patristics.info*, edited and formatted by Luke Wilson. Accessed July 06, 2022. https://patristics.info/justin-martyr-first-apology.html.

Keil, Carl Friedrich, and Franz Delitzsch. "Commentary on Genesis." In *Keil and Delitzsch Old Testament Commentary* (1854–1889). Accessed August 31, 2019. https://www.studylight.org/ commentaries/kdo/genesis-1.html.

Kirkpatrick, Lee A., and Phillip R. Shaver. "An Attachment-Theoretical Approach to Romantic Love and Religious Belief." *Personality and Social Psychology Bulletin* 18.3 (1992): 266–75. doi:10.1177/0146167292183002.

Kirkpatrick, Lee, and Phillip Shaver. "Attachment Theory and Religion: Childhood Attachments, Religious Beliefs, and Conversion." *Journal for the Scientific Study of Religion* 29.3 (1990): 315–34.

Klinenberg, Eric. *Going Solo: The Extraordinary Rise and Surprising Appeal of Living Alone*. New York: Penguin, 2012.

Köstenberger, Andreas J., and Margaret E. Köstenberger, *God's Design for Man and Woman: a Biblical–Theological Survey*. Wheaton: Crossway, 2014.

Laihonen, Aarno. "Trends in Households in the European Union: 1995–2025." *Statistics in Focus, Theme* 3, 24 (2003): 1–8. https://core.ac.uk/ download/pdf/148911875. pdf.

Lawson, Steven J. *Holman Old Testament Commentary: Job.* Nashville: Broadman and Holman Publishers, 2004.

Luther, Martin. *Works of Martin Luther*, vol. IV. Philadelphia: A. J. Holman Company and the Castle Press, 1931.

Mayers, Aviva M., and Martin Svartberg. "Existential Loneliness: A Review of the Concept, Its Psychosocial Precipitants and Psychotherapeutic Implications for HIV-Infected Women." *British Journal of Medical Psychology* 74 (2001): 539–53.

Mayers, Aviva M., Siek-Toon Khoo, and Martin Svartberg. "The Existential Loneliness Questionnaire: Background, Development, and Preliminary Findings." *Journal of Clinical Psychology* 58.9 (September, 2002): 1183–93.

McWhirter, Benedict T., and John Horan. "Construct Validity of Cognitive-behavioral Treatments for Intimate and Social Loneliness." *Current Psychology* 15.1 (Spring, 1996): 42–52. DOI: 10.1007/BF02686933.

Merriam Webster Dictionary. "Deprivation." Accessed December 6, 2022. https://www.merriam-webster.com/dictionary/deprivation.

Merriam Webster Dictionary. "Isolate." Accessed December 6, 2022. https://www.merriam-webster.com/dictionary/isolate.

Merton, Thomas. *Disputed Questions.* New York: Farrar, Straus and Cudahy, 1960.

Merton, Thomas. *No Man is an Island.* New York: Barnes and Noble Books, 2003.

Meyer, Heinrich August Wilhelm, ed. *Critical and Exegetical Hand-Book: to the Epistles to the Corinthians.* New York: Funk and Wagnalls Publishers, 1884.

Mills, Stella. "Loneliness: Do Interventions Help?" *Rural Theology* 1.2 (2017): 113–23. https://doi.org/10.1080/14704994.2017.1373474.

Moltmann, Jürgen. *The Coming of God: Christian Eschatology.* First Edition. Translated by Margaret Kohl. Minneapolis: Fortress Press, 1996.

Moltmann, Jürgen. *The Trinity and the Kingdom.* Translated by Margaret Kohl. San Francisco: Harper and Row, 1981.

Moon, Sarah L. "Religious Coping as a Moderating Variable." Doctor of Psychology Degree Diss., Wheaton, Illinois, October, 2013.

Moore, David George. *Holman Old Testament Commentary. Ecclesiastes, Song of Songs.* Nashville: Holman Reference, 2003.

Moore, Sebastian. *The Inner Loneliness.* New York: Cross Road, 1982.

Morgan, Leslie A. *After Marriage Ends: Economic Consequences for Midlife Women.* London: Sage, 1991.

Moustakas, Clark E. *Loneliness.* Englewood Cliffs: Prentice-Hall, 1961.

Origen, *Homilies on Joshua.* Translated by Barbara J. Bruce, edited by Cynthia White. Washington: The Catholic University of America Press, 2002.

Oxford Learner's Dictionaries. "Hermit." https://www.oxfordlearnersdictionaries.com/definition/english/hermit.

Paine, David R., and Steven J. Sandage. "More Prayer, Less Hope: Empirical Findings on Spiritual Instability." *Journal of Spirituality in Mental Health* 17.4 (2015): 224–31. https://doi.org/10.1080/19349637.2015.1026429.

Pargament, Kenneth I., Bruce W. Smith, Harold G. Koenig, and Lisa Perez. "Patterns of Positive and Negative Religious Coping with Major Life Stressors." *Journal for the Scientific Study of Religion* 37.4 (1998): 710–24.

Pargament, Kenneth, Joseph Kennell, William Hathaway, Nancy Grevengoed, Jon Newman, and Wendy Jones. "Religion and the Problem-Solving Process: Three Styles of Coping." *Journal for the Scientific Study of Religion* 27.1 (1988): 90–104. Doi: 10.2307/1387404.

Pesikta Rabbati: Homiletical Discourses for Festal Days and Special Sabbaths. Translated by William George Braude. Vol. 2. New Haven: Yale, 1968.

Putman, Anna Ruth. "The Loneliness of Koheleth." In *Loneliness. Boston University Studies in Philosophy and Religion*, edited by Leroy S. Rouner, 143–59. Vol. 19. Notre Dame: University of Notre Dame Press, 1998.

Reis, Harry T. "The Role of Intimacy in Interpersonal Relations." *Journal of Social and Clinical Psychology* 9.1 (1990): 15–30. https: //doi.org/10.1521/jscp.1990.9.1.15.

Reynolds, Jill, Margaret Wetherell, and Stephanie Taylor. "Choice and Chance: Negotiating Agency in Narratives of Singleness." *The Sociological Review* 55.2 (2007): 331–51. https://doi.org/10.1111%2Fj.1467-954X.2007.00708.x.

Robertson, Archibald, and Alfred Plummer, eds. *The International Critical Commentary. 1 Corinthians*. Edinburgh: T&T Clark, 1957.

Rokach, Ami. "Cultural Background and Coping with Loneliness." *The Journal of Psychology* 133.2 (1999): 217–29. https://doi.org/10.1080/00223989909599735.

Rokach, Ami. "Effective Coping with Loneliness: A Review." *Open Journal of Depression* 7 (November 2018): 61–72. https://doi.org/10.4236/ojd.2018.74005.

Rutledge, Fleming. *The Crucifixion: Understanding the Death of Jesus Christ*. Grand Rapids / Cambridge, U.K: Eerdmans 2015.

Sailhamer, John H. *Expositor's Bible Commentary: Genesis*. Vol. 1, edited by T. Longman III, and D. E. Garland. Grand Rapids: Zondervan, 2008.

Sandage, Steven J., Peter Jankowski, Sarah A. Crabtree, and Maria Schweer. "Attachment to God, Adult Attachment, and Spiritual Pathology: Mediator and Moderator Effects." *Mental Health, Religion and Culture* 18.10 (2015): 804–805. https://doi.org/10.1080/13674676.2015.1090965.

Sartre, Jean-Paul. *Kierkegaard Vivant: Collogue Organise par Unesko a Paris lu 21–23 April 1964* (Paris, 1966).

Schmidt, Nancy, and Vello Sermat. "Measuring Loneliness in Different Relationships." *Journal of Personality and Social Psychology* 44 (1983): 1038–47. https://psycnet.apa.org/doi/10.1037/0022-3514.44.5.1038.

Scholz, Piotr O. *Eunuchs and Castrati*. Translated by John A. Broadwin and Shelley L. Frisch. Princeton: Markus Wiener Publishers, 1999.

Schwarz, Christian A. *The 3 Colors of Ministry: A Trinitarian Approach to Identifying and Developing Your Spiritual Gifts*. St. Charles: ChurchSmart Resources, 2001.

Seccombe, Karen T., and Rebecca L.Warner. *Marriages and Families: Relationships in Social Context*. Belmont: Thomson/Wadsworth, 2004.

Seepersad, Sean. S. "Helping the 'Poor Get Richer' – Successful Internet Loneliness Intervention Programs." In vol. 1 of *Addressing Loneliness: Coping, Prevention and Clinical Interventions*, edited by A. Sha'ked and A. Rokach, 231–40. New York: Routledge, 2015.

Shaver, Phillip R., and Cynthia Hazan. "Adult Romantic Attachment: Theory and Evidence." In vol. 4 of *Advances in Personal Relationships*, edited by W. Jones and D. Perlman, 29–70. London: Jessica Kingsley, 1992.

Sheriff, Duane. "Who am I." YouTube series. Accessed December 20, 2022. https://www.youtube.com/watch?v=gPja9OQrlbsandlist=PLNEz4ajKSEZ9KmBw4R2LjSWHbhhbn4zKY.

Simpson, Roona. "Singleness and Self-identity: The Significance of Partnership Status in the Narratives of Never-Married Women." *Journal of Social and Personal Relationships* 33.3 (2016): 385–400. https://doi.org/10.1177/ 0265407515611884.

Simpson, Roona. "The Intimate Relationships of Contemporary Spinsters." *Sociological Research Online* 11.3. http://www.socresonline.org.uk/11/3/simpson.html.

Smith, Adam. *Theory of Moral Sentiments*, Sixth Edition. Sao Paulo: MexaLibri, 2006.

Spence, Canon H. D. M., and Joseph S. Exell, eds. *The Pulpit Commentary. 1 Corinthians*. New York and Toronto: Funk and Wagnalls Company, 1910.

Spero, Shubert. "A People That Shall Dwell Alone: Curse or Blessing?" *Jewish Bible Quarterly* 43.2 (April – June 2015): 1–26. https://jbqnew.jewish bible.org/assets/Uploads/432/jbq_432_sperodwell.pdf.

Sroka, Barbara. *One is a Whole Number*. Victor Books, 1978.

State Statistics Service of Ukraine, 2009–2019. "Marriages and divorces." Accessed December 6, 2022. http://database.ukrcensus.gov.ua/MULT/Dialog/statfile_c_files/ shlub.html.

Storr, Anthony. *Solitude*. London: Flamingo: An Imprint of Harper Collins Publishers, 1989.

Stott, John. *The Cross of Christ*. Downers Grove: InterVarsity, 1986.

Synodical Letter and Canons. "The Council of Gangra, Historical Note." In *Corpus Juris Canonici, Gratian's Decretum*, Pars I., Dist. XXX., C. V.

Tertullian, Kwint. "On Exhortation to Chastity." Chapter IX. https://ccel.org/ccel/s/schaff/anf04.xml.

Tertullian, Kwint. "To His Wife." In *Writers: The Works of The Fathers in Translation*, edited by Johannes Quasten and Joseph C. Plumpe. Translated and annotated by William P. Le Saint. Westminster: The Newman Press, 1956.

The Pulpit Commentary. "Genesis." Accessed January 17, 2018. http://biblehub.com/commentaries/pulpit/genesis/1.htm.

Thomas, Virginia, and Margarita Azmitia. "Motivation matters: Development and Validation of the Motivation for Solitude Scale – Short Form (MSS-SF)." *Journal of Adolescence* 70 (2019): 33–42.

Thoreau, Henry D. *Walden*. A Fully Annotated Edition. London: New Haven, Yale University Press, 2004.

Toonstra, Rob. *Naked and Unashamed: Exploring the Way the Good News of Jesus Transforms Sexuality*. Oro Valley: Doulos Resources, 2014.

Tozer, Aiden W. *The Best of A.W. Tozer*. Grand Rapids: Baker Book House Company, 1980.

Tozer, Aiden W. *The Root of the Righteous*. Camp Hill: Christian Publishing Inc., 1985.

Walsh, Joseph, and Patrick R. Connelly. "Supportive Behaviors in Natural Support Networks of People with Serious Mental Illness." *Health and Social Work* 21.4 (1996): 296–303. https://doi.org/10.1093/hsw/21.4.296.

Wehr, Kathryn. "Virginity, Singleness and Celibacy: Late Fourth-Century and Recent Evangelical Visions of Unmarried Christians." *Theology and Sexuality* 17.1 (2011): 75–99. https:// doi:10.1558/tse.v17i1.75.

Weiss, Robert. *Loneliness: The Experience of Emotional and Social Isolation*. Cambridge: MIT Press, 1975.

Well, Tara. "The Link between Loneliness and Smiling." *Psychology Today* (September 26, 2019). https://www.psychologytoday.com/us/blog/the-clarity/201909/the-link-between-loneliness-and-smiling.

Wiesel, Elie. "The Lonely Prophet." In vol. 19 of *Loneliness, Boston University Studies in Philosophy and Religion*, edited by Leroy S. Rouner, 127–42. Notre Dame: University of Notre Dame Press, 1998.

Wildman, Wesley J. "In Praise of Loneliness." In vol. 19 of *Loneliness, Boston University Studies in Philosophy and Religion*, edited by Leroy S. Rouner, 15–39. Notre Dame : University of Notre Dame Press, 1998.

Willard, Dallas. *The Divine Conspiracy. Rediscovering Our Hidden Life in God*, EPub Edition (Harper Collins ebook, 2009).

Williams, David T. "Who Will Go for Us? (Is.6 :8): The Divine Plurals and the Image of God." *Old Testament Essays* 12.1 (1999): 173–90.

Young, Emma. "Preliminary Evidence that Lonely People Lose the Reflex to Mimic Other People's Smiles Potentially Sustaining the Isolation." *Neuropsych* (June 23, 2019). https://bigthink.com/neuropsych/loneliness/.

Zahl, Bonnie Poon, and Nicholas J. S. Gibson. "God Representations, Attachment to God, and Satisfaction with Life: A Comparison of Doctrinal and Experiential Representations of God in Christian Young Adults." *International Journal for the Psychology of Religion* 22.3 (2012): 216.

Zimmerman, Johann Georg. *Solitude considered, with respect to its influence upon the mind and the heart*. London: C. Dilly, 1799.

Zizioulas, John D. "Human Capacity and Human Incapacity: A Theological Exploration of Personhood." *Scottish Journal of Theology* 28.5 (October, 1975): 408.

Zodgiates, Spiros, edited *Hebrew–Greek Key Word Study Bible*. Chattanooga: ANG International, 2008.

Августин Аврелий. "О Супружестве и Похоти." In *Трактаты о Любви: Сборник Текстов*, ред. Ольга Зубец. М.: Российская Академия Наук, 1994 [Augustine Aurelius, "On Marriage and Lust," in Treatises on Love: A Collection of Texts, eds. Olga Zubets (Moscow: Russian Academy of Sciences, 1994)].

Аристотель. *Сочинения. Политика*. Т. 4. Перевод О. Кислюка. М.: Мысль, 1983 [Aristotle, Works, Politics, T. 4, trans. O. Kislyuk (Moscow: Mysl, 1983)].

Бердяев, Николай. *Я и Мир Объектов. Опыт Философии Одиночества и Общения*. Париж: YMCA PRESS, 1934 [Berdyaev, Nikolai. Me and the World of Objects. An Experience of the Philosophy of Loneliness and Communication (Paris: YMCA PRESS, 1934)].

Браун, Пітер. *Тіло і Суспільство. Чоловіки, Жінки і Сексуальне Зречення в Ранньому Християнстві*. Переклад В. Т. Тимофійчука. К.: Мегатайп, 2003 [Brown, Peter. Body and Society. Men, Women and Sexual Renunciation in Early Christianity, Ukrainian transl. V. T. Timofiichuk (K.: Megatype, 2003)].

Валентей, Дмитрий И. ред., *Демографический Энциклопедический Словарь*. М.: Советская Энциклопедия, 1985 [Valentey, Dmitry I. ed., Demographic Encyclopedic Dictionary (Moscow: Soviet Encyclopedia, 1985)].

Винч, Гай Л. *Первая Психологическая Помощь*. ООО «Попурри», 2014 [Winch, Guy. Emotional First Aid. Rus. Transl.]. http://loveread.ec/view_global.php?id=47095.

Гасанова, Патимат Г., Марина К. Омарова. *Психология Одиночества*. Киев: Общество с Ограниченной Ответственностью "Финансовая Рада Украины", 2017 [Gasanova, Patimat G. and Omarova Marina K. Psychology of Loneliness (Kyiv: Limited Liability Company "Financial Rada of Ukraine," 2017)].

Григорий Богослов. "К монахам." In *Творения: Песнопения Таинственные*, 169–172. Т. 2 СПб.: Издательство П. П. Сойкина, 1912 [Gregory the Theologian, "To the Monks," in Creations: Mysterious Chants, vol. 2 (St. Petersburg: P. P. Soikin Publishing House, 1912)].

Григорий Палама. *Триады в Защиту Священно-Безмолвствующих*. М.: Канон, 1995 [Gregory Palamas. Triads for the Defense of Those Who Practice Sacred Quietude (Moscow: Kanon, 1995)].

Гриценко, Вікторія А. "Переживання Самотності й Особливості Духовно-Емоційної та Комунікативної Сфер Життя Старших Підлітків." In *Збірник наукових праць Кам'янец-Подільського національного університету імені Івана Огієнка*. Вип. XVIII. Ред. Л. П. Мельник, В. І. Співак. Кам'янец-Подільський: Медобори-2006, 2012 [Hrytsenko, Viktoriia A. "Experiences of Loneliness and Peculiarities of the Spiritual-Emotional and Communicative Spheres of Life of Older Adolescents," in Collection of Scientific Papers of the Ivan Ohienko Kamianets-Podilskyi National University. Vol. XVIII. Ed. L. P. Melnyk, V. I. Spivak (Kamyanets-Podilskyi: Medobory-2006, 2012)]. https://fkspp.at.ua/Bibl/18.pdf.

Гриценко, Вікторія А. "Соціально-Педагогічні Умови Подолання Стану Самотності Студентів Вищих Навчальних Закладів I-II Рівнів Акредитації." Дис. канд. пед. наук, ун-т ім. Бориса Грінченка, Київ, 2014 [Hrytsenko, Viktoriia A. "Social and Pedagogical Conditions for Overcoming the Loneliness of Students of Higher Educational Institutions of I-II Levels of Accreditation" (Dissertation of Candidate of Pedagogical Sciences, Borys Grinchenko University, Kyiv, 2014)]. https://nolonely.info/socio-pedagogical-conditions-overcoming-loneliness.pdf.

Гуляницкий, Августин. *Предисловие* к "Двум Окружным Посланиям св. Климента Римского о Девстве, или к Девственникам и Девственницам." [Gulyanitsky, Augustine, Bishop. Preface to the "Two Epistles of St. Clement of Rome on Virginity]. https://acathist.ru/en/literatura/item/ep-avgustin-gulyanitskij-dva-okruzhnykh-poslaniya-sv-klimenta-rimskogo-o-devstve-ili-k-devstvennikam-i-devstvennitsam.

Давыденков, Олег. "Догм. Богословие." Курс лекций [Davydenkov, Oleg. "Dogmatic Theology." Course of lectures]. Accessed December 20, 2022. https://azbyka.ru/perixorezis.

Держстат України, 2009–2019. "Шлюби та розірвання шлюбів." [State Statistics Service of Ukraine, 2009–2019. "Marriages and Divorces."] Accessed January 18, 2023. http://db.ukrcensus.gov.ua/mult/dialog/statfile_c_files/shlub.html.

Ивин, Александр А. ред. *Философия: Энциклопедический Словарь*. Accessed August 25, 2019. М.: Гардарики, 2004 [Ivin Alexander A., ed., Philosophy: Encyclopedic Dictionary (Moscow: Gardariki, 2004)]. https://dic.academic.ru/dic.nsf/enc_philosophy/890.

Ириней Лионский. *Против Ересей. Доказательство Апостольской Проповеди.* Перевод прот. П. Преображенского, Н.И. Сагарды. СПб.: Издательство Олега Абышко, 2008 [Irenaeus of Lyons, Against Heresies. The Demonstration of the Apostolic Preaching, trans. arch. P. Preobrazhensky, N.I. Sagardy, (St. Petersburg: Oleg Abyshko Publishing House, 2008)].

Каценельсон, Лев, Давид Г. Гинцбург. *Еврейская Энциклопедия*, ред. Т.4. СПб.: Тип. акц. общ. Брокгауз-Ефрон, 1906–1913 [Katsenelson, Lev, and David G. Gintsburg, Jewish Encyclopedia, eds. Т.4. (St. Petersburg: Brockhaus - Efron Publishing, 1906–1913)].

Козлов, Максим, Протоиерей. "О Практике Целибата в Русской Церкви." Молодежный Интернет Журнал МГУ "Татьянин День." [Kozlov, Maxim, Archpriest. "On the Practice of Celibacy in the Russian Church." Youth Internet Journal of Moscow State University "Tatyanin's Den."] Accessed December 27, 2010. http://www.taday.ru/text/814342.html.

Кон, Игорь С. *Многоликое Одиночество. Популярная Психология. Хрестоматия.* М.: Просвещение, 1990 [Kon, Igor S. Many Faces of Loneliness, Popular Psychology, Reader (Moscow: Prosveshchenye, 1990)].

Кьеркегор, Сьорен. *Страх и Трепет*. М.: Республика, 1993 [Kierkegaard, Søren. Fear and Trembling (Moscow: Republic, 1993)].

Мазуренко, Елена А. "Одиночество как Феномен Индивидуальной и Социальной Жизни." Автореф. дис. Архангельск: Поморский Государственный Университет Имени М. В. Ломоносова, 2006 [Mazurenko, Elena A. "Loneliness as a Phenomenon of Individual and Social Life," (Abstract diss., Arkhangelsk: Pomorsky State University named after M.V . Lomonosov, 2006)].

Покровский, Иосиф А. *История Римского Права*. Перевод с лат., науч. ред. и комм. А. Д. Рудокваса. СПб: Изд.-торг. дом «Летний сад», 1999 [Pokrovsky, Joseph A. History of Roman Law, trans. from Latin, scientific ed. and comm. A. D. Rudokvas (St. Petersburg: Publishing house "Letniy Sad," 1999)].

Пузанова, Жанна. "Социологическое Измерение Одиночества." Автореф. дисс. док. социол. наук. Москва, 2009 [Puzanova, Zhanna. "The Sociological Dimension of Loneliness" (Abstract of diss. doc. sociology. Moscow, 2009)].

Разумовский, Олег С. "Реляционизм и Изоляционизм: Пролог к Теории Систем." *Полигнозис* 4 (1999) [Razumovsky, Oleg S. "Relationism and Isolationism: A Prologue to Systems Theory," Polygnosis 4 (1999)]: 1–30.

Романова, Нелли. "Социальный Статус Одиноких Женщин в Современном Российском Обществе: Теоретико-Методологический Анализ на Материалах Забайкалья." Дисс. док. социол. наук, Улан-Удэ: Бурятский Государственный Университет, 2006 [Romanova, Nelli. "The Social Status of Single Women in Modern Russian Society: Theoretical and Methodological Analysis on the Materials of Transbaikalia" (Diss. Doctor of Sociology, Buryat State University, Ulan-Ude, 2006)].

Санніков, Сергій В. *Популярна Історія Християнства. Двадцять Століть у Дорозі*. К.: Самміт-Книга, 2012 [Sannikov, Serhii V. Popular History of Christianity. Twenty Centuries on the Road (Kyiv: Summit-Knyga, 2012)].

Свендсен, Ларс Фр. Г. *Філософія Самотності*. Переклад Софії Волковецької. Київ: Ніка-Центр, 2017 [Svendsen, Lars Fr. G. A Philosophy of Loneliness, Trans. Sofia Volkovetskoy (Kyiv: Nika-Center, 2017)].

Хайдеггер, Мартин. *Основные Понятия Метафизики: Мир-Конечность-Одиночество*. Перевод В. В. Бибихина, Л. В. Ахутина, А. П. Шурбелева. СПб: Владимир Даль, 2013 [Heidegger, Martin. The Fundamental Concepts of Metaphysics: World-Finitude-Solitude, trans. V. V. Bibikhina, L. V. Akhutina, A. P. Shurbeleva (St. Petersburg: Vladimir Dal, 2013)].

Чорнобай Валерія. "Богословське Осмислення Феномена Самотності." Дис. канд. філос. наук, Київ: НПУ Драгоманова, 2020 [Chornobai, Valeriia. "Theological Reflections on the Phenomenon of Loneliness" (PhD Diss. of Philosophical Sciences, Kyiv: Drahomanova National University, 2020)].

Чорнобай, Валерія А. "Стратегії Подолання Самотності Християн: Соціально-Релігійний Аспект." *Практична Філософія* 68. 2 (2018) [Chornobai, Valeriia.

"Strategies to Overcome Loneliness of Christians: Socio-Religious Aspect," Practical Philosophy 68. 2 (2018)]: 193–99.

Шагивалеева, Гузалия Р. "Культурологическое и Психологическое Понимание Феномена Одиночества." *Концепт, Спецвыпуск* 1 (2013): 10 [Shagivaleeva, Guzaliya R. "Culturological and Psychological Understanding of the Loneliness Phenomenon," Concept, Special Issue 1 (2013)].

Энциклопедия Социологии 'Академик.' "Изоляция." [Encyclopedia of Sociology Academician "Isolation."] Accessed August 25, 2019. https://dic.academic.ru/dic.nsf/socio/1177.

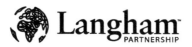

Langham Literature and its imprints are a ministry of Langham Partnership.

Langham Partnership is a global fellowship working in pursuit of the vision God entrusted to its founder John Stott –

> *to facilitate the growth of the church in maturity and Christ-likeness through raising the standards of biblical preaching and teaching.*

Our vision is to see churches in the Majority World equipped for mission and growing to maturity in Christ through the ministry of pastors and leaders who believe, teach and live by the word of God.

Our mission is to strengthen the ministry of the word of God through:
- nurturing national movements for biblical preaching
- fostering the creation and distribution of evangelical literature
- enhancing evangelical theological education

especially in countries where churches are under-resourced.

Our ministry

Langham Preaching partners with national leaders to nurture indigenous biblical preaching movements for pastors and lay preachers all around the world. With the support of a team of trainers from many countries, a multi-level programme of seminars provides practical training, and is followed by a programme for training local facilitators. Local preachers' groups and national and regional networks ensure continuity and ongoing development, seeking to build vigorous movements committed to Bible exposition.

Langham Literature provides Majority World preachers, scholars and seminary libraries with evangelical books and electronic resources through publishing and distribution, grants and discounts. The programme also fosters the creation of indigenous evangelical books in many languages, through writer's grants, strengthening local evangelical publishing houses, and investment in major regional literature projects, such as one volume Bible commentaries like *The Africa Bible Commentary* and *The South Asia Bible Commentary*.

Langham Scholars provides financial support for evangelical doctoral students from the Majority World so that, when they return home, they may train pastors and other Christian leaders with sound, biblical and theological teaching. This programme equips those who equip others. Langham Scholars also works in partnership with Majority World seminaries in strengthening evangelical theological education. A growing number of Langham Scholars study in high quality doctoral programmes in the Majority World itself. As well as teaching the next generation of pastors, graduated Langham Scholars exercise significant influence through their writing and leadership.

To learn more about Langham Partnership and the work we do visit **langham.org**

Milton Keynes UK
Ingram Content Group UK Ltd.
UKHW020614061023
430059UK00012B/435